PLANNING

Architects' technical reference

PLANNING Ninth Edition

Other volume titles

PLANNING

Volume 1
Architects' technical reference

Edited by
EDWARD D. MILLS, C.B.E., F.R.I.B.A., M.S.I.A.

LONDON
ILIFFE BOOKS

THE BUTTERWORTH GROUP

ENGLAND
Butterworth & Co (Publishers) Ltd
London: 88 Kingsway, WC2B 6AB

AUSTRALIA
Butterworth & Co (Australia) Ltd
Sydney: 586 Pacific Highway, Chatswood, NSW 2067
Melbourne: 343 Little Collins Street, 3000
Brisbane: 240 Queen Street, 4000

CANADA
Butterworth & Co (Canada) Ltd
Toronto: 14 Curity Avenue, 374

NEW ZEALAND
Butterworth & Co (New Zealand) Ltd
Wellington: 26–28 Waring Taylor Street, 1

SOUTH AFRICA
Butterworth & Co (South Africa) (Pty) Ltd
Durban: 152–154 Gale Street

First published in 1936 by Architect & Building News
Second edition 1937
Third edition 1938
Fourth edition 1939
Fifth edition published for Architect & Building News
by Gilbert Wood & Co Ltd 1947
Sixth edition 1949
Seventh edition published for Architect & Building News
by Iliffe & Sons Ltd 1953
Eighth edition published for Architect & Building News
by Iliffe Books Ltd 1959
Ninth edition, Volume 1, published by Iliffe Books, an imprint
of the Butterworth Group 1972

© E. D. Mills, 1972

ISBN 0 592 00243 8

Filmset by V. Siviter Smith Ltd, Birmingham

Printed in England by Clarke, Doble & Brendon Limited, Plymouth

FOREWORD

By Gontran Goulden, Director General of the Building Centre Group

The construction industry becomes daily more complicated and to attempt to abstract the relevant information from the mass of literature available is no easy task. It is now almost impossible for one man to know even the main sources of technical information by heart.

For nearly forty years *Planning* has been a leader among the books that list, discuss and illustrate all those vital facts and figures that are not to be found in one place elsewhere. The man on the drawing board, whether a beginner, experienced in general or specialised practice, or about to burst into computerised building design will always need simple basic information of the kind that packs the pages of Volume One of this entirely new edition of *Planning*.

The whole question of information for the construction industry still awaits a satisfactory solution. It is doubtful even whether it is capable of being solved to meet everyone's demands. At one end of the scale there are those who demand comprehensive lists of manufacturers and products, corrected up to the minute and covering every conceivable detail of each item. Others require research information in the greatest depth with all available sources equally up to date and comprehensive. We know that this problem can be dealt with by computers, at a price. We know too that various attempts and exercises have been and are being made to turn this major undertaking into a financially possible service.

Only time will show whether the user can be trained to realise that time spent in his office on research costs money and that the answer could be available in less time, thereby saving him money. A small proportion of users are prepared to pay for information, most still think it should be free and paid for by the other fellow. Comprehensive information for the industry will require a nationally co-ordinated effort. So far there is little or no sign of this.

In the meantime the need for the right information continues in all branches of the industry. In addition to major outside-the-office sources each one of us has his own particular favourite reference books and catalogues. This personal preference will always be there wherever comprehensive systems develop.

Planning has filled many people's personal information needs for years. With a mass of useful data, and as a guide to the form of construction industry information generally, this first volume of a series of five should, like its predecessors, prove invaluable and I wish it every success.

1972   *Gontran Goulden*

ACKNOWLEDGEMENTS

The publishers are grateful to the Controller of Her Majesty's Stationery Office for allowing them to reproduce the following figures, tables and brief extracts:

Extracts on pages 35 and 36 on Urban Roads System, Bus Stops, Junction Spacing and Slip Roads, taken from *Roads in Urban Areas*; and pages 56 and 57 on Dimensional Co-ordination, from *Going Metric in the Construction Industry*.

Thanks are also gratefully tendered to the publishers, William Heinemann, London, for permission to include the following illustrations and tables from *Techniques of Landscape Architecture*, edited by Professor A. E. Weddle for the Institute of Landscape Architects:

The publishers would also like to thank the British Standards Institution for permission to re-produce the tables on pages 101–130. A similar acknowledgement is due to Messrs Marryat & Scott Ltd for permission to use Figs. 2.7–2.10 from their booklet *Recommended Dimensions and Metric Equivalents*, and to Thames & Hudson for Figs. 4.9 and 4.10 taken from *Room Outside, a New Approach to Gardening Design* by J. Brookes. Table 4.18 is based on information in *Trees for Town and Country* by B. Colvin (Lund Humphries).

CONTENTS

INTRODUCTION

Planning first appeared as a weekly feature in the *Architect and Building News* before World War II, to which two architects contributed under the pseudonym of E. & O.E. In 1936, the first bound volume of *Planning* was published and the authors were subsequently revealed as Rowland Pierce and Patrick Cutbush, later to be joined by Anthony Williams. Since that date successive editions have appeared and the general pattern has changed little over the years. The most recent edition (the eighth in 1959, with the third revised impression in 1969) contains a great deal of data that appeared in the original weekly *Architectural and Building News* features.

Nearly 40 years have passed since E. & O.E. began to make their weekly contributions to the *Architect and Building News* and today *Planning* is recognised throughout the world as one of the standard reference books for architects. There can be few architects' offices in the United Kingdom which do not possess and constantly use at least one copy, and in many architects' offices in the remote parts of the world a much used copy of *Planning* still holds pride of place on the bookshelf. Architectural students have always found the book to be an essential work of reference and many have started their architectural libraries with it and one or two of the other well-known books of reference.

The radical changes which are taking place in the world of building has led to a reappraisal of the place of *Planning* in the technical information field and in the way in which the valuable material it contained is presented. New techniques and disciplines are being developed in the Building Industry and these must be reflected in the technical information available. The Building Industry is becoming a more closely integrated one and *Planning* must therefore reflect this. It has, therefore, been re-structured so that it appeals to a wider cross-section of the industry including architects, builders, quantity surveyors, engineers, planners and students. With these considerations in mind, together with the change to metric in the Building Industry, the publishers decided that a completely new approach should be adopted, and this volume is the first of a series to reflect the new pattern.

The 1969 revised impression of the eighth edition of *Planning* consisted of three sections: (1) a general section dealing with information applicable to more than one type of building; (2) a section dealing with information applicable to specific building types and (3) metrication information to aid the conversion of imperial units to metric ones. In essence the ninth edition of *Planning* accepts this broad classification.

This volume is the first of a series of separate volumes which will include some of the basic data from the original book but also incorporate other material which will be of value to the various members of the building team.

Before the war, the *Architect and Building News* published, in association with the Architectural Association, *The Architects' Technical Reference*. This was an extremely useful volume of technical data, at one time combined with an architect's diary, which gave a considerable amount of information not found elsewhere, and was of considerable use to practising architects. Unfortunately this particular publication closed in 1948, but for some time it has been felt that the idea behind it was of sufficient value for its future to be reconsidered. The publishers therefore agreed to the amalgamation of *The Architects' Technical Reference* and *Planning* so that basic reference material of a technical nature could be incorporated in addition to planning data.

This volume (Architects' Technical Reference) therefore includes sections dealing with legislation, British Standards, materials, etc. as well as basic planning data which concern all types of building, such as car parking, circulation, sanitary requirements, storage requirements. All information contained in earlier editions which is still valid has been retained and a considerable amount of new material has been added. Future volumes will deal with specific building types and will cover a wide range of subjects under general groupings as laid down in the CI/Sfb Building Manual.

The unique characteristic of *Planning* is that it indicates how various types of buildings are planned by supplying information and data which are essential before planning can begin. It does not deal with the aesthetics of design, although future volumes dealing with particular building types will be illustrated not only by means of diagrams but by plans and photographs of actual completed buildings, either in part or whole showing the way in which particular problems have been solved.

The sources from which the material for Volume I has been gathered have been many and varied, and assistance has been rendered by many people in the preparation of this new volume. Books, periodicals, people and associations have all contributed in a very practical way and because it is impossible to set out a complete list of all those concerned this general acknowledgement is addressed to all those who have been associated with the preparation of the book and is an expression of the sincere thanks of the editor to all concerned.

However, particular thanks are due to Gontran Goulden, who contributed the Foreword in his private and personal capacity and has been concerned intimately with all aspects of building information, both in this country and abroad, for the past twenty-five years.

Finally, the editor would welcome any information from readers which would enable subsequent editions to be just as informative and up to date.

1972

Edward D. Mills

PUBLISHERS' NOTE

On metric projects during the changeover period, it may be necessary to continue to use products and components produced and sold in imperial sizes which are normally described by reference to their dimensions. This book follows the recommendations given in B.S.I. P.D.6031 which says in such cases the metric equivalent sizes (generally to the nearest millimetre) should be given in parentheses: for example 4 in (102 mm).

In a few instances where imperial dimensions have been changed to metric values, which may not in all cases be the exact metric equivalent, no equivalent imperial value is given.

The symbols for units of linear measure on drawings have been discarded in accordance with the following rules. Whole numbers indicate millimetres: for example, a length of 1500 millimetres would appear as just 1500. B.S.I. P.D.6031 recommends that where metres and millimetres are used on the same drawing, then metres should be given to three places of decimals: for example 1·500. This would be visually compatible with and could be used as an alternative. All other dimensions are followed by the unit symbol: for example 1·50 m or 3·5 mm.

1 HUMAN DIMENSIONS AND COMMON SIZES INCLUDING STORAGE EQUIPMENT

Information in this section is applicable to all building types. Dimensions given are for average men and women and variations may occur by reason of age and racial groups. All dimensions are minimum and clearance sizes need to be allowed.

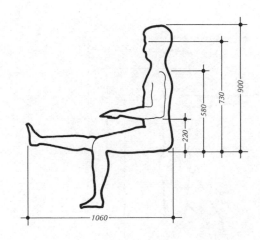

Fig. 1.1   Mean average dimensions of adult males

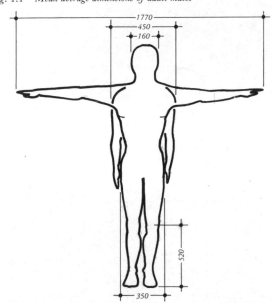

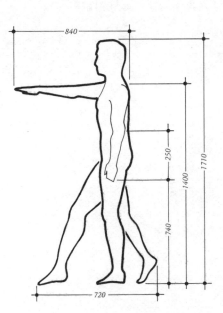

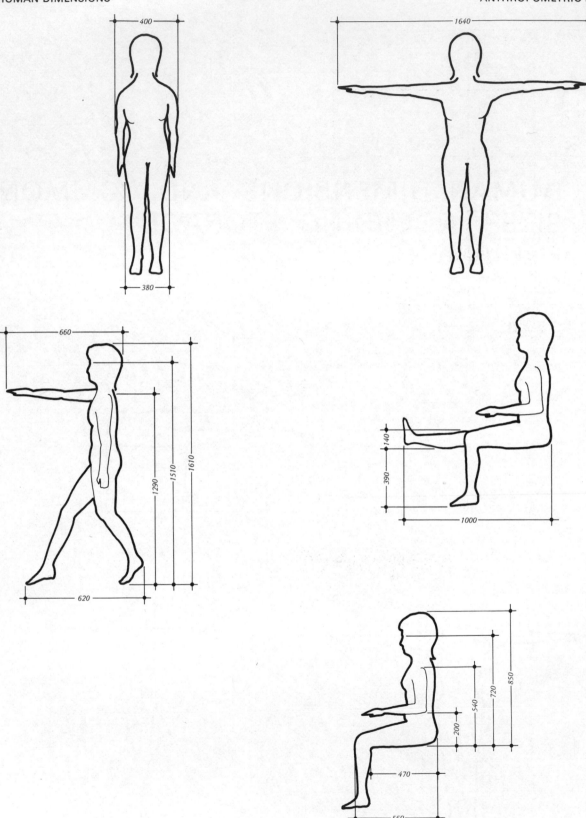

Fig. 1.2   Mean average dimensions of adult females

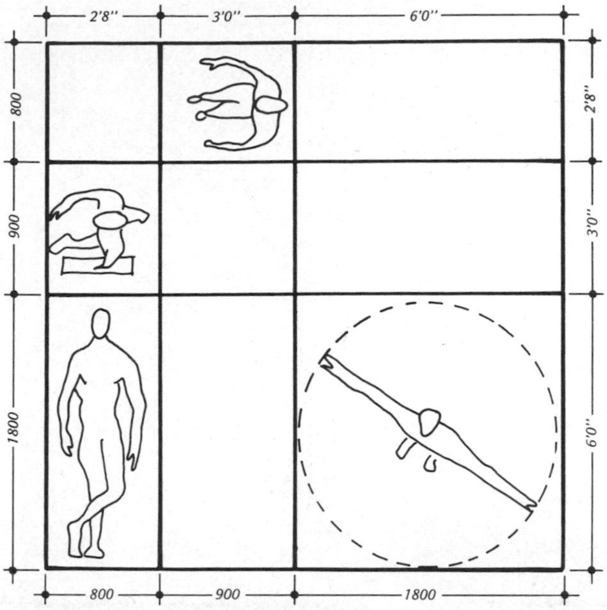

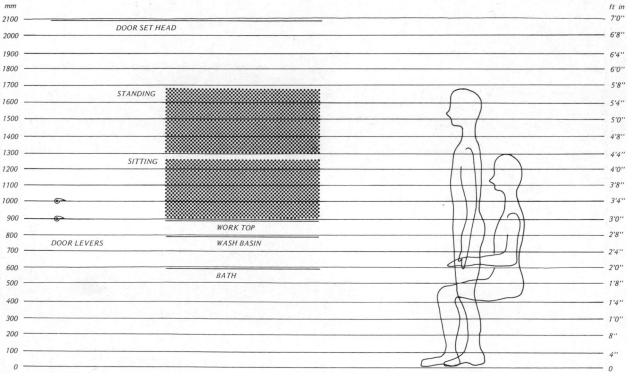

Fig. 1.3   Space for human activities

Fig. 1.4   Levels of human activity

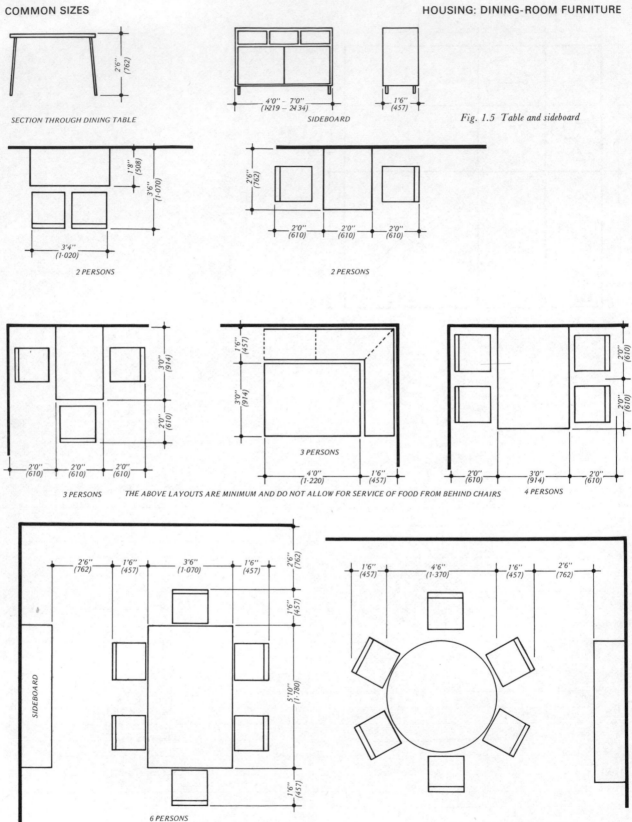

SECTION THROUGH DINING TABLE

SIDEBOARD

Fig. 1.5 Table and sideboard

2 PERSONS

2 PERSONS

3 PERSONS

3 PERSONS   THE ABOVE LAYOUTS ARE MINIMUM AND DO NOT ALLOW FOR SERVICE OF FOOD FROM BEHIND CHAIRS   4 PERSONS

6 PERSONS

MINIMUM LAYOUTS ALLOWING FOR SERVICE BEHIND CHAIRS

6 PERSONS

Fig. 1.6 Dining-room layouts for tables and seating

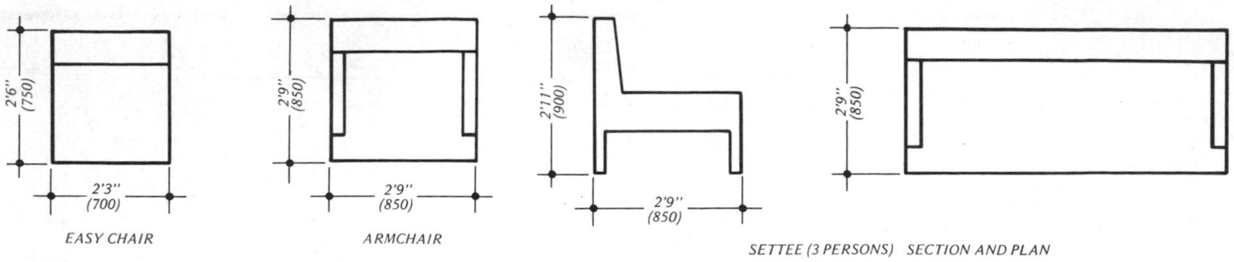

2'6"
(750)

2'3"
(700)

EASY CHAIR

2'9"
(850)

2'9"
(850)

ARMCHAIR

2'11"
(900)

2'9"
(850)

SETTEE (3 PERSONS) SECTION AND PLAN

2'9"
(850)

Fig. 1.7   Easy chair, armchair and settee

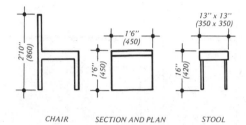

2'10"
(860)

CHAIR

1'6"
(450)

1'6"
(450)

SECTION AND PLAN

13" x 13"
(350 x 350)

16"
(420)

STOOL

Fig. 1.8   Chair and stool

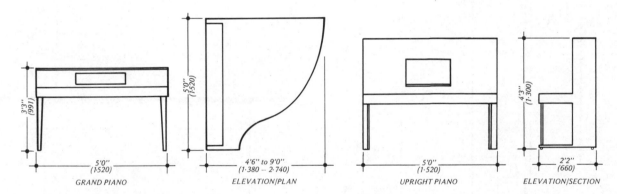

3'3"
(991)

5'0"
(1·520)

GRAND PIANO

5'0"
(1520)

4'6" to 9'0"
(1·380 − 2·740)

ELEVATION/PLAN

5'0"
(1·520)

UPRIGHT PIANO

4'3"
(1·300)

2'2"
(660)

ELEVATION/SECTION

Fig. 1.9   Grand piano, upright piano

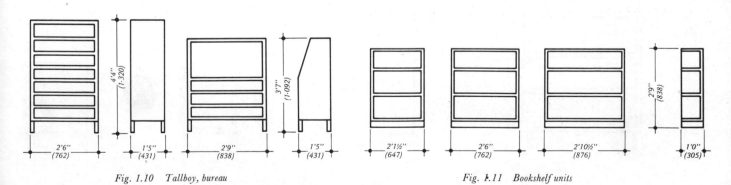

4'4"
(1·320)

2'6"
(762)

1'5"
(431)

2'9"
(838)

3'7"
(1·092)

1'5"
(431)

Fig. 1.10   Tallboy, bureau

2'1½"
(647)

2'6"
(762)

2'10½"
(876)

2'9"
(838)

1'0"
(305)

Fig. 1.11   Bookshelf units

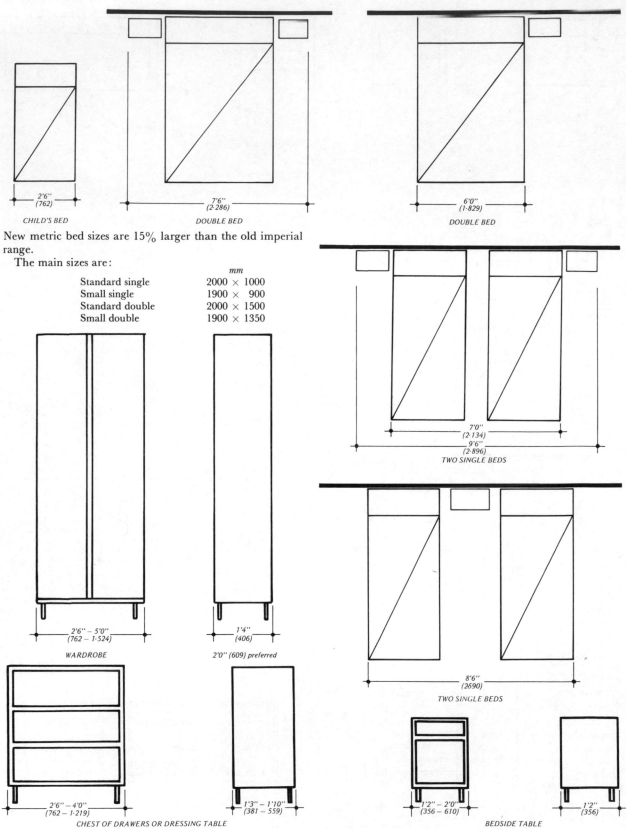

New metric bed sizes are 15% larger than the old imperial range.

The main sizes are:

	mm
Standard single	2000 × 1000
Small single	1900 × 900
Standard double	2000 × 1500
Small double	1900 × 1350

Fig. 1.12   Dimensions of typical bedroom furniture

SINKS, BATHS, SHOWER TRAYS: TYPICAL OVERALL SIZES

The range of sanitary fittings for all purposes is very considerable and there is very little dimensional standardisation. The dimensions given for sanitary fittings should therefore be regarded as average. Details of specialised sanitary fittings for specific buildings, i.e. factories, hospitals, etc., will be found in the volume of *Planning* dealing with these building types.

SINKS (TYPICAL SIZES)

Metal sinks—overall sizes	Width		Projection	
	in	mm	in	mm
Single draining board	36	915	18	455
	42	1065	18	455
	42	1065	21	535
	63	1600	21	535
Double draining board	54	1370	18	455
	63	1600	21	535
Two bowls	86	2132	21	535
Fireclay sinks—Belfast pattern				
	18	455	15	380
	24	610	18	455
	30	760	18	455

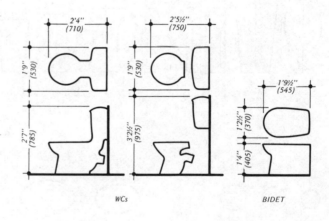

Fig. 1.13   Lavatory basins

BATHS (TYPICAL SIZES)

Length		Width	
in	mm	in	mm
66	1675	29	725
72	1830	29	725
66	1675	28	710
72	1830	28	710
60	1525	27	675
66	1675	27	675
60	1525	24	610

Height of bath from floor will vary from $17\frac{3}{8}$–$21\frac{1}{8}$ in (440–535 mm) according to type of trap employed.

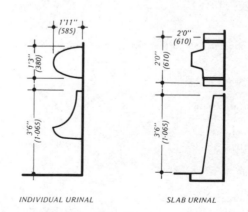

SHOWER TRAYS (FIRECLAY) TYPICAL SIZES

Length/Breadth/Depth
24 in × 24 in × 7 in   (610 mm × 610 mm × 180 mm)
30 in × 30 in × 7 in   (760 mm × 760 mm × 180 mm)
36 in × 36 in × 7 in   (915 mm × 915 mm × 180 mm)

Fig. 1.14   Wcs, bidets and urinals

SIZES OF BOTTLES

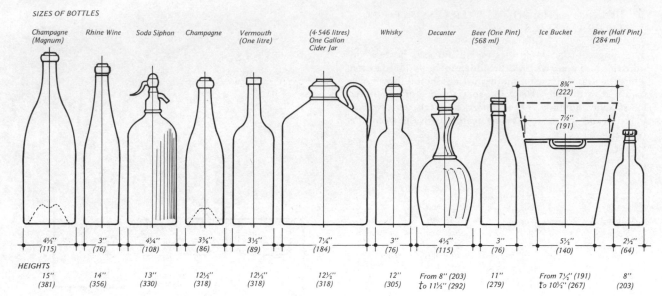

	Champagne (Magnum)	Rhine Wine	Soda Siphon	Champagne	Vermouth (One litre)	(4·546 litres) One Gallon Cider Jar	Whisky	Decanter	Beer (One Pint) (568 ml)	Ice Bucket	Beer (Half Pint) (284 ml)
Width	4½" (115)	3" (76)	4¼" (108)	3⅜" (86)	3½" (89)	7¼" (184)	3" (76)	4½" (115)	3" (76)	5½" (140)	2½" (64)
HEIGHTS	15" (381)	14" (356)	13" (330)	12½" (318)	12½" (318)	12½" (318)	12" (305)	From 8" (203) to 11½" (292)	11" (279)	From 7½" (191) to 10½" (267)	8" (203)

SIZES OF GLASSES

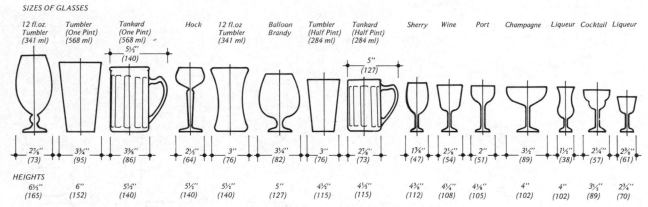

	12 fl.oz Tumbler (341 ml)	Tumbler (One Pint) (568 ml)	Tankard (One Pint) (568 ml)	Hock	12 fl.oz Tumbler (341 ml)	Balloon Brandy	Tumbler (Half Pint) (284 ml)	Tankard (Half Pint) (284 ml)	Sherry	Wine	Port	Champagne	Liqueur	Cocktail	Liqueur
Width	2⅞" (73)	3¾" (95)	3⅜" (86)	2½" (64)	3" (76)	3¼" (82)	3" (76)	2⅞" (73)	1⅞" (47)	2⅛" (54)	2" (51)	3½" (89)	1½" (38)	2¼" (57)	2⅜" (61)
HEIGHTS	6½" (165)	6" (152)	5½" (140)	5½" (140)	5½" (140)	5" (127)	4½" (115)	4½" (115)	4⅜" (112)	4¼" (108)	4⅛" (105)	4" (102)	4" (102)	3½" (89)	2¾" (70)

Fig. 1.15   Shape and sizes of bottles and glasses

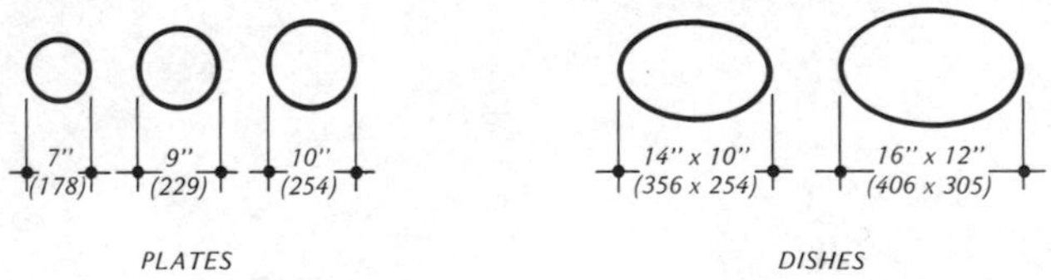

PLATES
7" (178)   9" (229)   10" (254)

DISHES
14" x 10" (356 x 254)   16" x 12" (406 x 305)

Fig. 1.16   Standard plate and dish sizes

Selected Drawing Paper Sizes

	in
Antiquarian	53 × 31
Double Elephant	40 × 27
Elephant	28 × 23
Imperial	30 × 22

Selected Stationery Paper Sizes

	in
Foolscap	13 × 8
Quarto	10 × 8
Demi-octavo	8 × 5

International Paper Sizes (trimmed)

	in	mm
A0	33⅛ × 46¾	841 × 1189
A1	23⅜ × 33⅛	594 × 841
A2	16½ × 23⅜	420 × 594
A3	11¾ × 16½	297 × 420
A4	8¼ × 11¾	210 × 297
A5	5⅞ × 8¼	148 × 210
A6	4⅛ × 5⅞	105 × 148
A7	2⅞ × 4⅛	74 × 105
A8	2 × 2⅞	52 × 74
A9	1½ × 2	37 × 52
A10	1 × 1½	26 × 37

The R.I.B.A. have recommended that building industry trade and technical literature be A4 size.

Post Office Preferred Envelope Sizes (POP)

Envelopes must fall within the maximum sizes of 120 × 235 mm

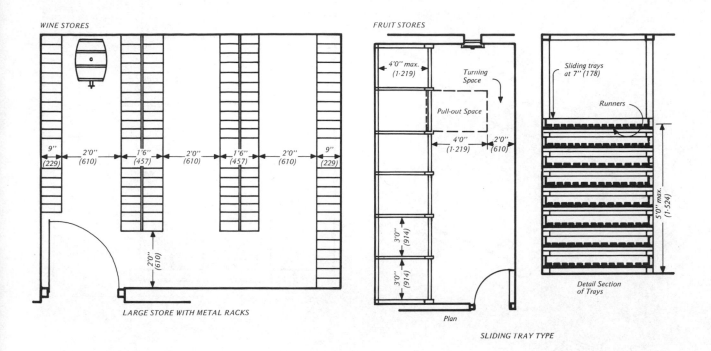

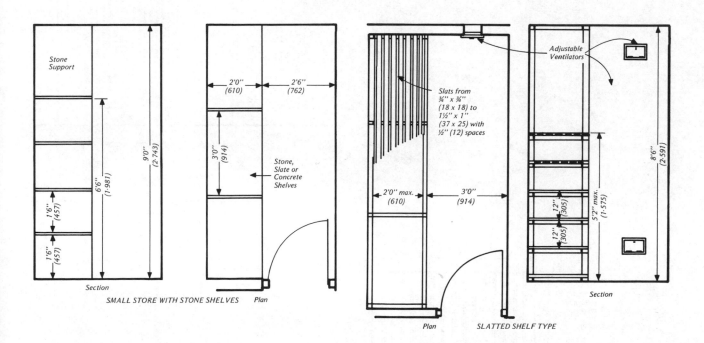

Fig. 1.17   Methods of storing wine and fruit

These sizes are approximate and are given as a guide only.

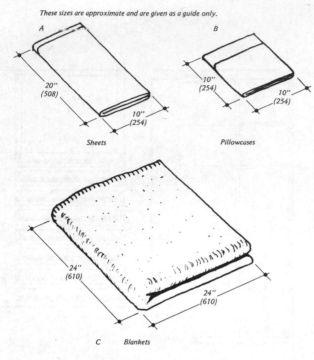

Fig. 1.18   Approximate sizes of folded linen

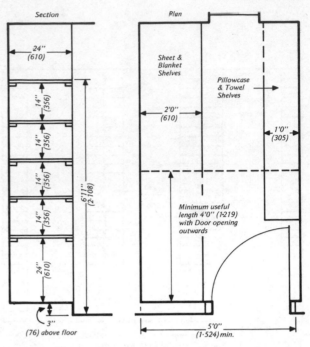

Fig. 1.20   Linen stores

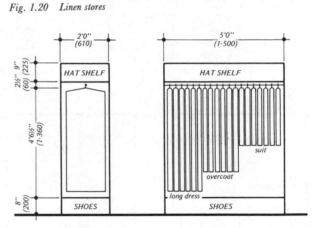

Fig. 1.21   Optimum hanging spaces for men and women

RECOMMENDED SIZES FOR BUILT-IN WARDROBES

	Homes for Today and Tomorrow	Scottish Housing Handbook
Main bedroom	No recommendation	8 ft 0 in (2·45 m) run of cupboard 2 ft 0 in (600 mm) minimum depth with 4 ft 0 in (1·20 m) of hanging rail and 4 ft 0 in (1·20 m) of shelves and drawers
Other bedrooms	2 ft 0 in (600 mm) of rail per occupier not less than 1 ft 9 in (55 mm) deep	2 ft 0 in × 2 ft 0 in (600 mm × 600 mm) wardrobe cupboard

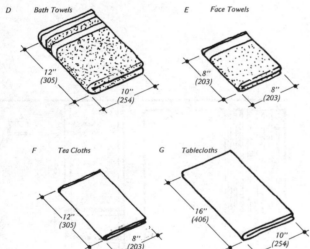

B = 2'6" (762) max.
This dimension
should always
be less than 'A'.

Fig. 1.19   Linen cupboards

BIBLIOGRAPHY

BRITISH STANDARDS INSTITUTION

Bathroom Equipment and Sanitary Appliances and Fittings

C.P. 305:1952   Sanitary appliances. Amendment P.D. 1847, Apr. 1954.

B.S. 219:1959   Soft solders. Amendments P.D. 4843, March 1963; P.D. 5087, Nov. 1963.

B.S. 441:1954   Rosin-cored solder wire, 'activated' and 'non-activated' (non-corrosive).

B.S. 504:1961   Drawn lead traps. Amendment P.D. 4448, Jan. 1962.

B.S. 1010:1959   Draw-off taps and stop valves for water services (screw-down pattern). Amendments P.D. 3493, Sept. 1959; P.D. 3739, Apr. 1960; P.D. 4367, Nov. 1961; P.D. 4767, Jan. 1963; P.D. 4867, Mar. 1963; P.D. 5225, May 1964; P.D. 5432, Jan. 1965; P.D. 5433, Jan. 1965; P.D. 5501, Mar. 1965; P.D. 5888, Aug. 1966; P.D. 6051, Mar. 1967; P.D. 6121, Apr. 1967; AMD 260, June 1969.

B.S. 1125:1969   W.C. flushing systems (including dual flush cisterns and flush pipes).

B.S. 1182:1955   Cast brass thimbles (spigot and socket) and tail pieces (for drainage connections).

B.S. 1184:1961   Copper and copper alloy traps. Amendment A.M.D. 201, Feb. 1969.

B.S. 1185:1963   Guards for underground stop valves.

B.S. 1188:1965   Ceramic wash basins and pedestals.

B.S. 1189:1961   Cast-iron baths for domestic purposes. Amendment P.D. 4534, Apr. 1962.

B.S. 1206:1945   Fireclay sinks (dimensions and workmanship) (confirmed 1954 and 1959). Amendments P.D. 330, Jan. 1952; P.D. 4644, Sept. 1962.

B.S. 1212:1953   Ballvalves (Portsmouth type) excluding floats. Amendments P.D. 1932, Aug. 1954; P.D. 2333, Nov. 1955; P.D. 2460, Apr. 1956; P.D. 3237, Jan. 1959; P.D. 3545, Nov. 1959; P.D. 5116, Jan. 1964; P.D. 5424, Jan. 1965; P.D. 5829, May 1966; P.D. 5933, Nov. 1966.

B.S. 1213:1945   Ceramic washdown w.c. pans (dimensions and workmanship). Amendments P.D. 769, Apr. 1948; P.D. 1750, Nov. 1953; P.D. 4462, Feb. 1962; P.D. 5509, Apr. 1965; A.M.D. 134, Nov. 1968; A.M.D. 443, Feb. 1970.

B.S. 1226:1945   Draining boards (confirmed 1954). Amendments P.D. 404, Oct. 1945; P.D. 1305, Dec. 1951.

B.S. 1229:1945   Fireclay wash tubs and sink sets (dimensions and workmanship). Amendment P.D. 1361, Apr. 1952.

B.S. 1244:1956   Metal sinks for domestic purposes. Amendment P.D. 6361, Mar. 1968.

B.S. 1254:1945   W.C. seats (plastics). Amendments P.D. 1415, June 1952; P.D. 5250, May 1964; P.D. 6000, Jan. 1967.

B.S. 1255:1953   Brackets and supports for lavatory basins and sinks.

B.S. 1291:1946   Ferrous traps for baths.

B.S. 1329:1956   Metal lavatory basins for domestic purposes. Amendment P.D. 5367, Oct. 1964.

B.S. 1390:1947   Sheet steel baths for domestic purposes (confirmed 1954). Amendment P.D. 772, Apr. 1948.

B.S. 1415:1955   Mixing valves (manually operated) for ablutionary and domestic purposes. Amendment P.D. 5235, May 1964.

B.S. 1876:1952   Automatic flushing cisterns for urinals (confirmed 1959). Amendment P.D. 3150, Aug. 1958.

B.S. 1968:1953   Floats for ballvalves (copper). Amendments P.D. 3220, Nov. 1958; P.D. 4667, Sept. 1962.

B.S. 2081:1954   Portable closets for use with chemicals.

B.S. 2089:1954   W.C. seats (wooden) (confirmed 1966). Amendments P.D. 1887, May 1954; P.D. 5822, Apr. 1966.

B.S. 2456:1954   Floats for ballvalves (plastics) for cold water. Amendments P.D. 2953, Jan. 1958; P.D. 3917, Sept. 1960; P.D. 6065, Mar. 1967.

B.S. 2879:1957   Draining taps (screw-down pattern). Amendment P.D. 3841, July 1960.

B.S. 3380:——   Wastes for sanitary appliances and overflows for baths.
Part 1: 1961 Wastes (excluding skeleton sink wastes) and bath overflows. Amendment P.D. 5634, Aug. 1965.
Part 2: 1962 Skeleton sink wastes.

B.S. 3402:1969   Quality of vitreous china sanitary appliances.

B.S. 3457:1962   Materials for water tap washers. Amendments P.D. 4543, Apr. 1962; P.D. 5525, May 1965.

B.S. 3943:1965   Plastics waste taps. Amendment A.M.D. 32, Aug. 1968.

B.S. 3974:——   Pipes supports.
Part 1: 1966 Components for rod-type pipe hangers for uninsulated and insulated steel and cast-iron pipes.

B.S. 4118:1967   Glossary of sanitation terms. Amendment A.M.D. 356, Oct. 1969

B.S. 4305:1968   Baths for domestic purposes made from cast acrylic sheet.

Storage Fitments and Equipment

B.S. 826:1955   Adjustable steel shelving (angle-post type). Amendment P.D. 2986, Mar. 1958.

B.S. 1292:1945   Storage fitments for living-rooms and bedrooms. Amendment P.D. 1437, July 1952.

B.S. 1396:1947   Gas meter cupboards (withdrawn).

2 INTERNAL CIRCULATION

GENERAL

Information given in this section does not relate to one particular building type, but is a general guide to the internal circulation within a building.

The following pages consist of such planning data as corridors, stairs, ramps, lifts and escalators. A list of British Standards, Codes of Practice, Design Bulletins and Building Research Station Digests pertaining to circulation, will be found at the end of the section.

Factors to be considered include the anticipated traffic flow, the direction of the flow, the position and number of entrances and exits, the illumination and the design and positioning of directional signs.

Average space allowance per person in circulation areas may be based on 1 yd² (0·8 m²) per person for general design purposes.

Table 2.1 MINIMUM AREAS PER PERSON IN VARIOUS TYPES OF BUILDING

Building type	Floor area per person ft²	m²
Theatre or similar closely spaced audience	5	0·46
Circulating gangway in large stores, supermarkets, etc.	5	0·46
Dance hall	6	0·56
Restaurant	12	1·11
Shop or showroom	50	4·64
Offices	100	9·29
Warehouse	300	27·87
Workroom	400	37·16

Figures taken from the London Building Acts (1930–39)

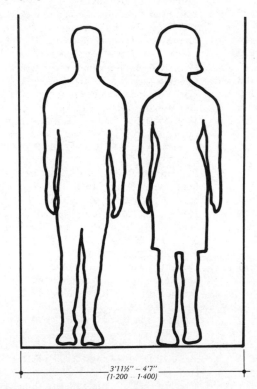

3'11½" – 4'7"
(1·200 – 1·400)

Fig. 2.1   Corridor widths for two persons passing

CORRIDORS

The design of corridors or passageways should ensure the expeditious flow of traffic, both human and vehicular.

RAMPS

Ramps, or inclined passageways, should not exceed an inclination of 20°, the ideal being 15°. The walking surface should be non-slip under all conditions. Handrails are desirable, and essential if the ramp has open sides. Where ramps lead to stairways, they should terminate with a level section, at least 3 ft (914 mm) in length.

STAIRWAYS

Definitions—National Building Regulations 1965

Common stairway means an internal, or external, stairway of steps, with straight nosings on plan, which forms part of a building and is intended for common use in connection with two or more dwellings.

Notional Width has the meaning that where a stairway contains consecutive tapered steps of differing widths, all such tapered steps shall be deemed to have a notional width equal to the width of the narrowest part of those tapered steps, measured from the side of the stairway where the treads are narrower.

Parallel step means a step, of which the nosing is parallel to the nosing of the step, or landing, next above it.

Pitch line means a notional line drawn from the floor, or landing, below a stairway, to connect the nosings of all the treads in a flight of stairs.

Private stairway means an internal, or external, stairway of steps, with straight nosings on plan, which forms part of a building and is either within a dwelling, or intended for use solely in connection with one dwelling.

Tapered step means a step, the nosing of which is not parallel to the nosing of the step, or landing, next above it.

PRIVATE STAIRWAYS

Private stairways should have a minimum clearance of 5 ft 0 in (1·52 m) and a minimum headroom of 6 ft 6 in (1·98 m). In practice, it will be found that with an angle of pitch above 39° 43 ft (13·11 m), the clearance of 5 ft 0 in (1·52 m) is critical. Every step between consecutive floors must have an equal rise and going. The rise must not exceed 8 in (203 mm), and the going must not be less than 8½ in (216 mm), with a maximum angle of pitch of 42°, nor must the sum of twice the rise, plus the going in inches, be less than 22½ in (571 mm), or more than 25 in (635 mm).

Where open-type stairways are used, without solid risers, the nosing of each tread must overlap the back edge of the tread below by at least ⅝ in (15·9 mm).

Domestic stairways should be designed to allow the movement of large items of furniture, etc.; removable balustrades can be used in suitable circumstances.

COMMON STAIRWAYS

The requirements for common stairways are generally as laid down for private stairways, but with a reduced angle of pitch of 38°. The rise of each step must not exceed 7½ in (190 mm), and the minimum tread is 9 in (229 mm). Very long, unbroken flights of stairs are dangerous, and the maximum number of risers in any one flight should, therefore, be limited to sixteen.

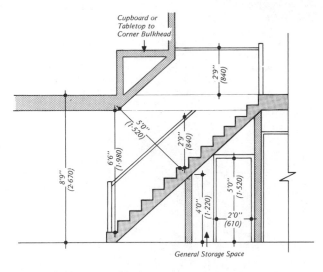

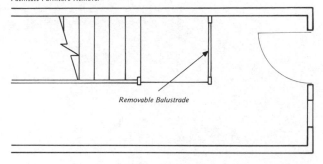

Plan of Typical Hall Showing Removable Balustrade to Facilitate Furniture Removal

Removable Balustrade

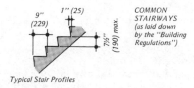

Typical Stair Profiles

Fig. 2.2 Typical key dimensions for staircases in housing

TAPERED STEPS

The National Building Regulations, 1965, allow these in both common and private stairways, provided the following rules are observed. The pitch line must be taken at a point 10½ in (266 mm) from the extremities of the width of the stairway. If the stairway is of varied width, the pitch line is taken at the 'notional width', i.e. the narrowest part of the tapered steps, measured from the narrower edge of the treads. The pitch line is located 10½ in (266 mm) from the extremities of this 'notional width'. The maximum going for tapered steps is '2 × rise + going', namely 28 in (711 mm); where the angle of taper is 10° or less the maximum going is 2 × rise + going, namely 25 in (635 mm). The minimum going should be 2 × rise + going, i.e. 22½ in (571 mm).

Table 2.2 PRIVATE AND COMMON STAIRWAYS

Stairways	Min. clearance		Min. headroom			Rise not to exceed		Going not less than		Dimensional limits for rise and going
	ft	m	ft	in	m	in	mm	in	mm	Max. angle of pitch (°)
Private	5	1·52	6	6	1·98	8	203	8½	216	42
Common	5	1·52	6	6	1·98	7½	190	9	229	38

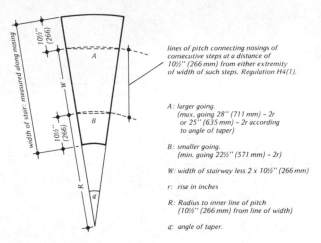

lines of pitch connecting nosings of consecutive steps at a distance of 10½'' (266 mm) from either extremity of width of such steps. Regulation H4(1).

A: larger going.
(max. going 28'' (711 mm) – 2r or 25'' (635 mm) – 2r according to angle of taper)

B: smaller going.
(min. going 22½'' (571 mm) – 2r)

W: width of stairway less 2 x 10½'' (266 mm)

r: rise in inches

R: Radius to inner line of pitch (10½'' (266 mm) from line of width)

a: angle of taper.

Fig. 2.3   Calculations for tapered steps

PUBLIC STAIRWAYS

Where these are used for the purpose of escape from a building, they should be totally enclosed with fire-resisting materials. The National Building Regulations, 1965, define such enclosures as 'protected shafts', and the provisions apply to stairshafts, lifts, escalators, or any other form of chute or shaft which enable people, things or air, to pass vertically through a building.

A 'protected shaft' may also be used for a pipe duct, or for toilet accommodation. Such an enclosure must have at least 1 hr fire resistance, and surface finishes must be satisfactory, regarding flame spread. Openings, i.e. doors, should be at least 4 ft 6 in (1·37 m) wide in the clear, and self-closing. They should open in the direction of the escape route, and swing clear of the normal passageway, to avoid reducing the width of the escape route.

Doors in stairshafts, above ground level, should have suitable fire resistance, according to the type of building, with a minimum of half an hour.

Air ducts may not pass through a stair shaft and the National Building Regulations prohibit gas or oil pipes.

Escape stairs must be well lit by natural or artificial means. The edges of the treads should be easily definable. All stairways should have adequate ventilation.

BALUSTRADES

All private and common stairways and their landings must be guarded on both sides. This protection may be in the form of a wall, screen, balustrade or railing not less than 2 ft 9 in (838 mm) in height above the pitch line in the case of a stairway, and similar protection to a height of not less than 3 ft (914 mm) is required for landings to private stairways, where these overlook the stairs. This dimension is increased to 3 ft 6 in (1·07 m) in the case of a common stairway. Balustrades must be securely fixed and be capable of taking a lateral load of 25 lb (11·34 kg) per foot run for private stairways, and 50 lb (22·68 kg) per foot run for common stairways.

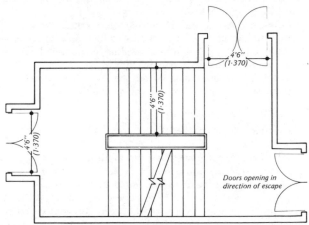

Doors opening in direction of escape

Fig. 2.4   Typical escape stair with recessed entrances (stairs in buildings used by the public)

The width of the staircase will often depend upon the maximum number of persons liable to use it for escape purposes.

width of staircase

passageway of not less than 3'0'' (914)

Preferred   Minimum

Fig. 2.5   Typical escape stair without recessed entrances

Table 2.3 RECOMMENDED MINIMUM WIDTHS OF STAIRS, SIZES OF RISERS AND TREADS

Type of use	Minimum width of stair		Min. width of tread		Max. height of rise	
			in	*mm*	*in*	*mm*
Housing	2 ft 11 in	889 mm	8½	216	8	203
Private houses	3 ft 3 in	991 mm	8½	216	8	203
Flats; entrance	3 ft 6 in	1 067 mm	9	229	7	178
Offices	3 ft 6 in for 200 persons, 4 ft 6 in for over 200 persons, plus 6 in per 100 persons over 400	1 067 mm for 200 persons, 1 372 mm for over 200 persons, plus 152 mm per 100 persons over 400	9	229	7	178
Schools	3 ft 6 in	1 067 mm	10	254	6½	165
Stores	4 ft 6 in; allow 12 in per 1 000 ft² floor area	1 372 mm; allow 305 mm per 92·90 m² floor area	10	254	6½	165
Municipal: Main	5 ft 0 in	1 524 mm	11	279	6	152
Secondary	4 ft 0 in	1 219 mm	9	229	7	178
Factories	3 ft 6 in	1 067 mm	9	229	7	178

Table 2.4 NUMBER OF RISERS AND FLIGHTS, HEIGHTS OF HANDRAILS AND HEAD CLEARANCE, ETC.

	ft	in	mm
Minimum number of risers in a flight		3	
Maximum number of risers in a flight without a landing		16	
Maximum number of risers in a flight, if there is no change between two flights		12	
Maximum number of flights without a change of direction		2	
Minimum height of handrail measured vertically from a line joining the nosings	2	9	838
Minimum height of handrail for external escape stairs	3	6	1 067
Minimum height of handrail when horizontal—(housing)	2	9	838
(public)	3	0	914
Minimum head clearance measured vertically	6	6	1 981
or measured at right angles to a line joining the nosings	5	0	1 524
Maximum width of stair without a centre handrail	5	6	1 676

LADDERS

Inclines of 50–90° involve the use of ladders, which should have flat heads where the angle of incline is between 50° and 75°, and rungs at angles of 75–90°. The average vertical distance between rungs or steps should be approximately 12 in (305 mm), with a minimum width of 18 in (457 mm) vertical (90°). Ladders exceeding 20 ft (6·10 m) in height should be provided with suitable guards to form an enclosure. Shallow ladders should be provided with balustrades, and all ladders should have suitable hand grips; in the case of ladders with rungs, the main ladder support can be used.

LIFTS

PASSENGER LIFTS

General: The National Building Regulations, 1965, specify the requirements for the construction of lift shafts. These are classified as 'protected shafts' and the requirements are outlined in the foregoing notes on stairways. Non-self-closing doors may be used in certain circumstances, such as hospitals and factories. In such cases, special fire protection must be incorporated. Lift shafts may have openings to allow cables to pass into the motor room and they must have permanent and unobstructed ventilation equal to at least 1 ft² (0·09 m²) per lift. Pipes or ducts should not be housed in lift shafts.

POSITIONING OF LIFTS

Lifts should be grouped together, wherever possible, in order to make the maximum use of lift wells and machine rooms.

Only in exceptional circumstances should the machine room for electrically operated lifts be placed anywhere but immediately above the lift well. This position usually reduces loading on the structure, is less in first costs, allows a smaller lift well for a given size of car, and reduces maintenance costs, mainly in regard to suspension rope wear and shorter lengths of rope.

An exception to this rule is the oil hydraulic lift, which is operated by a hydraulic ram which pushes the lift car up the lift shaft. This type of lift is particularly suitable for heavy loads (i.e. garage, and hospital lifts) and has a travelling speed of up to 200 ft/min (1·00 m/s) for passenger lifts, 100 ft/min (0·50 m/s) for hospital lifts, and slower speeds for heavy goods lifts.

The machine room may be located adjacent to the lift shaft, or any other convenient place remote from the lift shaft, but must be on the same level as the bottom floor served. A roof-level motor room is, therefore, not required.

SOUND TRANSMISSION

The lift wheels should not back on to adjoining walls of rooms, in which people have to live and work. Everything possible should be done to reduce sound transmission from halls and lobbies; in addition, great care should be taken to insulate the lift machinery at source.

VENTILATION AND LIGHTING

Every lift car should be adequately illuminated and ventilated, and provided with a suitable escape hatch in case of emergencies.

FIRE PROTECTION

As with staircases, lifts generally have to be enclosed for their full height with fire-resisting material and have fire-resisting doors or fire shutters. The lift well should be carried up, if possible, above the roof and be vented to the open air through a louvred smoke vent. Machine rooms should be permanently ventilated by means of high-level air outlets and low-level air intakes and, if possible, should have natural lighting, without the necessity of leaving open access doors to roofs, when repairs or maintenance work are being carried out.

GENERAL CALCULATIONS

The size of a lift, the speed and its number is determined by the type of building in which it is to be installed.

To Calculate the Approximate Number and Size of Lifts

Calculation should be based on total estimated population, the desired waiting interval (from 20 to 60 s*, according to the type of building and its importance), the number of upper floors and any special services which may be needed. Specialist advice should be sought as the calculations are extremely complex.

NUMBER OF PERSONS IN A GIVEN TYPE OF BUILDING

Offices: general offices, one person per 60 ft² (5·57 m²); private offices, one person per 80 ft² (7·43 m²).
Hotels: one person per 100–150 ft² (9·29–13·94 m²).
Flats: one person per 250 ft² (23·23 m²).
Department stores, peak load: one person per 25 ft² (2·32 m²).

NORMAL SPEEDS FOR LIFTS IN A GIVEN TYPE OF BUILDING

Flats:
Low- or medium-rent, up to eight floors — 100 ft/min (0·50 m/s).
More than eight floors — 150–300 ft/min (0·75–1·50 m/s).

Offices:
Up to five floors — 100 ft/min (0·50 m/s).
Up to eight floors — 150–200 ft/min (0·75–1·00 m/s).
Up to twenty floors — 300–500 ft/min (1·50–2·50 m/s).
More than twenty floors — 500–800 ft/min (2·50–4·06 m/s).

Small stores — 150 ft/min (0·75 m/s).

Department stores — 300–500 ft/min (1·50–2·50 m/s).

Hospitals (for bed lifts) — 100–200 ft/min (0·50–1·00 m/s) (higher speeds are being considered for multi-storey hospitals).

ALLOWANCE FOR PASSENGERS ENTERING THE LIFT

One passenger to enter a lift — 2 s; allowance at each landing — 8 s; allowance at ground, or major floor — 20 s.

For calculations it is normal to expect a time interval between trips of 30 s and two-thirds the number of persons per floor.

CONSIDERATIONS IN SELECTING A LIFT

1 Service
2 Number of lifts required, load and number of persons
3 Speed
4 Travel in metres, number of floors served; entrances required
5 Type of equipment and electrical supply
6 Type of lift control required
7 Position of machine room
8 Size of well; type of well construction and enclosure; type of guides
9 Safety gear; buffers
10 Type of doors to car entrance and landing; architraves; locks
11 Size of car inside; platform size; finish of car
12 Type of car and landing indicators

*s = second

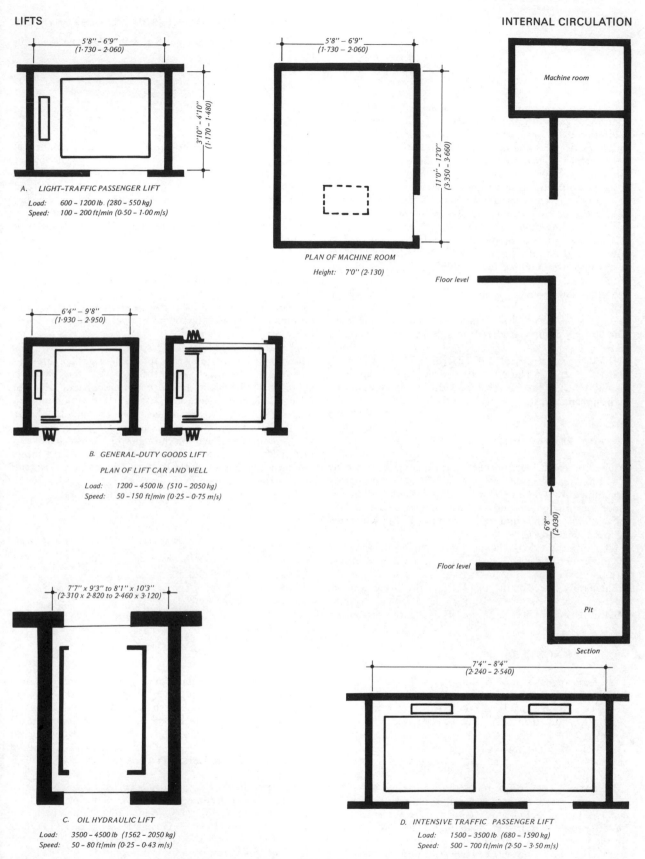

5'8'' – 6'9''
(1·730 – 2·060)

3'10'' – 4'10''
(1·170 – 1·480)

A.   LIGHT–TRAFFIC PASSENGER LIFT

Load: 600 – 1200 lb. (280 – 550 kg)
Speed: 100 – 200 ft/min (0·50 – 1·00 m/s)

5'8'' – 6'9''
(1·730 – 2·060)

11'0'' – 12'0''
(3·350 – 3·660)

PLAN OF MACHINE ROOM
Height: 7'0'' (2·130)

Machine room

Floor level

6'8''
(2·030)

Floor level

Pit

Section

6'4'' – 9'8''
(1·930 – 2·950)

B.   GENERAL–DUTY GOODS LIFT

PLAN OF LIFT CAR AND WELL

Load: 1200 – 4500 lb (510 – 2050 kg)
Speed: 50 – 150 ft/min (0·25 – 0·75 m/s)

7'7'' x 9'3'' to 8'1'' x 10'3''
(2·310 x 2·820 to 2·460 x 3·120)

C.   OIL HYDRAULIC LIFT

Load: 3500 – 4500 lb (1562 – 2050 kg)
Speed: 50 – 80 ft/min (0·25 – 0·43 m/s)

7'4'' – 8'4''
(2·240 – 2·540)

D.   INTENSIVE TRAFFIC PASSENGER LIFT

Load: 1500 – 3500 lb (680 – 1590 kg)
Speed: 500 – 700 ft/min (2·50 – 3·50 m/s)

Fig. 2.6 Types of lift for various buildings. Lift well sizes to vary with speed, type and capacity of lift

17

ESCALATORS

GENERAL

Escalators may be used in any building where there is a continuous heavy traffic flow, such as department stores, exhibition halls, race courses, holiday camps, stations, office buildings, airports and open streets. Escalators are particularly useful in office buildings where the hall floor is at a different level from the street.

New manufacturing techniques allow escalators to be made in a complete factory-tested unit, and it is usually possible to deliver the machine complete, saving time and expense in site erection and building attendance. To take advantage of this method, the site preparation should be completed in advance and an opening of about 11 ft² (1·02 m²) left for access into the building, installation usually being carried out at night.

Speed—The normal speed is 90–100 ft/min (0·46–0·50 m/s).

Angle of incline—30–35° angle escalators are available. The 35° type is not considered suitable for rises of over 20 ft (6·10 m).

Widths—Nominal widths are: 2 ft (610 mm), 3 ft (914 mm) and 4 ft (1·22 m). The 2 ft (610 mm) width is seldom used nowadays, while the 4 ft (1·22 m) width is only necessary for highest traffic density.

FIRE PROTECTION

Where fire regulations limit the cubic capacity of any section of a building to 250 000 ft³ (7079·20 m³), the escalators, being open from floor to floor, must be enclosed within fireproof construction, cutting off the escalator circulation from the remainder of the building at each floor, similar to methods adopted for staircases.

The important design factor is the point of intersection of the plane of the steps and the floor levels, on which the whole setting-out on the part of the engineers is based. The motors are generally placed on the top of each flight, but the amount of space, occupied below the floor level with usual floor heights, permits of placing showcases or counters beneath.

PATERNOSTERS

These are an early type of lift, still widely used on the Continent, which comprises a continuously moving chain of lift cars, each capable of taking two people at a speed of 50–60 ft/min (0·25–0·31 m/s). Cars are spaced approximately 10–14 ft (3·05–4·27 m) apart, from floor to floor. The well to house a typical paternoster installation is approximately 8 ft 6 in (2·59 m) wide by 5 ft 3 in (1·60 m) deep.

No doors are needed to either cars or shaft and there is no passenger control. Paternosters are claimed to have a low installation and maintenance cost, but are not suitable for buildings over about seven floors high. They are not practicable for elderly or infirm people, or where wheeled chairs are likely to be encountered. They tend to be noisy and, as the lift shaft has no cut-off at floor levels, the risk of smoke

and fire-spread is greater than with a conventional lift installation.

PASSENGER CONVEYORS

GENERAL

Passenger conveyors are designed to carry large numbers of people in a horizontal, or near, horizontal plan, where other methods of transportation are too costly or not practicable.

As both approach and landing surface are continuous, and special comb plates register with the grooved belt, the conveyor is safe and convenient for all classes of users, i.e. wheelchair, push-chair, pram, etc. The usual speed is 120 ft/min (0·61 m/s).

CIRCULATION FOR THE DISABLED

The movement of disabled persons around buildings requires adequate space, and the following points need to be borne in mind.

The standard Ministry of Health wheelchair, which is self-propelled and folding, occupies a floor area of approximately 7 ft² (0·65 m²), i.e. 3 ft 5 in × 2 ft 1 in (1041 × 635 mm). This means that a minimum corridor width of 2 ft 6 in (762 mm) is necessary, with a preferred minimum of 3 ft (914 mm). Electric wheelchairs are smaller, being 2 ft 1 in × 1 ft 9 in (635 × 533 mm).

The minimum dimension through which a wheelchair can turn a 90° corner necessitates a width of 3 ft (914 mm). Special requirements apply to those who can only use one arm for the operation of vehicles.

Passageways for disabled persons are as follows:

Type	Minimum width			Preferred minimum width		
	ft	in	mm	ft	in	mm
Stick user	2	4	711	2	6	762
Crutches	3	0	914	–	–	–
Walking aids	2	6	762	–	–	–

Small differences in floor levels should be avoided where there are disabled people. Steps less than 3 in (80 mm) are dangerous. Single and double steps should always be avoided. Stair risers should not be more than 7 in (178 mm) and treads not less than 10 in (254 mm). (Ministry of Housing and Local Government Design Bulletin recommends a going of 11·4 in (290 mm) and a rise of 6·6 in (167 mm). This gives an incline of 30°.)

All stairs should have handrails on both sides. No ramps for wheelchair users should exceed an incline of 1:12 (4½°), with a minimum width of 3 ft 6 in (1·07 m) and a preferred minimum of 4 ft (1·22 m). No ramp should be longer than 30 ft (9·14 m), with a preferred maximum length of 20 ft (6·10 m). Short ramps may have a gradient of 1:10 (5½°), but these should not exceed 8 ft (2·44 m) in length.

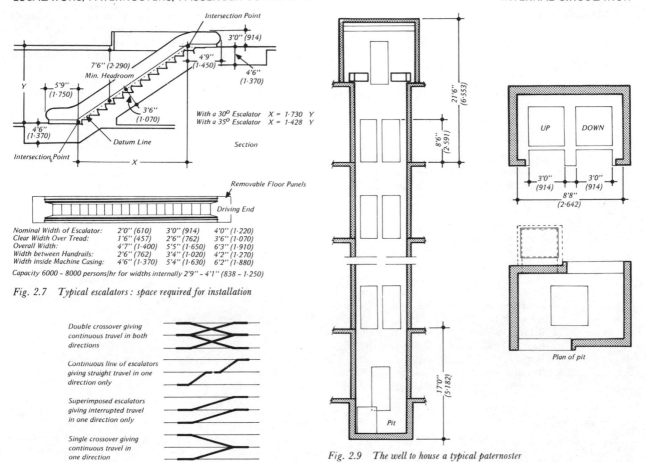

With a 30° Escalator   X = 1·730 Y
With a 35° Escalator   X = 1·428 Y

Section

Nominal Width of Escalator:	2'0" (610)	3'0" (914)	4'0" (1·220)
Clear Width Over Tread:	1'6" (457)	2'6" (762)	3'6" (1·070)
Overall Width:	4'7" (1·400)	5'5" (1·650)	6'3" (1·910)
Width between Handrails:	2'6" (762)	3'4" (1·020)	4'2" (1·270)
Width inside Machine Casing:	4'6" (1·370)	5'4" (1·630)	6'2" (1·880)

Capacity 6000 – 8000 persons/hr for widths internally 2'9" – 4'1" (838 – 1·250)

Fig. 2.7   Typical escalators : space required for installation

Double crossover giving continuous travel in both directions

Continuous line of escalators giving straight travel in one direction only

Superimposed escalators giving interrupted travel in one direction only

Single crossover giving continuous travel in one direction

Fig. 2.8   Types of escalators

Fig. 2.9   The well to house a typical paternoster

Fig. 2.10   Passenger conveyors

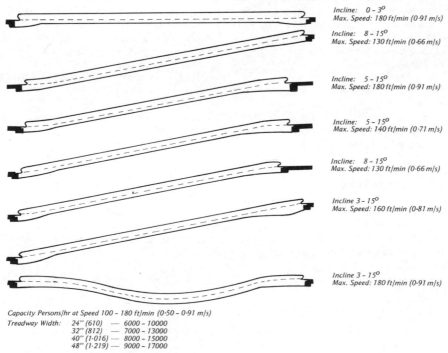

Incline: 0 – 3°
Max. Speed: 180 ft/min (0·91 m/s)

Incline: 8 – 15°
Max. Speed: 130 ft/min (0·66 m/s)

Incline: 5 – 15°
Max. Speed: 180 ft/min (0·91 m/s)

Incline: 5 – 15°
Max. Speed: 140 ft/min (0·71 m/s)

Incline: 8 – 15°
Max. Speed: 130 ft/min (0·66 m/s)

Incline 3 – 15°
Max. Speed: 160 ft/min (0·81 m/s)

Incline 3 – 15°
Max. Speed: 180 ft/min (0·91 m/s)

Capacity Persons/hr at Speed 100 – 180 ft/min (0·50 – 0·91 m/s)

Treadway Width:	24" (610)	—	6000 – 10000
	32" (812)	—	7000 – 13000
	40" (1·016)	—	8000 – 15000
	48" (1·219)	—	9000 – 17000

19

BIBLIOGRAPHY

BRITISH STANDARDS INSTITUTION

General Series

B.S. 205:—— Glossary of terms used in electrical engineering.
Part 7: 1943, Section 9. Lightning and surge phenomena.
Part 7: 1943, Section 10. Miscellaneous applications (including lifts, welding, X-rays, electromedical terms). Amendments P.D. 2187, Apr. 1955; P.D. 2188, May 1955.

B.S. 585:1956 Wood stairs.
B.S. 2655:—— Lifts, escalators, passenger conveyors and paternosters.
Part 1: 1970. General requirements for electric, hydraulic and hand-powered lifts.
Part 2: 1959. Single-speed polyphase induction motors for driving lifts. Amendments P.D. 3587, Dec. 1959; P.D. 3723, March 1960, A.M.D. 300, July, 1969.
Part 3: 1965. Outline dimensions. Amendment A.M.D. 301, July 1969.
B.S. 6977:1969 Braided travelling cables for electric and hydraulic lifts.

Codes of Practice

C.P. 114:1957 Structural use of reinforced concrete in buildings. Amendment Feb. 1965 (available separately ref. P.D. 5463) reset and reprinted including amendment No. 1, Feb. 1965.
C.P. 407.101:1951 Electric lifts for passengers, goods and service.
C.P. 407.301:1950 Hand-power lifts for passengers, goods and service.

MINISTRY OF HOUSING AND LOCAL GOVERNMENT

Design Bulletin No. 3, Part 2: Service cores in high flats. The selection and planning of passenger lifts.

BUILDING RESEARCH STATION

Digest No. 7 (second series). Noise in the home. (Appliances and installations: bathroom and w.c. plumbing; water hammer; storage tanks; noise transmission along pipes; central heating systems; lifts and other equipment; domestic power appliances; acoustic absorbents. Structural noises; squeaking floors and stairs; slamming doors; rain on metal roofs; noise transmission through floors.)
Digest No. 43 (second series). Safety in domestic buildings—1. (Precautions that can be taken in the design of domestic buildings to minimise the risk of accidents to occupants. The layout of kitchens and their equipment. Heating installations: the hazards of solid fuel; electricity, gas, portable oil heaters. Electrical installations, gas installations, laundry provisions, bathrooms, lifts.)

ACTS OF PARLIAMENT

Factories Act, 1961.

OTHER PUBLICATIONS

Staircases, Lifts, Elevators

ANNETT, F. A., *Elevators: Electric and Electrohydraulic Elevators, Escalators, Moving Sidewalks and Ramps*, McGraw-Hill, New York (1960)
B.W.M.A. Guide to Stair Design, British Woodwork Manufacturers Association (May 1965)
BUCKLEY, A., *Goods Lifts and Modern Industry*, Sawell Publications Ltd, London (1960)
CORNS, J. A., *Staircase Manual*, Cleaver-Hume, London (1959)
GATZ, KONRAD et al. (editors), *Entrances and Staircases*, Architect's 'Detail' Library, published for *The Architect and Building News* by Iliffe Books, London (1967)
KNIGHT, T. L., and DUCK, A. E., 'The Costs of Lifts in Multi-storey Flats for Local Authorities', reprinted from the *Chartered Surveyor* (March 1962)
MINISTRY OF PUBLIC BUILDING AND WORKS, *The Building Regulations, 1965 (Technical Memoranda: Fire, Stairs, Space and General Index)*, H.M.S.O. (1966)
MINISTRY OF TECHNOLOGY, *Lifts in Large Buildings:* Symposium held at the Building Research Station on 15th June 1966, Ministry of Technology B.R.S. (1966)
PHILLIPS, R. S., *Electric Lifts: A Manual on the Current Practice in the Design, Installation, Working and Maintenance of Lifts*, 5th edn, Pitman, London (1966)
STEINHOFEL, OTTO, *Holztreppen (Wooden Stairs)*, Handbook for the Construction of Wooden Stairs, George D. W. Callwey, Munich (English and French translation from p. 51 onwards) (1960)
YUKER, HAROLD, E., COHN, ALFRED and FELDMAN, MARTIN A., *The Development and Effects of an Inexpensive Elevator for Eliminating Architectural Barriers in Public Buildings*, Nempsted (1966)

3 EXTERNAL CIRCULATION, INCLUDING TRANSPORT

GENERAL

This section is concerned with external circulation and deals mainly with roads and the types of vehicles that use them.

TRANSPORT

The information deals with sizes and loading of private, commercial and public service vehicles. Turning circles and various layouts for parking are also suggested.

There are several Acts of Parliament and Statutory Regulations which relate to the subject, and these are listed, together with other relevant publications, at the end of the Section.

PUBLIC SERVICE, COMMERCIAL AND PRIVATE VEHICLES

LENGTH LIMITS

Table 3.1 LENGTH LIMITS

Type of vehicle	Max. length (a)		
	ft	in	m
Goods vehicles:			
4-wheeler	36	1	11
6- or 8-wheeler	36	1	11
Articulated (b)	49	2½	15
Trailer (c)	22	11½	7(e)
Trailer (c) and (d)	39	4¼	12(e)
Public service vehicles:			
All types	39	4¼	12

* Each point of law is identified by reference to the appropriate Act, Order or Regulation. For example 321/69/3(1) means sub-paragraph 1, Article 3 (for Orders) or Regulation 3 (for Regulations) of Statutory Instrument No. 321 of 1969. In succeeding references to the same Orders or Regulations in the same or following sentences, the references are often abbreviated to, for example, [3(1)].

(a) Overall length excludes any driving mirror, starting handle, any hood when down, any Post Office letter box (1 ft (305 mm) allowed), any telescopic fog lamp when extended, any ladder forming part of a turntable fire escape fixed to a vehicle, any container to hold a seal issued for Customs' clearance, and any snow-plough fixed in front of a vehicle [321/69/3(1)].*

(b) There is no overall length limit for an articulated vehicle constructed and normally used for the conveyance of indivisible loads of exceptional length. This is subject to the condition that all the wheels of the vehicle must be equipped with pneumatic tyres or, if solid tyred, the speed of the vehicle must not exceed 12 mile/h (19·30 km/h) [321/69/7(1) Proviso]. 'Indivisible' means a load which cannot without undue expense or risk be divided into two or more loads for conveyance on a road [3(1)].

(c) Excluding trailers constructed and normally used to carry indivisible loads of exceptional length, land implements, all semi-trailers, broken-down vehicles, and trolley vehicles in course of construction or delivery. Nor does the limitation apply to any trailer which is a drying or mixing plant for the production of asphalt or bitumen or tar macadam and used mainly for the construction, repair or maintenance of roads, or to any road planing machine so used, provided the overall length of vehicle and trailer does not in any case exceed 60 ft (18·28 m) [321/69/60(2)].

(d) The 12-metre trailer length applies to trailers with four or more wheels where the distance between the area of contact with the road of the foremost and rearmost wheels is not less than three-fifths of the trailer's overall length and provided that the unladen weight of the drawing vehicle is 2 tons or more [321/69/60(1) Proviso].

(e) Excluding drawbar and drawbar fittings [321/69/60(3)].

WIDTHS

The overall width of a locomotive must not exceed 2·75 m [321/69/34]; a motor tractor, 2·50 m [39]; a heavy motor-car, 2·50 m [43]; and a motor-car, 2·50 m [48]. Public service vehicles may be 2·50 m wide.

HEIGHTS

The maximum height of a public service vehicle is 15 ft (4·57 m) [321/69/8].

No height limit is laid down for goods vehicles or their loads, but the Ministry of Transport has fixed 16 ft (4·87 m) as the minimum clearance space underneath bridges over roads.

LADEN WEIGHT LIMITS [321/69/68 to 74 and 7th Sched.]

Table 3.2 LADEN WEIGHT LIMITS FOR PLATED GOODS VEHICLES*

Non-articulated heavy motor-cars, motor-cars, and trailers	On one axle Tons (a)	Distance apart of axles	Total laden weight Tons (d) (e)
2 axles	10(b) 9(c)	10 ft 8 in (3·25 m) but less than 12 ft (3·65 m)	15
2 axles	,, ,,	12 ft (3·65 m) or more	16
3 axles	,, ,,	18 ft (5·48 m) or more	22
4 axles	,, ,,	23 ft (7·00 m) but less than 26 ft (7·92 m)	26
4 axles	,, ,,	26 ft (7·92 m) or more	28
Articulated vehicles			
3 axles	,, ,,	Under 18 ft (5·48 m)	20
3 axles	,, ,,	18 ft (5·48 m) or more	24
4 axles	,, ,,	Under 23 ft (7·00 m)	24
4 axles	,, ,,	23 ft (7·00 m) but less than 26 ft (7·92 m)	26
4 axles	,, ,,	26 ft (7·92 m) but less than 32 ft (9·75 m)	28
4 axles	,, ,,	32 ft (9·75 m) but less than 38 ft (11·58 m)	30
4 axles	,, ,,	38 ft (11·58 m) or more	32
more than 4 axles	,, ,,	under 23 ft (7·00 m)	24
more than 4 axles	,, ,,	23 ft (7·00 m) but less than 26 ft (7·92 m)	26
more than 4 axles	,, ,,	26 ft (7·92 m) but less than 29 ft 6 in (8·99 m)	28
more than 4 axles	,, ,,	29 ft 6 in (8·99 m) but less than 32 ft (9·75 m)	30
more than 4 axles	,, ,,	32 ft (9·75 m) or more	32

* Many goods vehicles have to be plated and Ministry of Transport plates must indicate the gross weight for each vehicle.

Table 3.3 LADEN WEIGHT LIMITS FOR UNPLATED GOODS VEHICLES

	On one axle (a)	Total laden weight
4-wheeler	9 tons	14 tons
6-wheeler	9 tons	20 tons
8-wheeler	9 tons	24 tons
Trailer (four wheels or fewer)	9 tons	14 tons
Vehicle and trailer (d) (e) (f)	—	24 tons
Vehicle and trailer with power-assisted brakes	—	32 tons
Articulated (2-wheeled semi-trailer)	—	20 tons
Articulated (semi-trailer with four or more wheels)	—	24 tons

(a) Refers to two-wheeled axles [321/69/71, 72]; where there are more than two wheels in line across the vehicle or trailer chassis, the weight on all these wheels must not exceed 11 tons [75]. Two wheels are counted as one if their centres of contact with the road are less than 18 in (457 mm) apart [3(5)].

(b) Twin pneumatic tyres (with their centres of contact with the road not less than 12 in (305 mm) apart) or a wide tyre (with an area of contact with the road of at least 12 in (305 mm)) must be fitted.

(c) This axle weight limit applies when tyre equipment does not conform to (b) [321/69/71(2) and 72(3)].

(d) A plated vehicle drawing an unplated trailer cannot take advantage of the plated total laden weight scale [321/69/71(2) Proviso].

(e) The total laden weight of a trailer which has only a parking brake and overrun brakes must not exceed 3½ tons [321/69/72(4)].

(f) These figures are for combined weights; vehicle and trailer must still comply with requirements given above [71, 72]. The total weight of all trailers, laden or unladen, drawn by a locomotive (other than trailers not complying with C. and U. Regulations and used under Special Types Orders) must not exceed 40 tons [321/69/69].

The maximum laden 'axle' weight on single front wheel is 4½ tons for an unplated [71(1)] and 5 tons for a plated goods vehicle [71(2)].

Table 3.4 LADEN WEIGHT LIMITS FOR PUBLIC SERVICE VEHICLES [321/69/70]

	On one axle	Distance apart of axles	Total laden weight
(a) Prior 1968	10 tons	10 ft 8 in (3·25 m) but less than 12 ft (3·65 m)	15 tons
(b) Post 1968 (c) Temporarily imported		12 ft (3·65 m) or more	16 tons
(d) Other p.s.vs	9 tons	—	14 tons

(a) A p.s.v. in the heavy motor-car or motor-car class registered before January 1, 1968, with a main brake efficiency of at least 50% and a second brake, operated independently or as applied on a failure in a split braking system, with an efficiency of not less than 25%.

(b) A p.s.v. in heavy motor-car or motor-car class registered on or after January 1, 1968.

(c) A temporarily imported vehicle is a p.s.v. (heavy motor-car or motor-car) brought temporarily into Great Britain which is not registered, does not necessarily conform to specific C. and U. Regulations, and has brakes with efficiences detailed in (a) above.

(d) Other p.s.vs in the heavy motor-car class which are not included in (a), (b) or (c).

Laden weight of p.s.v. is total of vehicle with water, oil and fuel, plus 140 lb (63·50 kg) per seat (and in the case of 'standee' vehicles registered after December 31, 1954, an additional 140 lb (63·50 kg) for each standing passenger in excess of eight) and 140 lb (63·50 kg) each for the driver and conductor (if carried) [321/69/70(3)].

DRIVES AND TURNING CIRCLES

A commercial vehicle must be able to make a complete turn without reversing.

Single driveways must accommodate ordinary motor vehicles without the possibility of their having to reverse.

The legal maximum turning circles for public service vehicles are: Up to 65 ft 0 in (19·81 m) for 27 ft 0 in (8·22 m) length or under. Up to 71 ft 0 in (21·64 m) for over 27 ft 0 in (8·22 m) but not exceeding 36 ft 0 in (10·97 m) in length. Up to 78 ft 0 in (23·77 m) for over 36 ft 0 in (10·97 m) in length.

Table 3.5 gives the turning circles and weights for various vehicles; for private cars the minimum turning radius is 17 ft 6 in (5·33 m) to outside the roadway. Wherever possible a minimum of 25 ft 0 in (7·62 m) should be allowed for road

curves to reduce the risk of damage to kerbs, etc. Drives should not be less than 8 ft 0 in (2·44 m) wide, with a minimum gate width of 7 ft 9 in (2·36 m) in the clear.

Drives should be designed to take a minimum load of 2 tons (2·03 tonnes) and heavy-duty manhole covers, gully gratings, etc., should be used. A camber of $\frac{1}{2}$ in (12·70 mm) to each foot width, between the centre and edge of the roadway, should be provided. On private gravel drives, two lines of hard surfacing at approximately (4 ft 6 in (1·37 m) centres are adequate to take the track of the average motor vehicle. The average track width of a commercial vehicle is approximately 4 ft 8 in (1·42 m). The maximum gradient for a drive should not exceed 1:12 and this should terminate on a level area. A car washing space should be drained to a gully and should be a minimum of 10 ft 0 in wide × 20 ft 0 in (3·05 × 6·10 m) long.

Table 3.5 SIZES, TURNING CIRCLES AND WEIGHTS OF PRIVATE CARS: SELECTED DATA

Make of model	Wheelbase			Overall length			Overall width			Overall height			Turning circle			Weights (approx.) (unladen with petrol and water)	
	ft	in	m	ft	in	m	ft	in	m	ft	in	m	ft	in	m	lb	kg
Sunbeam Imp	6	10	2·08	11	7	3·53	5	0¼	1·52	4	4½	1·32	31	6	9·60	1625	737·1
Hillman Husky	6	10	2·08	11	8½	3·56	5	0¼	1·52	4	10½	1·47	30	6	9·30	1662	753·9
Singer Gazelle	8	2½	2·49	14	0	4·27	5	3½	1·60	4	8	1·42	34	0	10·36	2034	922·6
Hillman Imp	6	10	2·08	11	7	3·53	5	0¼	1·52	4	4½	1·32	30	6	9·30	1560	707·6
Sunbeam Rapier	8	2½	2·49	14	6½	4·42	5	4¾	1·63	4	7	1·40	34	0	10·36	2276	1032·4
Rover 2000	8	7	2·62	14	10	4·52	5	6	1·68	4	7	1·40	31	6	9·60	2770 with 5 gal petrol (22·73 l)	1256·6
Hillman Minx	8	2½	2·49	14	0	4·27	5	3½	1·60	4	8	1·42	34	0	10·36	2033	922·0
Humber Sceptre	8	2½	2·49	14	1½	4·29	5	4¾	1·63	4	8	1·42	34	0	10·36	2187	992·0
Mini 1275 GT	6	8	2·03	10	0¼	3·06	4	7½	1·40	4	5	1·35	28	6	8·69	1456	660·4
Hillman Hunter	8	2½	2·49	14	1½	4·29	5	3½	1·60	4	8	1·42	34	0	10·36	2036	923·5
Rolls Royce Phantom V	12	0	3·66	19	10	6·05	6	7	2·01	5	9	1·75	48	9	14·86	4368	1981·3

Table 3.6 SIZE, TURNING CIRCLE AND WEIGHT OF FIRE APPLIANCE

Make	Wheelbase			Overall length			Overall width			Overall height			Turning circle	Weight (laden with 100 gal (454·60 l) water) with fire-escape
	ft	in	m	ft	in	m	ft	in	m	ft	in	m		
Fire appliance	12	6	3·81	28	0	8·53	7	6	2·29	10	9	3·28	Under 55 ft (16·76 m)	9 ton 5 cwt (9·40 t)
														Unladen weight
														5 ton 6 cwt 2 qr (5·41 t)

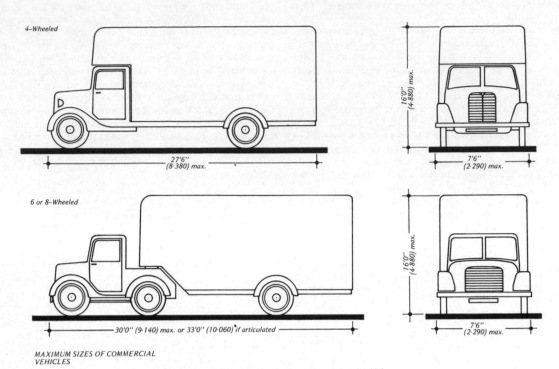

MAXIMUM SIZES OF COMMERCIAL
VEHICLES

Fig. 3.1a   Maximum sizes of commercial vehicles

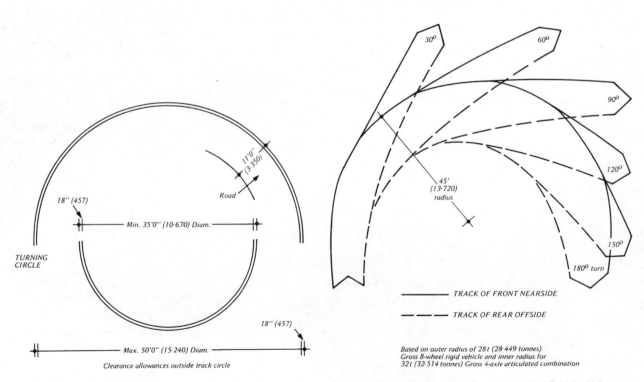

Fig. 3.1b   Turning circle for commercial vehicles

Fig. 3.2   Turning circle diagram for maximum-sized British vehicles

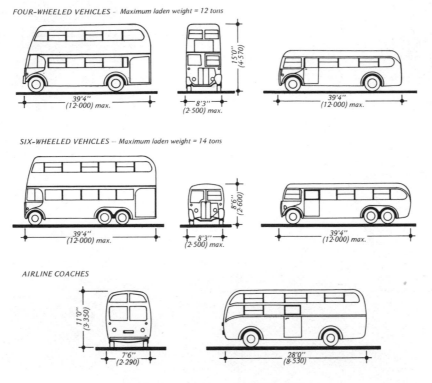

FOUR-WHEELED VEHICLES – Maximum laden weight = 12 tons

15'0''
(4·570)

39'4''
(12·000) max.

8'3''
(2·500) max.

39'4''
(12·000) max.

SIX-WHEELED VEHICLES – Maximum laden weight = 14 tons

39'4''
(12·000) max.

8'6''
(2·600)

8'3''
(2·500) max.

39'4''
(12·000) max.

AIRLINE COACHES

11'0''
(3·350)

7'6''
(2·290)

28'0''
(8·530)

TURNING CIRCLE FOR PUBLIC SERVICE VEHICLES

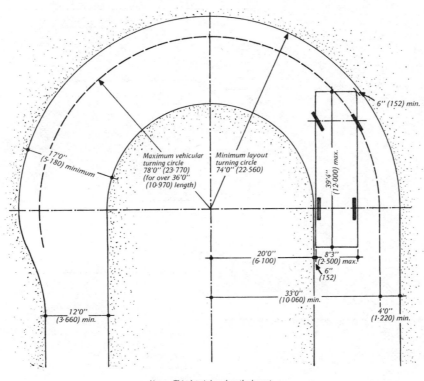

6'' (152) min.

7'0''
(5·180) minimum

Maximum vehicular
turning circle
78'0'' (23·770)
(for over 36'0''
(10·970) length)

Minimum layout
turning circle
74'0'' (22·560)

39'4''
(12·000) max.

20'0''
(6·100)

8'3''
(2·500) max.

6''
(152)

33'0''
(10·060) min.

12'0''
(3·660) min.

4'0''
(1·220) min.

Note: This data is based on the largest
Public-service vehicle in use

Fig. 3.3   Details of public service vehicles

MOTOR CYCLES

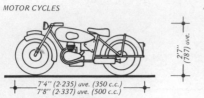

Fig. 3.4 *Average sizes of motor cycles*

SIZES OF MOTOR CYCLES: SELECTED DATA

Make	Wheelbase		Turning circle		
	in	mm	ft	in	m
Royal Enfield Bullet,					
500 c.c.	54	1372	12	9	3·886
Velocette Mac	52½	1333	16	0	4·877
B.S.A. B31	56	1422	14	3	4·343
Ariel Red Hunter,					
350 c.c.	56	1422	14	4	4·369
Norton ES2	56½	1435	16	6	5·029
Triumph Speed Twin	55½	1409	15	6	4·724
B.S.A. B33	54½	1384	15	0	4·572

Storage of motor cycles: racks at 3 ft 0 in centres

SIDECAR OUTFITS

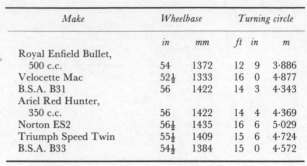

Fig. 3.5 *Average sizes of sidecar outfits*

SIDECAR OUTFITS: SELECTED DATA

Make	Turning circles				
	Left hand			Right hand	
	ft	in	m	ft	in	m
Norton 19S						
Canterbury Carmobile	14	6	4·420	19	0	5·791
Ariel Huntmaster						
Watsonian Ascot	15	4	4·674	18	8	5·690
Ariel VB						
Watsonian Maxstoke	14	9	4·496	19	0	5·791
Royal Enfield Meteor						
Canterbury Victor	14	9	4·496	20	6	6·248

SCOOTERS

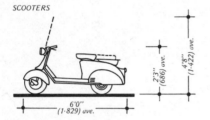

Fig. 3.6 *Average sizes of scooters*

SCOOTERS: SELECTED DATA

Make	Wheelbase		Turning circle		
	in	mm	ft	in	m
Progress 200 c.c.	55	1397	—		—
B.S.A. Dandy	45	1143	—		—
Lambretta 150 c.c.	50½	1282	—		—
Vespa 145 c.c.	46	1168	—		—
N.S.U. Prima	49½	1257	9	7	2·921
Zundapp Bella	51½	1308	13	6	4·115

MINIATURE CARS

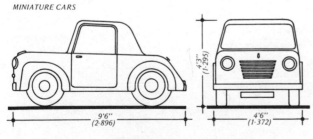

Fig. 3.7 *Average sizes of miniature cars*

MINIATURE CARS: SELECTED DATA

Make	Wheelbase			Turning circle		
	ft	in	mm	ft	in	m
Astra	6	2	1880	22	0	6·706
A.C. Petite	6	0	1829	—		—
Fairthorpe Atomota	6	9	2057	27	0	8·230
Goggomobil Regent 300	5	10¾	1800	24	6	7·468
Isetta 300 Standard	4	10	1473	30	0	9·144
Reliant Regal	6	2	1880	24	0	7·315

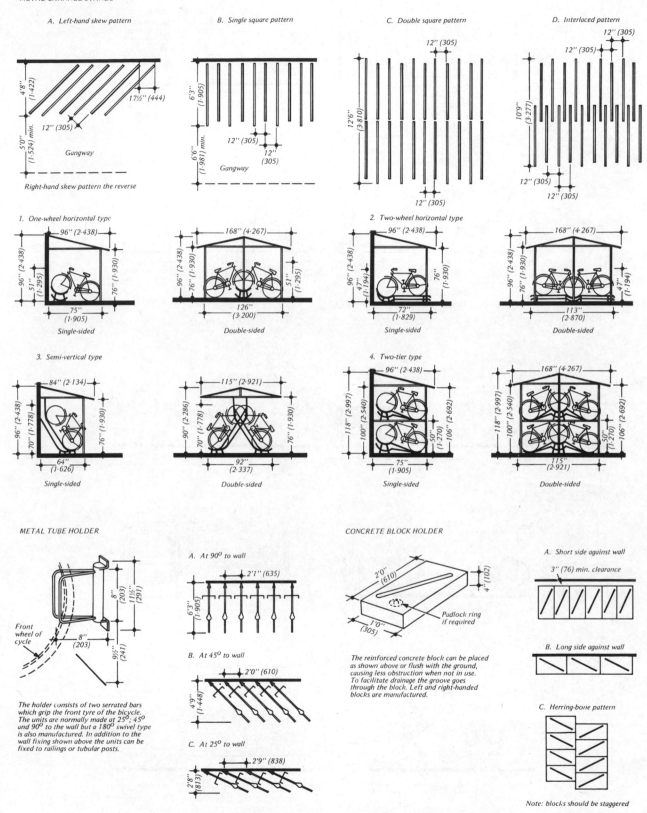

Fig. 3.8   Bicycle storage and parking: details of sheds, stands, etc.

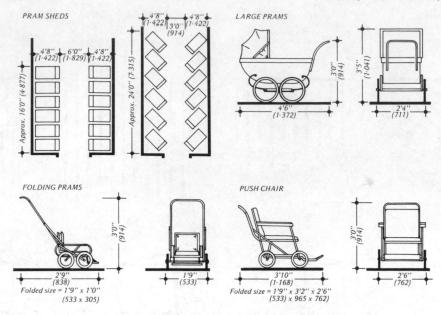

Fig. 3.9 Details of pram sheds, prams and push chairs

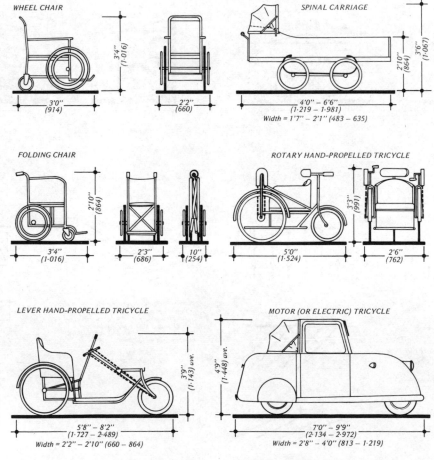

Fig. 3.10 Details of disabled persons vehicles

PARKING AREAS

The average private car requires a space of 8 ft 0 in × 16 ft 0 in (2·44 × 4·87 m) for comfortable parking, and a distance of 20 ft (6·10 m) should be allowed between rows of parked cars. Fig. 3.11 shows various alternative car parking layouts.

CAR PARKING STANDARDS

OFFICES AND SHOWROOMS

One car space per 2000 ft² (185·81 m²) of gross floor space should be allowed.

INDUSTRIAL BUILDINGS

With factory and office combined, two car spaces should be allowed for a gross floor area under 2500 ft² (232·26 m²) and three car spaces for a gross floor area between 2500 and 5000 ft² (232·26 and 464·52 m²). With combined or separate office space where the gross floor area is over 5000 ft² (464·52 m²) two car spaces basically, plus one space for every 2000 ft² (185·81 m²) of offices, and one space for every 5000 ft² (464·52 m²) of factory area should be allowed.

COMMERCIAL BUILDINGS

One lorry space of 500 ft² (46·45 m²) should be allowed for every 5000 ft² (464·52 m²) of gross floor space.

RESIDENTIAL DWELLING UNITS

(a) In density zones, up to and including 100 persons per acre, one garage or car space, per dwelling unit, must be provided.

(b) Where the full amount of parking space is unlikely to be needed for some years, provision of up to one half may be deferred, on condition that the layout allows for the eventual provision of the total required. (*N.B.* In the case of the London area this standard is subject to the G.L.C.'s consideration of any views expressed by the London Borough's Standing Joint Committee.)

HOMES AND HOSTELS PROVIDED UNDER NATIONAL ASSISTANCE ACTS, HOUSING ACTS AND THE CHILDREN'S ACT 1948 AND SIMILAR BUILDING PROVIDED BY PUBLIC AUTHORITIES AND PRIVATE ORGANISATIONS, AND FOR STUDENTS' HOSTELS AND NURSES' HOMES

One space for every 20 occupants must be provided.

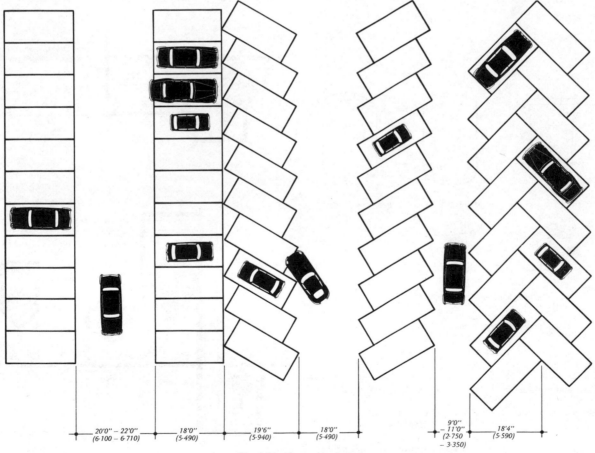

| 20'0"–22'0" (6·100–6·710) | 18'0" (5·490) | 19'6" (5·940) | 18'0" (5·490) | 9'0"–11'0" (2·750–3·350) | 18'4" (5·590) |

Fig. 3.11   Car parking layouts

SHOPPING, DEPARTMENTAL STORES AND LARGE RETAIL ESTABLISHMENTS

One car space for every 2500 ft² (232·26 m²) of gross floor space must be provided. This standard should be used mainly for premises in the central area. Parking provision for district and local shopping centres should normally be made in public car parks.

CINEMAS

One car space for every 60 seats must be provided.

THEATRES AND CONCERT HALLS

Car parking should be provided on the basis of one car space for every 30 seats.

Table 3.7 DUSTBINS (B.S. 792)

Capacity		Diameter		Height	
ft³	m³	in	mm	in	mm
1	0·03	14	356	14	356
2	0·06	16	406	20	508
2½	0·07	17	432	22	559
3¼	0·09	18	457	24	610

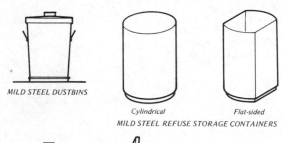

MILD STEEL DUSTBINS

Cylindrical   Flat-sided

MILD STEEL REFUSE STORAGE CONTAINERS

Closed   Open

MILD STEEL REFUSE OR FOOD WASTE CONTAINERS

Fig. 3.12   Dustbins and refuse containers

Table 3.8 FUEL STORAGE

Coal and anthracite	41 ft³ per ton (approx.) (1·4 m³/1000 kg)
Gas and hard coke	70–105 ft³ per ton (approx.) (2·1–3·1 m³/1000 kg)
Coalite	90 ft³ per ton (approx.) (2·5 m³/1000 kg)

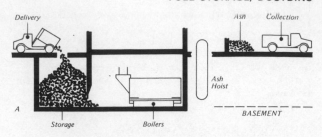

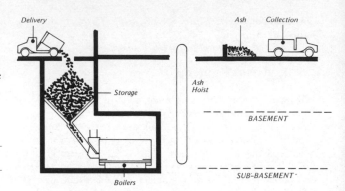

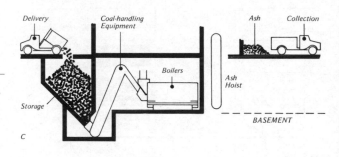

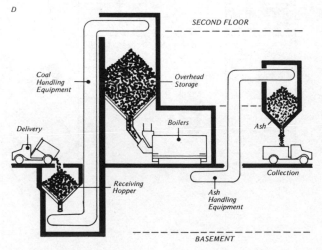

Fig. 3.13   Relationship of solid fuel storage to boilers

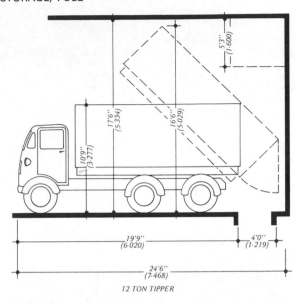

12 TON TIPPER

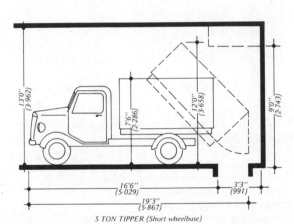

5 TON TIPPER (Short wheelbase)

Fig. 3.14   Bulk delivery vehicles

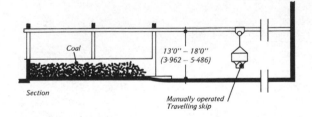

Coal

13'0" – 18'0"
(3·962 – 5·486)

Section

Manually operated
Travelling skip

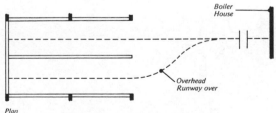

Boiler
House

Overhead
Runway over

Plan

Fig. 3.15   Layout and dimensions for open-air fuel storage

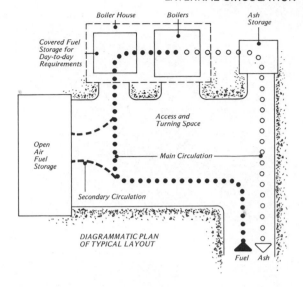

DIAGRAMMATIC PLAN
OF TYPICAL LAYOUT

Long Section

1'0" (305) Height
Lines to assist in
checking stock

Kerbs to protect
end walls of bays

Walls of bays to be min.
4" (102) concrete on 4½" (114) brickwork

Plan

Cross Section
OPEN AIR STORAGE BAYS

Fig. 3.16   Storage bays with overhead runway

Table 3.9 OIL TANK SIZES

Nominal capacity		Length			Height			Width		
gal	litre	ft	in	mm	ft	in	mm	ft	in	mm
300	1364	6	0	1829	4	0	1219	2	0	610
650	2955	6	6	1981	4	0	1219	4	0	1219
1250	5682	8	0	2438	5	0	1524	5	0	1524
2500	11364	8	0	2438	6	6	1981	8	0	2438
4000	18184	10	0	3048	8	0	2438	8	0	2438
6000	27276	10	0	3048	8	0	2438	10	0	3048

Table 3.10 REFUSE COLLECTION AND DISPOSAL

Table of sizes	M.S. refuse or food waste containers	Mild steel dustbins					M.S. refuse storage containers	
		A	B	C	D		Cylindrical	Flat-sided
Nominal capacity	0·5 ft³ (0·014 cm³)	1 ft³ (0·028 cm³)	2 ft³ (0·057 cm³)	2½ ft³ (0·071 cm³)	3¼ ft³ (0·092 cm³)		34 ft³ (0·963 cm³)	27 ft³ (0·765 cm³)
Internal diameter	8½ in bottom (0·215 m) 11¾ in top (0·298 m)	12 in bottom (0·305 m) 14 in top (0·356 m)	14 in bottom (0·356 m) 16 in top (0·406 m)	15 in bottom (0·381 m) 17 in top (0·432 m)	16 in bottom (0·406 m) 18 in top (0·457 m)		3 ft 0 in (0·914 m)	3 ft 0 in (0·914 m) 2 ft 6 in across (0·762 m)
Maximum width	13¾ in closed (0·520 m)	18 in (0·457 m)	20 in (0·508 m)	21 in (0·533 m)	22 in (0·559 m)		3 ft 5 in (1·041 m)	3 ft 5 in (1·041 m) 2 ft 6½ in across (0·882 m)
Internal height	10½ in (0·266 m)	14 in (0·356 m)	20 in (0·508 m)	22 in (0·559 m)	24 in (0·610 m)		4 ft 3 in (1·295 m)	4 ft 3 in (1·295 m)
Overall height	15½ in (0·196 m)	18 in (0·457 m)	24 in (0·610 m)	26 in (0·660 m)	28 in (0·711 m)		4 ft 4 in (1·321 m)	4 ft 4 in (1·321 m)
Net weight	5 lb 12 oz (2·608 kg)	13 lb (5·897 kg)	20 lb (9·072 kg)	23 lb (10·433 kg)	28 lb (12·701 kg)			

BIBLIOGRAPHY

BRITISH STANDARDS INSTITUTION

Refuse Disposal

C.P. 306:1960 The storage and collection of refuse from residential buildings.
B.S. 792:1947 Mild steel dustbins (confirmed 1957). Amendments P.D. 787, May 1948; P.D. 2817, June 1957; P.D. 3492, Aug. 1959; P.D. 5605, July 1965.
B.S. 1136:1956 Mild steel refuse storage containers. Amendments P.D. 3571, Nov. 1959; P.D. 4841, March 1963.
B.S. 1577:1949 Mild steel refuse or food waste containers.
B.S. 1703:—— Refuse chutes.
Part 1: 1967. Hoppers.
Part 2: 1968. Chutes.
B.S. 3495:1962 Aluminium refuse storage containers.
B.S. 3654:1963 Galvanised steel dustbins for dustless emptying.
B.S. 3735:1964 Rubber components for steel dustbins. Amendment A.M.D. 62, Aug. 1968.

ACTS OF PARLIAMENT

Highways Act, 1959
Public Service Vehicles (Travel Concessions) Act, 1955
Rights of Way Act, 1932
Road and Rail Traffic Act, 1933
Road Safety Act, 1967
Road Traffic (Amendment) Act, 1967
Road Traffic Regulations Act, 1967
Road Transport Lighting Act, 1967
Special Roads Act, 1949
Town and Country Planning Act, 1968
Transport Act, 1968

OTHER PUBLICATIONS

Transport

BURKE, JOHN (Editor), *Encyclopedia of Road Traffic, Law and Practice,* Vols. 1, 2 and 3, Sweet & Maxwell (1960 onwards)
KIDNER, GERALD (Editor) *Mahaffy and Dodson on Road Traffic,* Vol. 1 *Statutes,* Vol. 2 *Regulations and Service,* 3rd edition, Butterworths (1970)

4 EXTERNAL WORKS AND LANDSCAPE INCLUDING ROAD SERVICES

GENERAL

The basic factors relating to the design of roads are location, traffic flow, and safety. The most comprehensive recom- mendations concerning the detailed planning of roads are contained in the various publications of the Ministry of Transport and these are listed, together with other important references, at the end of the section.

Table 4.1 RECOMMENDED LANE WIDTHS

Road type	Single two-lane carriageway	Dual or divided carriageway with at least 4 lanes
Primary distributor		12 ft 0 in (3·65 m)
District distributor	12 ft 0 in (3·65 m)	12 ft 0 in (3·65 m) normally 11 ft 0 in (3·35 m) if the proportion of heavy commercial traffic is fairly low
Local distributor	12 ft 0 in (3·65 m) in industrial districts 11 ft 0 in (3·35 m) in principal business districts 10 ft 0 in (3·04 m) in residential districts	
Access road Principal means of access	12 ft 0 in (3·65 m) in industrial districts 11 ft 0 in (3·35 m) in principal business districts 9 ft 0 in (2·74 m) normally in residential districts	
Secondary means of access	10 ft 0 in (3·04 m) in industrial and principal business districts. On back roads in residential districts a two-lane width of 13 ft 0 in (3·96 m) will suffice if use is limited to cars	

Table 4.2 MINIMUM SIGHT DISTANCES

Design speed		Minimum overtaking distance (single carriageway)		Minimum stopping distance (single and dual carriageways)	
mile/h	km/h	ft	m	ft	m
50	80	1200	365·76	425	129·54
40	64	950	289·56	300	91·44
30	48	700	213·36	190	57·91
20	32	480	146·30	110	33·52

Table 4.3 MINIMUM SLIP ROAD RADII AND STOPPING DISTANCES

Design speed		Minimum radius		Minimum stopping sight distance	
mile/h	km/h	ft	m	ft	m
40	64	490	149·35	300	91·44
30	48	240	73·15	190	57·91
25	40	170	51·81	150	45·72
20	32	110	33·52	110	33·52
15	24	60	18·28	70	21·33

Table 4.4 ACCELERATION AND DECELERATION LANE LENGTHS

Design speed of major road		Gradient of major road	Acceleration lane length		Deceleration lane length	
mile/h	km/h	(%)	ft	m	ft	m
50	80	4% up	800	243·84	270	82·29
		level	560	170·68	300	91·44
		4% down	440	134·11	340	103·63
40	64	4% up	510	155·44		
		level	340	103·63	250	76·20
		4% down	250	76·20		
30	48	4% up				
		level	210	64·00	210	64·00
		4% down				

Table 4.5 SOME METHODS OF TRAFFIC SEGREGATION

Type of segregation	Method	Purpose
Segregation in relation to destination	By construction of by-passes	To separate through traffic from traffic requiring to enter the town and traffic circulating within it
	By provision of separate primary and distributory traffic networks	To separate longer distance urban traffic from local traffic
Segregation of types of traffic	By construction of urban motorways	To provide fast, high-capacity routes solely for motor traffic and eliminate accidents involving pedestrians and pedal cyclists
	By cycle tracks and cycle ways	To separate pedal cyclists from faster motor vehicles and from pedestrians
	By pedestrian ways and elevated footways	To obviate conflicts with faster traffic and give easy, direct access to various parts of the town
	By construction of back streets	To give separate access for goods and service vehicles, with facilities for loading and unloading
	By reserving some roads or traffic lanes for buses	To ensure rapid and direct public transport and reduce interference from other traffic
Segregation of traffic by grade separation	By construction of flyovers, underpasses and grade-separated junctions	To avoid conflicts between through and crossing or turning traffic streams
	By building special subways and bridges for pedestrians or cyclists	To eliminate conflicts with motor traffic
Segregation in relation to direction	By dual or divided carriageways and one-way streets	To reduce or eliminate the risk of conflict between opposing traffic streams
	By channelising islands at junctions	To separate traffic streams and points of possible conflict, thereby simplifying the driver's task
Segregation of moving vehicles from parked vehicles	By provision of off-street parking and prohibition of street parking	To increase street capacity and eliminate risks due to screening of pedestrians from view by stationary vehicles
Segregation by other controls	By traffic signals	Use of time segregation to eliminate or reduce traffic conflicts at junctions
	By banning right turns, closing side streets and limiting access points	To reduce the risk of conflict between through and turning or crossing traffic

URBAN ROAD SYSTEM

Primary Distributors

These roads form the primary network for the town as a whole. All longer-distance traffic movements to, from, and within the town should be channelled on to the primary distributors.

District Distributors

These roads distribute traffic within the residential, industrial and principal business districts of the town. They form the link between the primary network and the roads within environmental areas (i.e. areas free from extraneous traffic in which considerations of environment predominate over the use of vehicles).

Local Distributors

These roads distribute traffic within environmental areas. They form the link between district distributors and access roads.

Access Roads

These roads give direct access to buildings and land within environmental areas.

STAGES OF IMPROVEMENT

The Ministry of Transport in its Bulletin *Roads in Urban Areas* recommend the following sequence of events for the planned improvement of urban roads.

1. Prohibit or restrict waiting on primary and district distributors. During peak traffic periods prohibit the loading and unloading of commercial vehicles, and limit stopping to pick up or set down passengers as on urban clearways.

2. Take urgent action to provide off-street parking accommodation, consistent with a policy relating the availability of parking space to the capacity of the network. Site garages and car parks near the main centres of development, with easy access to distributor roads.

3. Construct secondary means of access to enable goods and service vehicles to load or unload at the rear of shops and other premises. Where it is not immediately possible to provide these to full vehicular width, the interim construction of rear alleyways wide enough for the operation of trolleys or fork-lift trucks should be considered. These alleyways should terminate at suitably sited loading bays on minor streets.

4. Prohibit or restrict street parking on local distributors and access roads, in conjunction with the planned provision of car park spaces and the availability of back streets for servicing shops, etc.

5. Construct or improve primary and district distributors to the required standards. This work should be carried out concurrently with stages (1) to (4) and programmed so that the most needed sections are completed first.

6. As the primary network is developed, introduce traffic control to canalise cross-town journeys on to primary distributors instead of local and district distributors.

DESIGN SPEEDS

Suggested design speeds for urban roads are shown in the following table:

Table 4.6 SUGGESTED DESIGN SPEEDS FOR URBAN ROADS

	mile/h	km/h
Primary distributor:		
urban motorway	50	80
all purpose	40	64
District distributor		
Local distributor	30	48
Important access roads		

Table 4.7 RECOMMENDED FOOTWAY WIDTHS

Type of road	Recommended minimum footway widths	
	ft	m
Primary distributor:		
Urban motorway	No footways	
All-purpose road	9*	2·74
District distributor:		
In principal business and industrial districts	9*	2·74
In residential districts	8*	2·44
Local distributor:		
In principal business and industrial districts	9*	2·74
In residential districts	6*	1·83
Access road (principal means of access):		
In principal business districts	9*	2·74
In industrial districts	6*	1·83
Normally in residential districts	6*	1·83
Adjoining shopping frontages	12–15	3·66–4·57
Access road (secondary means of access):		
Verge instead of footway on roads in principal business and industrial districts	3	0·91
Verge instead of footway on roads in residential districts	2	0·61

* If no footway is required provide verge at least 3 ft (0·91 m) wide

Table 4.8 CLEARANCES FROM THE CARRIAGEWAY

Design speed		Height of object on footway, verge or central reserve	Minimum clearance where carriageway is:								
			away from, or towards object but not steeper than 1 in 40			towards object but not steeper than 1 in 24			towards object and steeper than 1 in 24		
mile/h	km/h		ft	in	mm	ft	in	mm	ft	in	mm
30	48	Less than 10 ft 0 in (3·05 m)	1	6	457	1	9	533	2	0	610
		10 ft 0 in (3·05 m) and above	1	6	457	2	0	610	2	6	762
40 or 50	64 or 80	Less than 10 ft 0 in (3·05 m)	2	0	610	2	0	610	2	0	610
			Desirable clearance where conditions permit: 4 ft 0 in (1·22 m)								
		10 ft 0 in (3·05 m) and above	3	0	914	3	0	914	3	0	914
			Desirable clearance where conditions permit: 5 ft 0 in (1·52 m)								

BUS STOPS

A bus stop on the approach to an intersection should be far enough away to ensure that:

1. A waiting bus does not restrict visibility leftwards from the main road to the side road or, to the right, from the side road to the main road.
2. Traffic wishing to turn left is not obstructed by the bus (if buses turn left at the junction it may be possible to incorporate a bus bay at the beginning of an additional lane for left-turning traffic.
3. Waiting buses do not interfere with the efficient working of traffic signs, or the movement of traffic at a roundabout.

JUNCTION SPACING

As a rough guide, suggested minimum spacings along various types of road are given below:

Primary distributor (urban motorway)	1800 ft (548·64 m)
Primary distributor (all-purpose motorway)	900 ft (274·32 m)
District distributor	700 ft (213·36 m)
Local distributor or access road	300 ft (91·44 m)

SLIP ROADS

DESIGN SPEED

This should normally be between two-thirds and a half the speed of the traffic on the more important major roads at the junction.

WIDTH

Slip road carriageways should normally carry one-way traffic only. One-lane slip roads should have a 14 ft (4·27 m) carriageway, bounded on the left-hand side by a 1 ft (305 mm) marginal strip or lip kerb and a paved verge not less than 5 ft (1·52 m) wide, and on the right-hand side a raised kerb and a verge wide enough to give clearances as indicated in Table 4.8. Where traffic flows warrant the provision of two-lane slip roads, the carriageway should be increased to 24 ft (7·32 m).

CURVE RADII

Minimum radii for various design speeds are given in Table 4.3 on page 33.

SIGHT DISTANCES

Minimum stopping distances for various design speeds are given in Table 4.3. Stopping distances should be checked between points 3 ft 6 in (1·07 m) above the carriageway along a line 6 ft (1·83 m) from both the nearside and offside edges of the carriageway.

GRADIENTS

Slip road gradients should preferably not exceed 5° and should nowhere be steeper than 8°. Where a slip road carries a large volume of heavy commercial traffic, its gradient should desirably be limited to 4°.

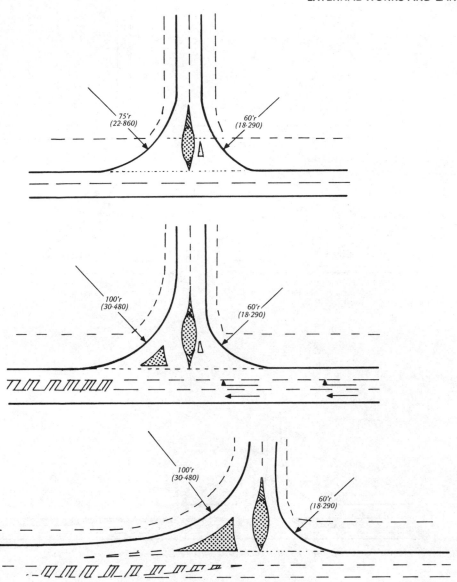

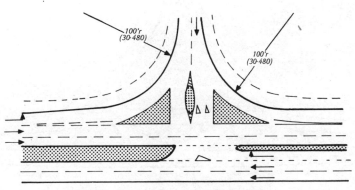

Fig. 4.1 Geometric dimensions applied to junctions

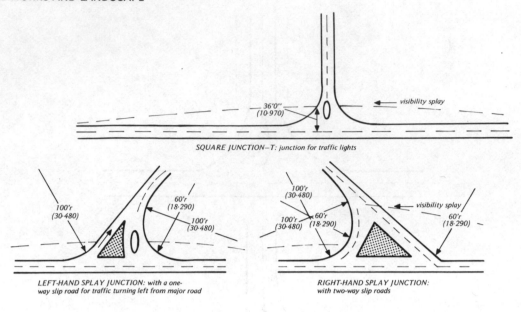

SQUARE JUNCTION—T: junction for traffic lights

LEFT-HAND SPLAY JUNCTION: with a one-way slip road for traffic turning left from major road

RIGHT-HAND SPLAY JUNCTION: with two-way slip roads

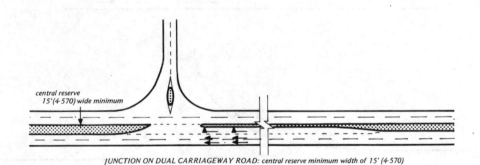

JUNCTION ON DUAL CARRIAGEWAY ROAD: central reserve minimum width of 15′ (4·570)

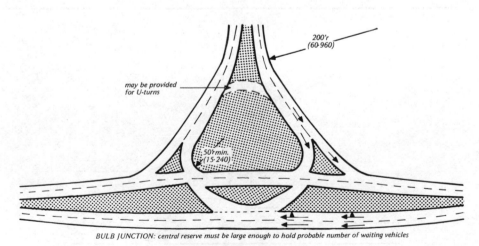

BULB JUNCTION: central reserve must be large enough to hold probable number of waiting vehicles

Fig. 4.2   Design of T-junctions

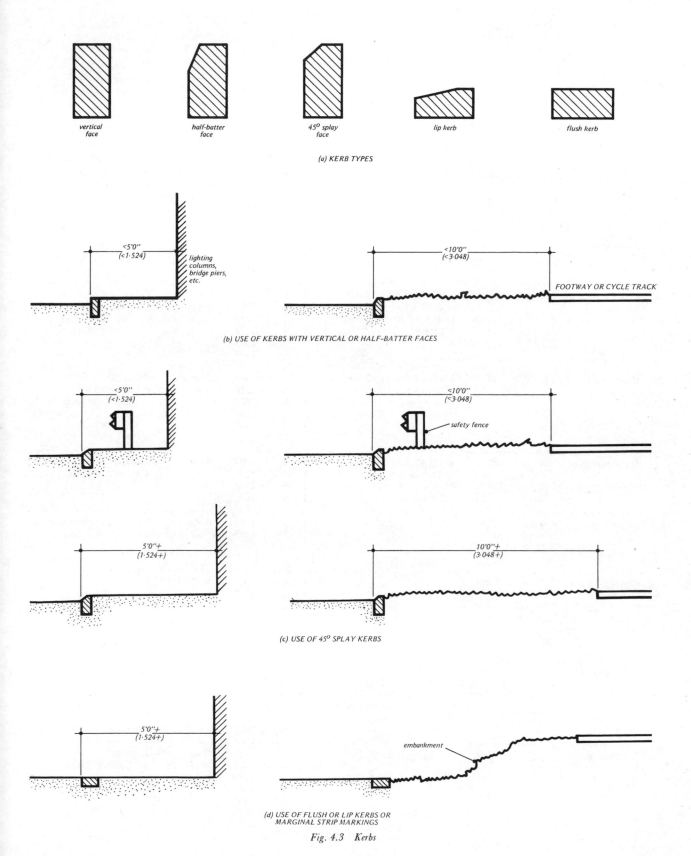

(a) KERB TYPES

vertical face

half-batter face

45° splay face

lip kerb

flush kerb

(b) USE OF KERBS WITH VERTICAL OR HALF-BATTER FACES

(c) USE OF 45° SPLAY KERBS

(d) USE OF FLUSH OR LIP KERBS OR MARGINAL STRIP MARKINGS

Fig. 4.3   Kerbs

Table 4.9 TYPES AND SIZES OF FENCES FOR VARIOUS USES

Types of fence	Maximum distance apart of uprights			Depth of posts in ground	Heights of fences			Materials for posts	Heights of fences for various uses
	ft	in	mm		ft	in	mm		
Chain link	10	0	3048	Up to 4 ft 6 in (1372 mm) 2 ft 0 in (609 mm) Over 4 ft 6 in (1372 mm) 2 ft 6 in (762 mm)	3 3 4 4 5 5 6	0 6 0 6 0 6 0	914 1067 1219 1372 1524 1676 1829	Concrete Steel Wood	Housing 3 ft 0 in (914 mm) min.
Woven wire	12	0	3658	2 ft 0 in (609 mm)	2 2 3 3 4	6 8 0 9 0	762 813 914 1143 1219	Concrete Steel Wood	Estate boundaries 4 ft 0 in (1219 mm)
Strained wire	10	0	3048	2 ft 0 in (609 mm)	3 4 4	6 0 6	1067 1219 1372	Concrete Steel Wood	Playgrounds 4 ft 0 in (1219 mm) min.
Cleft chestnut pale	10	0	3048	Up to 4 ft 6 in (1372 mm) 2 ft 0 in (609 mm) Over 4 ft 6 in (1372 mm) 2 ft 6 in (762 mm)	3 3 4 4 5 6	0 6 0 6 0 0	914 1067 1219 1372 1524 1829	Concrete Wood	Public buildings 6 ft 0 in (1829 mm)
Close boarded	9	0	2743	Up to 4 ft 6 in (1372 mm) 2 ft 0 in (609 mm) Over 4 ft 6 in (1372 mm) 2 ft 6 in (762 mm)	3 4 4 5 5 6	6 0 6 0 6 0	1067 1219 1372 1524 1676 1829	Concrete Wood	Highways 4 ft 6 in–5 ft 0 in (1372–1524 mm)
Wooden palisade	9	0	2743	Up to 4 ft 6 in (1372 mm) 2 ft 0 in (609 mm) Over 4 ft 6 in (1372 mm) 2 ft 6 in (762 mm)	3 4 4 5	6 0 6 6	1067 1219 1372 1676	Wood	Railways 4 ft 6 in (1372 mm)
Post and rail	9 0 mortised 6 0 nailed		2743 1829	2 ft 6 in (762 mm)	3 4	9 3	1143 1295	Wood	Commercial buildings 6 ft 0 in (1829 mm)
Continuous bar	3	0	914	1 ft 6 in–2 ft 0 in (457–609 mm)	3 4 4	6 0 6	1067 1219 1372	Steel	Pigs 2 ft 8 in–3 ft 0 in (813–914 mm) Sheep 3 ft 0 in–6 ft 0 in (1143–1829 mm)
Unclimbable	9	0	2743	4 ft 0 in–4 ft 6 in (1219–1372 mm) 1 ft 9 in (533 mm) 5 ft 0 in–6 ft 0 in (1524–1829 mm) 2 ft 0 in (609 mm) 7 ft 0 in (2134 mm) 2 ft 6 in (762 mm)	4 4 5 5 6 7	0 6 0 6 0 0	1219 1372 1524 1676 1829 2134	Steel	Cattle 3 ft 9 in (1143 mm) Horses 4 ft 0 in (1219 mm)
Interwoven	6	4	1930	2 ft 0 in (609 mm)	3 3 4 4 5 5 6	0 6 0 6 0 6 0	914 1067 1219 1372 1524 1676 1829	Concrete Wood	Rabbits 3 ft 6 in (1067 mm)

COMMON TYPES OF FENCING

Wattle fencing
Interwoven fencing
Closeboarded and oak pale fencing
Palisade fencing
Horizontal boarded fencing
Cleft chestnut fencing
Chestnut spile fencing
Chestnut pale fencing
Post and rail fencing
Post and wire fencing
Continuous bar fencing
Unclimbable fences
Light border hurdles
Vertical-bar wall fencing
Steel-angle unclimbable fencing
Corrugated-steel pale fencing
Guard rail
Post and chain barrier
Chain-link fencing
Woven-wire fencing
Welded-mesh fencing
Expanded-metal fencing
Perforated-metal sheeting
Hexagonal-mesh wire fencing

Table 4.10 VARIOUS SIZES AND SHAPES OF CONCRETE SLABS

$1\frac{1}{2}$ in (40 mm) thick	1 ft 0 in × 6 in (305 × 152 mm)
	1 ft × 1 ft (305 × 305 mm)
2 in (50 mm) thick	9 in × 9 in (228 × 228 mm)
	1 ft 6 in × 9 in (457 × 228 mm)
	1 ft 6 in × 1 ft (457 × 305 mm)
	2 ft × 1 ft or 1 ft 3 in (610 × 305 or 381 mm)
	1 ft 6 in × 1 ft 6 in (457 × 457 mm)
	2 ft × 1 ft 6 in (610 × 457 mm)
	3 ft 0 in × 1 ft 6 in (914 × 457 mm)
	2 ft × 2 ft (610 × 610 mm)

Table 4.11 AREA COVERED BY PAVING MATERIALS

Quantity	Material*	Area covered (approx.)	
		yd²	m²
1 ton (1·02 t)	York stone in slabs 2 in (50 mm) thick	11	9·19
1 ton (1·02 t)	York stone in slabs $2\frac{1}{2}$ in (63 mm) thick	9	7·52
1 ton (1·02 t)	concrete paving slabs $1\frac{1}{2}$ in (40 mm) thick	15	12·54
1 ton (1·02 t)	concrete paving slabs 2 in (50 mm) thick	12	10·03
1 ton (1·02 t)	concrete paving slabs $2\frac{1}{2}$ in (63 mm) thick	10	8·36
1 ton (1·02 t)	slate in slabs 1 in (25 mm) thick	17	14·21
1 ton (1·02 t)	gravel well rolled 2 in (50 mm) thick	15	12·54
1 ton (1·02 t)	gravel well rolled 3 in (76 mm) thick	10	8·36
1 ton (1·02 t) setts 6 in × 4 in × 4 in (152 mm × 102 mm × 102 mm)		$4\frac{1}{2}$	3·34
1000 bricks in simple rows, on edge		20	16·72
1000 bricks in simple rows, flat		30	25·08
1000 bricks in pattern, with cutting, on edge		18	15·05
1000 bricks in pattern, with cutting, flat		27	22·57

The above table allows for normal jointing, but not for cutting to boundaries, breakage or waste.

PAVING

Table 4.12 PLANTING IN PAVED AREAS

Problem	Solution
Frost pockets—these occur in low areas without air drainage	Leave gaps in enclosing walls
Draught funnels—common amongst tall buildings	Use wind-hardy plants, and avoid north-east draughts
Waterlogged areas—often in clay in peaty areas	Provide drainage, or use raised beds
Vandalism—this is normally experienced in towns, and can be acute in housing areas	Use grouped planting away from access points, tough, spiny plants, and semi-mature trees rather than saplings. Good staking and tree guards will help
Excessive drying out—urban areas are usually warmer than country areas	Seek or provide shelter. Protective wrappings for delicate plants and young tree-trunks. Transpiration retarders, spraying and irrigation are needed during the establishment period

Table 4.12 PLANTING IN PAVED AREAS *(continued)*

Problem	Solution
Overshadowing by buildings	Use shade-bearing plants
Atmospheric pollution—*direct:* by solids and sulphur, diesel and petrol fumes; *indirect:* by light restriction	Use plants which are known for their resistance to urban conditions
Run-off pollution from paved areas—salt, petrol, oil, tar, soapy water, etc.	Use kerbs, and provide proper traps if used for irrigation
Drips from overhead cables; copper wires	Avoid these positions
Gas main leaks—even a small one caused by traffic vibrations can be harmful	—
Animals—urination, scratching and digging	—
Root restriction and amputation—due to hard pavings and excavations for trenches, services and buildings	Careful planning of pipes and planting. Leave ventilation spaces in paving

Table 4.13 SOIL CONTENT

Type of soil	Organic matter %	Clay %	Sand %	Lime %	Potash %	Phosphoric acid %	Alkalies %
Fertile loam*	4·38	18·09	76·16	1·37	0·49	0·12	—
Orchard soil	11·70	48·39	35·95	1·54	0·91	0·08	—
Marl**	11·08	52·06	24·53	11·53	0·32	0·12	—
Heavy clay	4·87	72·29	9·26	1·15	0·06	1·37	—
Sterile sandy soil	5·36	4·57	89·82	0·25	—	(trace)	0·49

* A mixture of clay, sand and silt in fairly balanced proportions
** A mixture of clay and chalk

Table 4.14 TREATMENT OF PROBLEMATIC SOILS FOR TURF FORMATION

Soil	Problems	Treatment
Clay and clay loams	Heavy, compacted, waterlogged in winter, cracked in summer; earthworms	Difficult. If possible cover with several inches of good loam, otherwise dress with sharp sand
Sandy soils	Inadequate humus and minerals; summer drought	Readily improved by working in compost or peat Adjust pH with lime
Infertile heath	Mineral shortage, poor drainage, acidity	Break up 'iron pan' in subsoil to improve drainage; add lime, compost and fertilisers. Irrigate in dry weather
Chalky soils	Shallowness, alkalinity, excessive drainage	Break up subsoil, add sulphate of ammonia (or other acid fertiliser) and compost
Derelict land (slag heaps, etc.)	Debris, unweathered rock, sometimes acidity	This takes time, clear the worst debris, break up the soil and allow to weather. Preferably import top soil

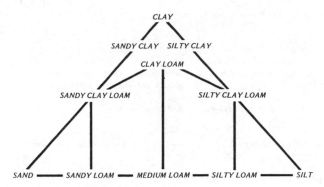

Fig. 4.4   Textural composition of soils

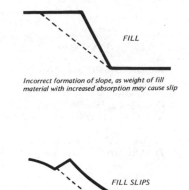

FILL

Incorrect formation of slope, as weight of fill
material with increased absorption may cause slip

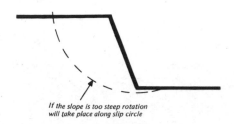

If the slope is too steep rotation
will take place along slip circle

FILL SLIPS

Slip of fill material along original formation

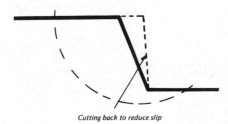

Cutting back to reduce slip

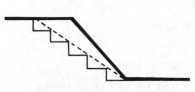

*FAILURE ON SLIP
CIRCLE*

Movement along slip surface of the original formation

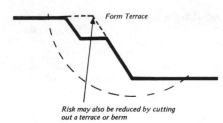

Form Terrace

Risk may also be reduced by cutting
out a terrace or berm

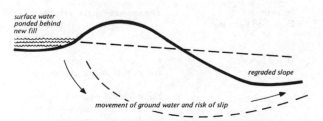

Correct procedure, benching cut into original
slope to prevent failure

Fig. 4.6   Formation of slopes with fill

surface water
ponded behind
new fill

regraded slope

movement of ground water and risk of slip

Fig. 4.7   Undrained areas behind new fill may lead to movement of ground
water, excessive loading on regraded slopes and consequent slip

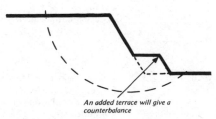

An added terrace will give a
counterbalance

Fig. 4.5   Formation of slopes in cut

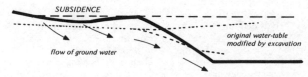

SUBSIDENCE

original water-table
modified by excavation

flow of ground water

Fig. 4.8   Subsidence resulting from fine material being (indicated by
arrows) carried away by the flow of ground water due to modified water-table
resulting from excavation. Interceptor drains are needed at top and foot of slope

Table 4.15 PLANT NUTRIENTS AND THEIR EFFECTS ON GRASS SWARDS

Element	Normal source	Effects of deficiency	Effects of excess
Nitrogen	Ammonium salts and nitrates, mostly in soil solution	Plants small, bright-tinted, with pale older leaves	Soft flabby growth, a risk of mechanical damage and disease
Phosphorus	Organic and inorganic phosphates in soil, not all available to grass	Poor roots, weak bluish or purplish shoots, wearing badly	Encourages clover
Calcium	Limestone, chalk, soil solution. Plentiful except in very acid soil	Growing points fail. Leaf tips yellow or stunted	Causes iron shortage, favours weeds
Potassium	Potash salts in soil solution, only scarce in peat, chalk or sands. Also in minerals e.g. feldspar	Growing points fail, shoots die back. Risk of disease	Seldom met with

Table 4.16 FERTILISERS AND MANURES FOR PLANTING AREAS

Material	Notes	Rate of application	Time and method of application
Bulky organic manures	All bulky organics vary in composition according to source. Obtain analysis before ordering		
Farmyard manure	Should be well rotted	1 yd³ to 25 yd² (0·76 m³ to 20·90 m²)	Mix with top soil during preliminary cultivation or apply as top dressing and lightly fork in during early spring
Poultry manure	Store before use	4 oz/yd² (130 g/m²)	
Sewage sludge (dried)		1 yd³ to 50 yd² (0·76 m³ to 41·80 m²)	
Sewage sludge (activated)		4 oz/yd² (130 g/m²)	
Spent mushroom beds	Contains lime and is not suitable for plants needing an acid soil	1 yd³ to 50 yd² (0·76 m³ to 41·80 m²)	
Concentrated organic manures: Bone meal Hoof and horn meal	The coarser the texture, the more slowly nutrients become available	2–4 oz/yd² (65–130 g/m²)	Spread on surface after cultivation and rake in
Dried blood	Expensive, but quick acting and safe. Good for evergreens	2–4 oz/yd² (65–130 g/m²)	Spread on surface after cultivation and rake in
Lime	Do not apply within 3 weeks of manuring as it reacts with many fertilisers and manures		
Carbonate of lime	Safe and slow in action	4–8 oz/yd² (130–260 g/m²)	Thoroughly work into top 3–4 in (76–102 mm) of soil during initial cultivation
Hydrated lime	Pure and fine; comparatively expensive	4–8 oz/yd² (130–260 g/m²)	
Peat Coarse sedge peat	High water-holding capacity	4–6 lb/yd² (2·16–3·25 kg/m²)	Soak very dry soil before adding peat. Mix with top soil at time of planting or use as a mulch after

Table 4.17 PLANTING GUIDE

Trees	Planting season	Plant	Distance apart		No. of plants/ yd² (0·836m²)
			in	mm	
Deciduous trees and shrubs	End of October– end of March	Dwarf and slow-growing shrub	18–24	457– 610	2–4
		Medium-growing shrub	36–48	914–1219	1
		Vigorous-growing shrub	60–72	1524–1828	2–3
Evergreen shrubs and conifers	End of September– early May	—	—	—	—
Herbaceous perennials	End of September– end of April	Vigorous-growing shrub	24–48	610–1219	1–3
		Average-growing shrub	12–18	305– 457	4–9
Alpines and rock plants	End of August–end of October or early March–end of April	—	—	—	—
Pot-grown plants and plants in containers	Throughout the year, preferably September– early May	—	—	—	—
Water lilies and marginal aquatics	Mid-March–early June			—	
Bulbs	Early September– October	Large bulbs, e.g. Narcissus	8–12	203– 305	9–25
		Small bulbs, e.g. Crocus	6–8	152– 203	25–36

Table 4.18 TREE GROWTH

Tree	Height in 20 yrs.		Height in 50 yrs.		Growth	Soil	Climate	Habitat/Use
	ft	m	ft	m				
Acacia (Locust)	40	12	70	21	Very fast in early stages	Light, poor soils, neutral or slightly acid reactions	Hardy plant, requires shelter from winds and sunshine	In England used for street planting and ornamental purposes. Hates shade from other trees
Ailanthus (Tree of Heaven)	20–40	6–12	55	16	Fast and vigorous	Deep, rich, permeable loam, of acid rather than alkaline tendency	Hardy against frost in winter, but prefers sunny districts and sheltered positions	Usually found in open, isolated positions
Alder (Almus Glutinosa)	20–40	6–12	60	18	Fairly fast in early stages	Any moist soil, except highly acid peat	Very hardy, quite firm against wind, but its partiality for low damp ground usually precludes its use as a windscreen	Frequently used for holding river banks against erosion
Almond	Under 20	Under 6	Under 40	Under 12	Fairly fast, under good conditions	Grows best in well-drained light loam, overlying chalk or limestone	Warm, sheltered positions	Grows well at considerable heights, and is probably a tree of developing scrub on steep slopes

45

Table 4.18 TREE GROWTH (*continued*)

Tree	Height in 20 yrs.		Height in 50 yrs.		Growth	Soil	Climate	Habitat/Use
	ft	m	ft	m				
Arbutus (Strawberry tree)	Under 20	Under 6	Under 40	Under 12	Slow	Light, well-drained loams; best on acid or neutral soils	Not very hardy and often suffers badly from late spring frosts in inland districts	In England occurs on margins of oak and birch woods
Ash (*Fraxinus Excelsior*)	25	7·6	60	18	Fairly fast in early stages	Chalk, limestone and any alkaline soils. Dislikes acid soils	Generally hardy, except in extreme north of Scotland	Woodland tree on moist hillsides
Beech (*Fagus Sylvatica*)	20–40	6–12	60	18	Fairly fast	Well-drained soil but chiefly on chalk	Survives low winter temperatures, but spring foliage is liable to damage by late frost	Chalk and limestone hills
Birch (Silver Birch)	25	7·6	60	18	Fast at younger stages	Light, sandy loam	Very hardy, enduring wind and frost	Grows at higher altitudes than other trees
Blackthorn (Sloe)	Under 20	Under 6	–	–	Rapid in early stages	Well-drained, alkaline or neutral soils. Light loam, sand, gravel or chalk	Very resistant to frost	Chalk cliffs by the sea
Catalpa (Indian Bean)	Under 20	Under 6	40	12	Rather slow	Deep moist loam	Endures moderate frost, but dislikes wind	Low altitudes. Does well in the south and east
Cedar of Lebanon (*Cedrus Lebani*)	20	6	60	18	Slow growth	Light sands and calcareous formations. Best on neutral valley loams, deep and well drained	Though hardy, succeeds best in warmer parts of Britain	Mixed woods
Japanese cherry	Under 20	Under 6	30	9	—	Deep alkaline loam, but tolerant of other soils	Hardy against frost, but must have shelter if flowers are to give of their best effect	—
Wild cherry	Under 20	Under 6	60	18	Medium rate	Alkaline loams of fairly open texture, but tolerant of other soils	Hardy against frost and wind. Grows in shade or sun	Woodland or chalk or limestone
Horse chestnut	25	7·6	60	18	Vigorous and fairly fast in young stages	Likes good depth of soil and prefers a deep, moist, but well-drained loam	Hardy against frost, but best in sheltered situations	Elevations between 300–400 ft (91·44–121·92 m) in moist shady valleys
Red chestnut	20–40	6–12	40	12	Less vigorous than horse chestnut	Well-drained loams and valley soils	Sheltered position	Suitable for town, street, lawn
Spanish chestnut	25	7·6	60	18	Slow, flowers only at maturity	Well-drained sandy soils. Dislikes clay, peat or chalk soils	Open sunny positions. Best in south and east	Grown for its timber—forms pure forest in some places

Table 4.18 TREE GROWTH *(continued)*

Tree	Height in 20 yrs.		Height in 50 yrs.		Growth	Soil	Climate	Habitat/Use
	ft	m	ft	m				
Crab apple	20	6	30	9	Fairly fast, foliage of medium density	Preference for limestone and chalk subsoils with good loam topsoil	Hardy, requires shelter from wind in order to make good growth	Commonly found along lanes and roadsides, and on edge of woods
Lawson cypress	30	9	60	18	Fairly fast growing	Deep, moist loam of neutral reaction	Hardy against wind and frost	Below 3000 ft (914·40 m) and 3–15 miles (4·83–24·14 km) from the coast./Needs full sun to grow vigorously
Swamp cypress	20	6	45	13·7	Narrow and pyramidal	Good, deep loam preferably near water—acid soils	Hardy and wind firm	Suitable for waterside
Cornish elm	20–40	6–12	40–60	12–18	Fairly fast	Prefers alluvial silt or moist gravel		
English elm	35	76	40–60	12–18	Fairly fast	Deep, well-drained valley loam and silt. Preference for soils that are slightly alkaline in reaction	Hardy against frost and wind	Wild in south of England
Wych elm	Under 40	Under 12	40–60	12–18	Vigorous	Rich loam and heavy soils, especially overlying limestone	Very hardy against frost and wind	Used as shade tree for pastures. Grows at considerable elevations
Eucalyptus (Blue gum)	20	6	30–40	9–12	Very rapid in early stages	Moist and well drained	Endures frost	Coast and waterside
Douglas fir	50	15	Over 60	Over 18	Fast	Moist	Hardy against frost, but dislikes windy positions	Coast, lawn, woodland
Gleditschia (Honey locust)	Under 20	Under 6	40	12	Rather slow	Light, rich loam or alluvial silt	Warmer parts	Streams, valleys
Hawthorn	Under 20	Under 6	30	9	Slow in height, rapid in thickness	Tolerant of all but wet or acid soils	Endures wind and cold	Hedge and plant
Holly	20	6	Under 40	Under 12	Slow	Any	Dislikes extremes of moisture or drought	Woodland
Hornbeam	20	6	Over 40	Over 12	Slow	Best on silt or gravel overlying heavier subsoil	Hardy against frost and wind	Lowland
Judas tree	20	6	–	–	Vigorous	Light well-drained loam or sandy soils	Sun and shelter from spring frosts	–
Laburnum	15	4·6	20	6	Fast in early stages	Calcareous soils	Very hardy	Edge of woodland
Larch	Under 40	Under 12	60	18	Vigorous and rapid	Best on good loamy soils with plenty of moisture	High rainfall	Higher slopes and as windscreens

Table 4.18 TREE GROWTH (*continued*)

Tree	Height in 20 yrs.		Height in 50 yrs.		Growth	Soil	Climate	Habitat/Use
	ft	*m*	*ft*	*m*				
Lime	20	6	Over 50	Over 15	Fairly fast	Deep, moist soil	Hardy and fairly wind firm	Woodland
Magnolia Conspicua (Yulan)	20	6	Over 30	Over 9	Rather slow	Moist, well aerated soil	Warm situations free from late frost	Open woodland forest glades
Maidenhair tree	30	9	Over 40	Over 12	Erratic	Deep, well-drained loam	Very hardy against frost but requires shelter	Lawn
Field maple	20	6	35	7·6	Rather slow	Alluvial soils	Hardy against frost	Woodland
Silver maple	20–40	6–12	60	18	Fastest growing maple	Rich, moist loam or alluvial silt	Hardy against frost	Open positions
English oak	Under 20	Under 6	40–60	12–18	Normally slow	Stiff loams overlying clay	Hardy against wind and frost	Woodland
Evergreen oak	Under 20	Under 6	Over 40	Over 12	Rather slow	Deep, warm, alkaline loams	Not hardy in north of Britain	Coastal areas
Scarlet oak	25	7·6	40	12	Vigorous in suitable soils	Moist, well drained soil	Warm, sheltered positions	—
Turkey oak	Over 20	Over 6	Over 40	Over 12	Faster than other oaks	Strong, stiff loam	Hardy against frost and wind	Low altitudes
Willowleaf pear	Under 20	Under 6	30	9	Rather slow	Rich, well-drained loam	Very hardy against frost and wind	—
Corsican pine	41	12	Over 60	Over 18	Slow at first, then rapid	Well-drained soil	Warm, dry sunny positions	Coast
Scots pine	–	–	40–60	12–18	Fairly fast	Light, well-drained acid soil	Very hardy	Coast, woodland, windscreen
Plane	Over 20	Over 6	40–60	12–18	Fairly fast	Deep loam or gravelly silt	Warm sunny positions	Domesticated
Black Italian poplar	Over 40	Over 12	Under 100	Under 30	Very fast in early stages	Moist loam	Very hardy	Riverside, valleys
Grey poplar	Over 40	Over 12	Under 100	Under 30	Fast	Moist, light loam	Very hardy	Damp woods
Lombardy poplar	Over 40	Over 12	Over 80	Over 24	Very fast in early stages	Moist, rich silt	Hardy	Windbreaks
Rowan (mountain ash)	20–40	6–12	Over 25	Over 7·6	Rather slow	Light, sandy or peaty loams	Hardy	Highland districts of north and west
Norway spruce	Over 20	Over 6	Over 60	Over 18	Fast between 6–40 years	Moist, deep alluvial loam	Moist conditions and can endure frost and wind	Windscreen, woodland
Serbian spruce	20–40	6–12	60	Over 18	—	Light, moist soils	Hardy against frost	Windscreen, woodland
Sycamore	20–40	6–12	Over 60	Over 18	Rapid	Prefers gravel lying over clay	Very hardy	Woodland, windscreen

Table 4.18 TREE GROWTH *(concluded)*

Tree	Height in 20 yrs.		Height in 50 yrs.		Growth	Soil	Climate	Habitat/Use
	ft	*m*	*ft*	*m*				
Giant thuya	Over 40	Over 12	Over 60	Over 18	Fast in early stages	Moist, well-drained sandy loams	Prefers moist atmosphere	Woodland, windscreen
Tulip tree	Over 40	Over 12	Over 80	Over 24	Fast	Deep, rich loam	Hardy but requires sunny conditions	Forest tree, river valleys
Walnut	20–40	6–12	40–60	12–18	Slow in early stages	Deep, light loam over chalk or limestone. Good drainage	Full sun, as not very hardy	—
Wellingtonia	40	12	Approx 100	Approx 30	Very vigorous	Any soil of neutral reaction	South sheltered positions preferred	—
Whitebeam	Under 20	Under 6	Under 40	Under 12	Slow in early stages	Light, well-drained loams	Hardy against frost and wind	Well developed on chalk hills
Weeping willow	20–40	6–12	40–60	12–18	Fast in young stages	Moist, valley loam	Open, sunny position	Banks of rivers and canals
White willow	20–40	6–12	40–60	12–18	Rapid	Moist, valley loam	Hardy	Low altitude, watersides
Yew	10	3	Under 40	Under 12	Slow	Preference for chalk and limestone	Very hardy	Woods

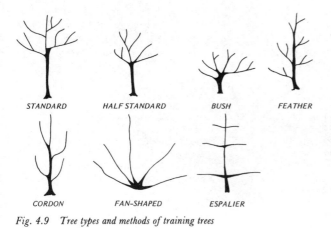

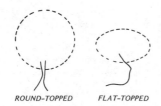

Fig. 4.9   Tree types and methods of training trees

STANDARD   HALF STANDARD   BUSH   FEATHER

CORDON   FAN-SHAPED   ESPALIER

Table 4.19 RECOMMENDED SIZES FOR TREES AND BUSHES

Form	Height from ground level to lowest branch		Diam. of stem measured to lowest branch between 2 ft 0 in–3 ft 0 in (610 mm–914 mm) from ground	
	in	*mm*	*in* (*minimum*)	*mm*
Bush	12–30	305– 762	—	—
Half standard	42–54	1067–1372	$\frac{3}{4}$	19·1
Three-quarter standard	57–63	1448–1600	$\frac{3}{4}$	19·1
Standard	66–72	1676–1829	$\frac{3}{4}$	19·1
Tall standard	75–84	1905–2134	1	25·0
Weeping standard	66	1676	$\frac{3}{4}$	19·1

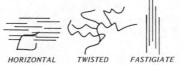

ROUND-TOPPED   FLAT-TOPPED   WEEPING   HORIZONTAL   TWISTED   FASTIGIATE   PYRAMIDAL

Fig. 4.10   Tree shapes

49

SERVICES

ELECTRICITY

Cables are laid directly in the ground. Where this is not possible, they are drawn through 4 in (102 mm) diameter earthenware ducts (older 3 in (76 mm) ducts are still in use). Low voltage cables must be laid at a minimum depth of 1 ft 6 in (457 mm) below ground, and runs are usually restricted to 400 ft (122 m).

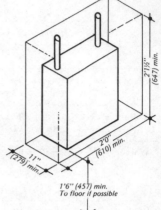

GAS

	Depth below ground
Mains: cast iron or steel 4 in (102 mm) minimum diameter	2 ft 0 in–2 ft 6 in (610–762 mm)
Service pipes: steel 1 in (25 mm) minimum diameter	1 ft 6 in–2 ft 0 in (457–610 mm)

Cover sizes are: 9 in (228mm)

Fig. 4.11   Meter sizes for domestic gas supply

WATER

	Diameter
Mains: cast iron, steel and occasionally asbestos	2–132 in (0·05–3·35 m)
Communication pipes: lead or polythene	½–1 in (12·7–25 mm)

Mains	Depth below ground
½–1 in (12·7–25 mm)	2 ft 6 in (762 mm)
2–12 in (51–305 mm)	3 ft 0 in (914 mm)
1–2 ft (305–610 mm)	3 ft 6 in (1·07 m)
Over 2 ft (610 mm)	4 ft 0 in (1·22 m)

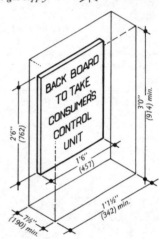

Fig. 4.12   Consumer control for domestic electricity supply

Table 4.20 SERVICES

Services	Materials and access needs	Minimum depth
Water mains	Mainly 4 in (102 mm) dia. cast iron, steel or asbestos (3–12 in (76–305 mm) dia. common; largest is 11 ft 0 in (3·35 m))	3 ft (914 mm) depth (up to 12 in (305 mm) dia.) 3 ft 6 in (1·07 m) depth (up to 24 in (610 mm) dia.)
Branches	½–2 in (12·7–51 mm) dia. Polythene useful, unaffected by soils or frost	2 ft 6 in (762 mm) depth
Gas mains Service Branches	4 in (102 mm) dia. min.; cast iron or steel 1 in (25 mm) dia. min.; W.I. steel ¼ in (6·25 mm) dia. min. Fall to main	2 ft 0 in–2 ft 6 in (610–762 mm) 1 ft 6 in–2 ft 0 in (457–610 mm)
Electricity mains (high voltage)	Low voltage is wasteful on long runs so street lights are run off spurs from mains below ground. The cables are laid direct in the ground or drawn through 4 in (102 mm) earthenware ducts in busy areas	1 ft 6 in (457 mm) or by agreement with the Highway Authority
Feeders (low voltage) (to lights, kiosks, etc.)	400 ft (122 m) length usual maximum. Armoured cable with tile covers	Just below paving
G.P.O. telephones	Polythene cables in ground or in ducts 2–3½ in (51–88·9 mm) asbestos and PVC ducts encased in concrete 170 yd (155 m) max. between surface junction boxes	9 in (228 mm) (protected cable), 1 ft 2 in (356 mm) (steel or self-aligning duct), 1 ft 6 in (457 mm) (3⅝ in (92·07 mm) earthenware ducts with 1, 2, 4, 6 and 9 ways)

Table 4.21 EXTERNAL LAMPS AND LIGHTING

	Tungsten	Mercury/fluorescent	Sodium	Fluorescent	Tungsten halogen
Colour	Yellow/white	Green/white	Yellow (monochromatic)	White	White
Colour rendering	Very good	Good	Poor	Very good	Very good
Lamp wattage range	40–1500	50–2000	45–200	40–125	750–1500*
Normal life (h)	1000	5000	4000	5000	2000
Lamp dimensions	Normal domestic size approx. 7 in (178 mm) long	Similar to tungsten	Approx. 12 in (305 mm) long	Sizes vary from 1–8 ft (0·30–2·43 m); circular and bulkhead fitting available	Between approx. 2–10 in (51–254 mm) in length, diameter of only approx. $\frac{1}{2}$–$\frac{3}{4}$ in (17·7–19·1 mm)
Lantern types	All types	Similar to tungsten: choke and capacitation usually housed in column base	Medium-sized lantern	Large lantern	Small flood lighting lantern
Cost of typical 15 ft (4·57 m) column and lantern†	£15–17	£15–20	£20–25	£25–30	—

* Lower wattages for special applications.
† Cost of electric service will be dependent on site conditions and availability of existing supply. The figures given in this table only outline the principal characteristics of various lighting sources; detailed information is available from manufacturers.

G.P.O. TELEPHONES

Polythene cables are laid in ducts or straight in the ground. Earthenware ducts with $3\frac{5}{8}$ in (92·07 mm) bore are most commonly used. Asbestos cement ducts with 2 in (51 mm) to $3\frac{1}{2}$ (88·90 mm) bore and 2 in (51 mm) P.V.C. ducts are used on housing estates. Polythene cables of up to 100 pairs are often used without ducts. The minimum depth for protected cables is 9 in (228 mm) and for steel self-aligning ducts (one-way) 14 in (356 mm). Multiple-way ducts below the footway are 18 in (457 mm) and below the carriageway 24 in (610 mm). Cover sizes are 10 in × 2 ft 4 in (254 × 711 mm) to 7 ft 6 in × 2 ft 4 in (2286 × 711 mm).

SEWERS

These cannot be grouped with other services. They have to be laid in straight lines of uniform gradient between manholes.

DRAIN AND SEWER SIZES AND FALLS

Drains should have a minimum velocity of 3 ft (914 mm) per second. Maguire's rule: Where D = internal diameter in millimetres, the fall should be 1:100. Manholes should not be spaced more than 120 ft (36·57 m) apart to facilitate rodding.

Table 4.22 VELOCITY AND DISCHARGE: VITRIFIED CLAY PIPES

Diameter of drains		Area		Fall	Velocity		Full discharge	
in	mm	in²	mm²		ft/s	mm/s	gal/min	litres/min
4	102	12·57	8062	1:60	3·02	914	99	450
				1:40	3·70	933	121	550
				1:30	4·28	1225	140	636
6	152	28·27	18071	1:100	3·07	914	225	1023
				1:80	3·45	926	253	1150
				1:60	3·97	1219	291	1323
				1:40	4·86	1239	355	1614
9	228	63·62	40659	1:120	3·68	932	610	2773
				1:90	4·25	1225	702	3192
				1:60	5·21	1530	860	3910
12	305	113·10	72903	1:260	3·03	914	892	4055
				1:120	4·46	1231	1310	5956

EXTERNAL WORKS AND LANDSCAPE

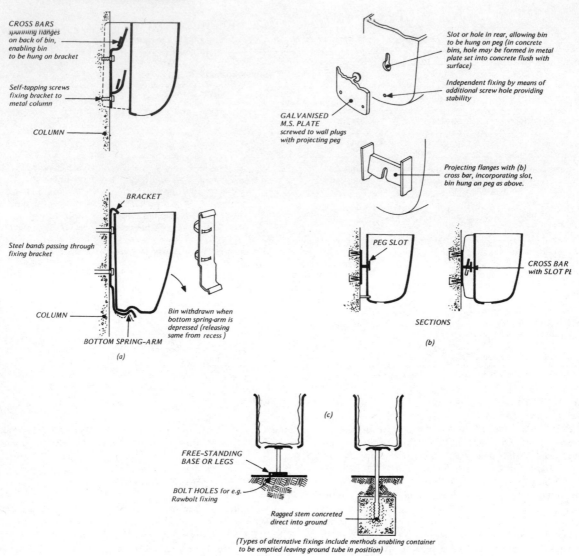

Fig. 4.13 Different types of litter bin. (a) Fixing to columns; (b) fixing to wall or vertical surface; (c) freestanding and fixed to ground

BIBLIOGRAPHY

BRITISH STANDARDS INSTITUTION

Paving, Roads, External Works and Features

B.S. 63:1951 — Single-sized roadstone and chippings. Amendments P.D. 1587, March 1953; P.D. 2009, Oct. 1954; P.D. 3488, Aug. 1959; A.M.D. 6, May 1968.

B.S. 76:1964 — Tars for road purposes.

B.S. 340:1963 — Specification for precast concrete kerbs, channels, edgings and quadrants.

B.S. 368:1956 — Precast concrete flags. Amendment P.D. 4896, Apr. 1963.

B.S. 435:1931 — Granite and whinstone kerbs, channels, quadrants and setts. Amendment P.D. 3538, Nov. 1959.

B.S. 594:1961 — Rolled asphalt (hot process). Amendments P.D. 4566, May 1962; A.M.D. 4, May 1968.

B.S. 706:1936 — Sandstone kerbs, channels, quadrants and setts (confirmed 1960). Amendment P.D. 3670, Feb. 1960.

B.S. 802:1967 — Tarmacadam with crushed rock or slag aggregate. Amendment P.D. 6125, Apr. 1967.

B.S. 892:1967 — Glossary of highway engineering terms.

B.S. 1241:1959 — Tarmacadam and tar carpets (gravel aggregate).

B.S. 1242:1960 Tarmacadam and 'tar paving' for footpaths, playgrounds and similar works. Amendment P.D. 6241, Aug. 1967.

B.S. 1324:1962 Asphalt tiles for paving and flooring (natural rock asphalt). Amendment P.D. 5811, March 1966.

B.S. 1373:1967 Clothes-line posts.

B.S. 1446:1962 Mastic asphalt (natural rock asphalt aggregate) for roads and footways. Amendment P.D. 5945, Nov. 1966.

B.S. 1447:1962 Mastic asphalt (limestone aggregate) for roads and footways. Amendment P.D. 5935, Nov. 1966.

B.S. 1623:1950 Hand rollers for road and constructional engineering (confirmed 1958).

B.S. 1716:1963 Cycle stands.

B.S. 1984:1967 Gravel aggregates for surface treatment (including surface dressings) on roads.

B.S. 2040:1953 Bitumen macadam with gravel aggregate (confirmed 1960).

B.S. 2542:1960 Recommendations for the use of bitumen emulsion (anionic) for roads.

B.S. 3690:1970 Bitumens for road purposes.

B.S. 3969:1965 Recommendations for turf for general landscape purposes.

B.S. 3975:—— Glossary for landscape work.
Part 4:1966. Plant description.

B.S. 4008:1966 Cattlegrids on private roads.

Street Furniture

B.S. 1308:1970 Concrete street lighting columns.

B.S. 1788:1964 Street lighting lanterns for use with electric lamps. Amendments P.D. 6276, Nov. 1967; A.M.D. 241, Apr. 1969; A.M.D. 533, June 1970.

B.S. 1840:1960 Steel columns for street lighting.

B.S. 3989:1966 Aluminium street lighting columns.

C.P. 1004:—— Street lighting, Parts 1 and 2: 1963. Part 1 General principles. Part 2 Lighting for traffic routes.
Part 3: 1969. Lighting for lightly trafficked roads and footways (Group B).
Part 4: 1967. Lighting for single-level road junctions including roundabouts.
Part 6: 1967. Lighting for bridges and elevated roads (Group D).
Part 8: 1967. Lighting for roads with special requirements (Group F).
Part 9: 1969. Lighting for town and city centres and areas of civic importance (Group G).

Fencing and Gates

B.S. 1485:1948 Galvanised wire netting.

B.S. 1722:—— Fences.
Part 1: 1963. Chain-link fences. Amendments P.D. 5318, Aug. 1964; P.D. 5579, July 1965; P.D. 6089, March 1967.
Part 2: 1963. Woven wire fences. Amendments P.D. 5000, Aug. 1963; P.D. 5319,

Aug. 1964; P.D. 5581, July 1965; P.D. 6109, March 1967.
Part 3: 1963. Strained wire fences. Amendments P.D. 5001, Aug. 1963; P.D. 5580, July 1965; P.D. 6110, March 1967.
Part 4: 1963. Cleft chestnut pale fences. Amendments P.D. 5320, Aug. 1964; P.D. 5582, July 1965; P.D. 6113, March 1967.
Part 5: 1963. Close-boarded fences including oak pale fences. Amendments P.D. 5002, Aug. 1963; P.D. 5321, Aug. 1964; P.D. 5583, July 1965.
Part 6: 1963. Wooden palisade fences. Amendments P.D. 5003, Aug. 1963; P.D. 5584, July 1965.
Part 7: 1963. Wooden post and rail fences. Amendments P.D. 5322, Aug. 1964; P.D. 6114, March 1967; P.D. 6417, May 1968.
Part 8: 1966. Mild steel or wrought iron continuous bar fences.
Part 9: 1963. Mild steel or wrought iron unclimbable fences with round or square verticals and flat standards and horizontals.
Part 10: 1963. Anti-intruder chain link fences. Amendments P.D. 5356, Oct. 1964; P.D. 6115, March 1967; A.M.D. 644, Dec. 1970.
Part 11: 1965. Woven wood fences.

B.S. 3470:1962 Field gates and posts. Amendments P.D. 4682, Oct. 1962; P.D. 4931, May 1963; P.D. 5327, Sept. 1964.

B.S. 3854:1965 Farm stock fences. Amendment P.D. 6111, March 1967.

B.S. 4092:—— Domestic front entrance gates.
Part 1: 1966. Metal gates.
Part 2: 1966. Wooden gates.

B.S. 4102:1967 Steel wire for fences.

Landscape Work

B.S. 3882:1965 Recommendations and classification for top soil.

B.S. 3936:—— Nursery stock.
Part 1: 1965. Trees and shrubs. Amendment P.D. 6026, March 1967.
Part 2: 1966. Roses. Amendments P.D. 5886, July 1966; P.D. 6303, Jan. 1968.
Part 3: 1965. Fruit.
Part 4: 1966. Forest trees.

B.S. 3969:1965 Recommendations for turf for general landscape purposes.

B.S. 3975:—— Glossary of terms for landscape work.
Part 4: 1966. Plant description.

B.S. 3998:1966 Recommendations for tree work.

B.S. 4043:1966 Recommendations for transplanting semi-mature trees.

B.S. 4132:1967 Winkle clinker for landscape work.

Services

C.P. 3:—— Code of basic data for the design of buildings. Chapter 7: 1950. Engineering and utility

	services. Amendments P.D. 1468, Aug. 1952; P.D. 5362, Oct. 1964; A.M.D. 636, Nov. 1970.
C.P. 99:1965	Frost precautions for water services. Amendment P.D. 6416, May 1968.
C.P. 310:1965	Water supply. Amendment A.M.D. 665, Dec. 1970.
C.P. 321:1965	Electrical installations.
C.P. 331:——	Installation of pipes and meters for town gas. Part 1: 1957. Service pipes. Amendments P.D. 3115, July 1958; P.D. 5606, Aug. 1965. Part 3: 1965. Installation pipes.
C.P. 332:——	Selection and installation of town gas space heating.
C.P. 333:——	Selection and installation of town gas hot water supplies. Part 1: 1964. Domestic premises. Amendment P.D. 5608, Aug. 1965. Part 2: 1948. Schools. Amendment P.D. 5609, Aug. 1965.

OTHER PUBLICATIONS

Gardens—Landscape

ANON, *Landscaping for Modern Living*, Sunset Publishers, Meulo Park, California, Lane Book Company (1961)

BEAZLEY, ELIZABETH, *Design and Detail of the Space Between Buildings*, Architectural Press, London (1960)

BRADBURY, ELIZABETH, *Trees as a Medium of Design* (R.I.B.A. Silver Medal Essay 1963–64 (commended) (mainly photographs)), (Library R.I.B.A.)

BRETT, L., *Landscape in Distress*, Architectural Press, London (1965)

CHADWICK, G. F., *The Park and the Town*, Architectural Press, London (1966)

CIVIC TRUST, *Street Improvement Schemes* (Practice Notes for Co-Ordinating Architects) (1967)

CULLEN, GORDON, *Townscape*, Architectural Press, London (1961)

ECKBO, GARRETT, *The Art of Home Landscaping*, F. W. Dodge, New York (1956)

ECKBO, GARRETT, *The Landscape We See*, McGraw-Hill, New York (1969)

ECKBO, GARRETT, *Urban Landscape Design*, McGraw-Hill, New York (1964)

HADFIELD, MILES, *Landscape with Trees*, Country Life, London (1967)

JELLICOE, G. A., *Studies in Landscape Design*, Oxford University Press, London (1960)

LINDER, WERNER, *Bauwerk und Umgebung (Buildings and Their Surroundings)*. Problems of siting buildings in the countryside, village and town. Report of the German Heimatbundes, **2**, Wasmuth, Tubingen (1964)

MINISTRY OF HOUSING AND LOCAL GOVERNMENT, *Landscaping for Flats: The Treatment of Ground Space on High Density Housing Estates*, Design Bulletin No. 5, H.M.S.O.

NAIRN, IAN, *The American Landscape: A Critical View*, Random House, New York (1965)

ORMSBEE SIMONDS, JOHN, *Landscape Architecture: The Shaping of Man's Natural Environment*. Published in Great Britain for *The Architect and Building News* by Iliffe Books (1961)

WEDDLE, A. E., 'Landscape with Figures', *Reprint from the Town Planning Review*, **39**, No. 4 (1969). (Based on the inaugural address given by Professor Weddle on 16th October 1968 in the University of Sheffield, Liverpool University Press, p. 307–318

WEDDLE, A. E. (editor), *Techniques of Landscape Architecture*, edited for The Institute of Landscape Architects, Heinemann, London (1967)

Roads

Association of Street Lighting Equipment Contractors, *Code of Practice for Street Lighting Equipment* (1959)

BREWSTER SNOW, W., *The Highway and the Landscape*, N. J. Rutgers, University Press, New Brunswick (1959)

British Road Federation, *Finance and Roads*, London (1963)

British Road Federation, *Roads: A New Approach; Summary of Report by a Working Party on Road Finance Administration* (summary of main report) (1968)

Cement and Concrete Association, Library Bibliography of Prestressed Concrete Roads and Runways

CROSS, C. A. and GARNER, J. F., *Highway Law including the Highways Act 1959*, annotated. Sweet and Maxwell, London (1960)

CROWE, SYLVIA, *Landscape of Roads*, Architectural Press (1960)

CROWE, SYLVIA, *Tomorrow's Landscape*, Architectural Press (1956)

Greater London Council, *London Roads: A Programme for Action* (1967)

HARRISON, GODFREY, narrative by, *Highway Needs: A Brief Summary of a Survey in South Wales and Monmouthshire* (Summary of Detailed Survey instituted by the Industrial Association of Wales and Monmouthshire), British Road Federation

Institution of Civil Engineers, *Proceedings of Conference on the Highway Needs of Great Britain*, London (1958)

JONES, JOHN HUGH, *The Geometric Design of Modern Highways* (Spons Civil Engineering Series edited by W. Fisher Cassie), E. and F. N. Spon, London (1961)

Metropolitan Boroughs Standing Joint Committee, *Practice Notes for Street Lighting in London* (1958)

MINISTRY OF TRANSPORT et al., *Specification for Roads and Bridgeworks*, H.M.S.O. (1969)

MINISTRY OF TRANSPORT, *Highways Act 1959*, H.M.S.O. Paving Patterns, *Building Materials*, London (1964)

ROGERS, W. T., *What Shall We Do About Roads?* Fabian Research Series 206 (1959)

SCHREUDER, D. A., *Lighting of Vehicular Traffic Tunnels*, MacMillan (1964)

SCOTTISH DEVELOPMENT DEPARTMENT, *Scottish Housing Handbook 2, Roads and Services*, H.M.S.O. (1963)

THORNHILL, PATRICK, *Roads and Streets*, illustrated by James Arnold, Get to Know Series for Local Studies, Methuen, London (1959)

TUNNARD, CHRISTOPHER and BOVIS, PUSHKAREV, *Man-Made America—Chaos or Control?* An Enquiry into Selected Problems of Design in the Urbanised Landscape, Yale University Press, Newhaven (1963)

WILLIAMS ELLIS, CLOUGH, *Roads in the Landscape*, H.M.S.O. (1967)

Trees

BODDY, F. A., *Highway Trees,* Clarke & Hunter, Gilford (1968)
CABORN, J. M., *Shelter Belts and Windbreaks,* Faber, London (1965)
CIVIC TRUST, 'Large Tree Transplanting', *Reprint from Industrial Architecture,* No. 3, p. 161–164 (March 1965)
CIVIC TRUST, *Moving Big Trees* (1967)
CIVIC TRUST, *Practice Notes on the Transplanting of Semi-mature Trees* (1967)
COLLINS, PETER (drawn by Badmin, S. R.), 'Trees of Britain', *Sunday Times* (1960)
COLVIN, B., *Trees for Town and Country,* Lund Humphries Publishers Ltd, London (1961)
Economic Forestry Group, Landscape Division, *Instant Trees,* Herts Economic Forestry Group 'Instant Trees Ltd', Berkhamstead (1967)
EDWARDS, PAUL, *Trees and the English Landscape,* Bell, London (1962)
HICKS, PHILIP, 'The Care of Trees on Development Sites', Advisory leaflet No. 3, Arboricultural Association (1968)
MINISTRY OF AGRICULTURE AND FISHERIES, 'Commercial Glass Houses', Bulletin No. 115, 4th edn., H.M.S.O. (1964)
MINISTRY OF AGRICULTURE AND FISHERIES, 'Soil Sterilisation', Bulletin No. 22, H.M.S.O.
MINISTRY OF HOUSING AND LOCAL GOVERNMENT, *Trees in Town and City,* H.M.S.O. (1958)
MORLING, RONALD J., *Trees, Including Preservation, Planting, Law, Highways,* Estates Gazette, London (Second revised edition) (1963)
PEARCE, S. A., *Ornamental Trees for Garden and Roadside Planting.* Chapters on diseases by Derek A. Reid, and Insect Pests by Joyce Van Konyenburg, W. H. and L. Collingridge (1961)

Electricity

Association of Supervising Electrical Engineers, Regulations for the Electrical Equipment of Buildings, Illustrated Guide to the I.E.E., 14th edn (1966)
British Electrical Development Association, *Electrical Data for Architects* (1957)
CRISP, J., 'Use of Mains Electricity on Building Sites', *Reprinted for Electrical Times* (1962), Department of Scientific and Industrial Research B.R.S.
Electrical Commissioners, *Electricity Supply Regulations,* H.M.S.O. (1937)
GRANT, BRIAN, *Electrical Installations,* A Handbook for Architects and Assistants, Architectural Press, London (1957)
HOLFORD, SIR WILLIAM, 'Electricity and the Landscape', Reprint from *The Guardian* Survey of Britain's Power Supplies, Central Electricity Generating Board, Newsletter No. 12 (1961)
JAY, PETER and HEMSLEY, JOHN, *Electrical Services in Buildings,*
Elsevier Architectural Science Series, Amsterdam (1968)
OSBORNE, A. L., *Electricity in Building,* B. T. Batsford, London (1957)
WHITFIELD, J. F., *Electrical Installations and Regulations,* Commonwealth and International Library, Electrical Engineers Division No. 2368 (1966)

Gas

Gas Council, 'Gas Handbook for Architects and Builders', Reprinted from Gas Council Supplements in *The Architects' Journal* (1956–60)

Water Supply, Sanitation, Drainage and Sewerage

ANDERSON, EDWIN P., *Audel's Domestic Water Supply and Sewage Disposal Guide: A Practical Treatise,* Audel, New York (1960)
ASHER, S. J., *Water Supply and Main Drainage,* Crosby Lockwood, London (1961)
BLAKE, E. H. and JENKINS, W. R. (revised by Gumbrell, Leonard B. and Smith, J. Francis), *Drainage and Sanitation,* 11th edn, Batsford, London (1956)
CRIMP, W. SANTO and BRUGES, W. E., (Revised by W. E. Bruges), *Tables and Diagrams for Use in Designing Sewers and Water Mains,* 3rd edn, Municipal Publications, London (1964)
DAVIES, A. G., *Public Cleansing: Present and Future,* Spon, London (1961)
ESCRITT, L. B., 'Sewage and Sewage Disposal, Calculations and Designs', *Contractors' Record,* London (1956)
GILLET, R. T., 'The Sanitation of Tall Buildings', reprinted from H.M. Ministry of Works for the Instute of Health Engineers (1961)
GLANVILLE GOODIN, F. and DOWNING, J., *Domestic Sanitation,* Estate Gazette Ltd, London (1959)
MINISTRY OF HOUSING AND LOCAL GOVERNMENT, *Metric Units with Reference to Water, Sewage and Related Subjects, Reprint of Working Party,* H.M.S.O. (1968)
MINISTRY OF HOUSING AND LOCAL GOVERNMENT, *Model Byelaws, Series 1, The Removal of House Refuse and the Cleansing of Earth Closets, Privies, Ashpits and Cesspools,* H.M.S.O. (1958)
MINISTRY OF HOUSING AND LOCAL GOVERNMENT, *Model Water Byelaws,* H.M.S.O., 2nd edn (1966)
MITCHELL, G. ERIC (revised by Thrower, S. E.), *Sanitation, Drainage and Water Supply,* George Newnes, London (1960)
'The Sizing of Building Drainage', *Booklet No. 8,* Institute of Plumbing, London (1968)
TWORT, A. C., *A Text Book of Water Supply,* Arnold, London (1963)
WEBSTER, SYDNEY, *Plumbing in Building,* Batsford, London (1957)
WISE, A. F. E., *Drainage Pipework in Dwellings: Hydraulic Design and Performance,* Department of Scientific and Industrial Research, H.M.S.O. (1959)

5 DIMENSIONAL CO-ORDINATION

Dimensional co-ordination is a tool by which compatibility may be achieved between the processes of design, manufacture and assembly of buildings and components to increase productivity. Its success will depend upon the balance being achieved between the needs of: the designer—who requires choice of components to satisfy the requirements of his clients and flexibility in the application of the components; the manufacturer—who requires variety reduction of components to meet the demands of economic production; and the contractor—who requires simplicity in order to reduce the number of operations in estimating, ordering, handling and assembling components.

METRIC EQUIVALENTS

During the transitional period it will be necessary to use imperial products in metric projects. When imperial sizes are converted to metric they should be rounded off to an appropriate degree of accuracy. These sizes are then referred to as metric equivalents.

SENSIBLE METRIC SIZES

Products that are to be modified but do not require to be dimensionally co-ordinated may have their sizes changed to rounded metric sizes to suit metric tools and gauges. These are normally referred to as sensible metric sizes.

CO-ORDINATED SIZES

Dimensionally co-ordinated sizes are derived from the preferences given in B.S. 4011. In selecting these first preference should be given to multiples of 300 mm and second preference to multiples of 100 mm. For sizes not exceeding 300 mm a third preference may be given to multiples of 50 mm and a fourth preference to multiples of 25 mm.

Table 5.1 SYMBOLS USED IN DIMENSIONAL CO-ORDINATION

Reference lines	Normally indicated as a continuous line.	
Centre and axial lines	Are normally also reference lines and are indicated as a thin chain line.	
Controlling lines	Indicated by a circle at the end of a reference line.	
Modular space	Diagrammatic representation of a basic space.	
Basic size	The symbol for a basic size of basic space which is a co-ordinated size.	
Work size	The size for the manufacture of a component or location of a component which is not a basic size.	

ASSEMBLY: SETTING-OUT

BASE LINES

Base lines should be related to the key planes of a building and set out in the normal manner.

CONTROLLING LINES

From the base lines one or more controlling lines can be established in order to locate zones for loadbearing walls or columns.

LOADBEARING WALLS WITH COLUMNS

Loadbearing walls and columns may then be constructed within the zones.

COMPONENTS

Components may then be located by reference to critical grid lines or controlling lines, taking into account the actual space achieved and the degree of tolerance, to which the components have been designed.

ACTUAL LOCATION

Once the first components are assembled on site, the dimensional framework is represented by tangible objects. The actual location of a component or assembly of components will vary within the limits specified, according to its actual size when manufactured and the accuracy with which it is positioned.

SEQUENCE OF ASSEMBLY

The accuracy with which the first components are assembled is therefore most important and will determine the space available to later components. This may either be larger or smaller than the basic space allocated to the components on the drawings.

SIZING AND TOLERANCES

The sizing and tolerances given to components have to be designed to accommodate these variations.

JOINTS

The joint design then has to be capable of accommodating the resulting gap sizes. A range of sizes of jointing components may therefore be necessary.

6   LEGISLATION

BUILDING REGULATIONS

On 1st July 1966, the responsibility for building regulations was transferred from the Minister of Public Building and Works to the Minister of Housing and Local Government for England, and the Secretary of State for Wales; for Wales and Monmouthshire. However, it is the responsibility of the Minister of Housing and Local Government only, to make (and to amend) building regulations.

The first set of regulations (S.I. 1965, No. 1373) came into force everywhere in England and Wales, except the Inner London Boroughs on 1st February 1966. These have been amended by Building (2nd Amendment) Regulations 1966 (S.I. 1966, No. 1144), which came into operation on 1st November 1966, and superseded the Building (1st Amendment) Regulations, 1965.

Administration and enforcement are the responsibility of local authorities in the first instance and regulation A9 requires plans and/or other particulars to be deposited with them wherever a person: (a) erects or re-erects a building which is not exempt from all or some of the regulations; (b) carries out alterations or extensions to such a building; (c) carries out work of drainage or sanitation, constructs wells or rainwater tanks for storing water for human consumption, or installs heat-producing appliances or incinerators in connection with such a building; or (d) effects certain changes in the use to which such a building is put.

INNER LONDON BOROUGHS

Legislation in the Inner London Boroughs is controlled by the London Building Act 1930; London Building Act (Amendment) Act 1935 and London Building Acts (Amendment) Act 1939. Memoranda on these acts are available from the G.L.C.

LOCAL ACTS OF PARLIAMENT

Since the Building Regulations came into operation, most provisions of local Acts of Parliament, which formerly covered the same ground, have been repealed. Some local authorities, however, may still have local Acts with provisions which are additional to those in the Regulations, or which modify the provisions of the Public Health Acts 1936 and 1961. As the authorities concerned consider that they play an essential part in the machinery of control in their areas, it has been agreed that they may continue in force for the time being.

NATIONAL ACTS AND BILLS AFFECTING BUILDING WORK

ADMINISTRATION

City of London (Various Powers) Act, 1958
Greater London Council (General Powers) Act, 1965
L.C.C. General Powers' Acts, 1931, 1933, 1945, 1954, 1955, 1958, 1962
Local Government Acts, 1888, 1929, 1933, 1958
Local Government (Miscellaneous Provisions) Act, 1953
London Government Act, 1963
Metropolis Management Act, 1855
Metropolis Management Act, 1862, Amendment Act, 1890
Metropolis Management Amendment Act, 1862
Metropolis Management and Building Acts, Amendment Act, 1878
Statutory Orders (Special Procedure) Act, 1945
Surrey County Council Act, 1931
Tribunals and Enquiries Act, 1958

AGRICULTURE AND HORTICULTURE

Agriculture Acts, 1947 and 1957
Agriculture and Horticulture Act, 1964
Agriculture (Safety, Health and Welfare Provisions) Act, 1956
Agriculture (Miscellaneous Provisions) Act, 1941
Agricultural Holdings Act, 1948
Agricultural Land (Removal of Surface Soil) Act, 1953
Horticulture Act, 1960

ANIMALS

Animal Boarding Establishments Act, 1963
Pet Animals Act, 1951
Riding Establishments Act, 1964

Slaughterhouses Acts, 1954 and 1958
Street Offences Act, 1959

ARBITRATION

Arbitration Acts, 1889, 1934 and 1950
County Courts Act, 1959
Criminal Justice Act, 1925
Supreme Court of Judicature (Amendment) Act, 1959
Supreme Court of Judicature (Consolidation) Act, 1925

BUILDING CONTROL, GENERAL

Building Control Act, 1966
Building Regulations, 1965
  Part A. General
  Part B. Materials
  Part C. Preparation of site and resistance to moisture
  Part D. Structural stability
  Part E. Structural fire precautions
  Part F. Thermal insulation
  Part G. Sound insulation
  Part H. Stairways and balustrades
  Part J. Refuse disposal
  Part K. Open space, ventilation and height of rooms
  Part L. Chimneys, flue pipes, hearths and fireplace recesses
  Part M. Heat-producing appliances and incinerators
  Part N. Drainage, private sewers and cesspools
  Part P. Sanitary conveniences
  Part Q. Ashpits, wells, tanks and cisterns
Building Restrictions (War-time Contravention) Act, 1946
Control of Offices and Industrial Development Act, 1965
London Building Act, 1930
London Building Act (Amendment) Acts, 1935 and 1939
London Building Constructional Byelaws, 1952–65

CEMETERIES AND CREMATORIA

Burial Act, 1857
Cremation Act, 1902
Disused Burial Grounds Act, 1884

ECCLESIASTICAL PROPERTY AND LAND

Cathedrals Measure, 1963
Church Property (Miscellaneous Provisions) Measure, 1960
Ecclesiastical Dilapidation 1923–29 (Amendment) Measure, 1951
Loans (Incumbents of Benefices) Amendment Act, 1918
New Housing Areas (Church Buildings) Measure, 1954
New Parishes Measure, 1943
Parsonages Measures, 1938 and 1947

EMPLOYMENT AND INDUSTRIAL PREMISES

Contracts of Employment Act, 1963
Control of Office and Industrial Development Act, 1965

Distribution of Industry Act, 1945
Factories Acts, 1937, 1948, 1959 and 1961
Factory and Workshop (Cotton, Cloth Factories) Act, 1929
Local Employment Acts, 1960 and 1963
Offices Act, 1960
Offices, Shops and Railway Premises Act, 1963
Sea Fish Industry, 1938
Shops Act, 1950

FINANCE AND LOANS

Compulsory Purchase Act, 1965
Finance (1909–10) Act, 1910
Finance Acts, 1895, 1914, 1931, 1954, 1962, 1965
Housing (Financial Provisions) Act, 1958
Loans (Incumbents of Benefices) Amendment Act, 1918
Local Government (Financial Provisions) Act, 1963
Local Loans Act, 1875
L.C.C. Loans Act, 1955
National Loans Act, 1939
Public Works Loans Act, 1875

HISTORIC BUILDING AND MONUMENTS

Ancient Monuments Act, 1931
Ancient Monuments Consolidation and Amendment Act, 1913
Ancient Monuments Protection Act, 1882
Historic Buildings and Ancient Monuments Act, 1953
Local Authorities (Historic Buildings) Act, 1962

HOUSING

House Purchase and Housing Act, 1959
Housing Acts, 1949, 1957, 1961 and 1964
Housing (Financial Provisions) Act, 1958
Housing Repairs and Rents Act, 1954
Housing (Slum Clearance Compensation) Act, 1965
Housing (Underground Rooms) Act, 1959
Small Dwellings Acquisition Acts, 1899–1923
Small Tenements Recovery Act, 1838

LAND

Acquisition of Land (Assessment of Compensation) Act, 1919
Acquisition of Land (Authorisation Procedure) Act, 1946
Agricultural Land (Removal of Surface Soil) Act, 1953
Improvement of Land Act, 1864
Land Charges Act, 1925
Land Commission Act, 1966
Land Compensation Act, 1961
Land Drainage Act, 1930 and 1961
Land Registration Act, 1825
Lands Clauses Consolidation Act, 1845
Lands Tribunal Act, 1949
Local Authorities (Land) Act, 1963
Requisitioned Land and War Works Acts, 1945, 1948
Settled Land Act, 1925

LEGISLATION

MINES AND QUARRIES

Coal Mines Act, 1911
Coal Mining (Subsidence) Act, 1957
Mineral Workings Act, 1951
Mines and Quarries Act, 1954
Mines (Working Facilities and Supports) Act, 1966
Opencast Coal Act, 1958

OIL AND PETROLEUM

Oil in Navigable Waters Act, 1955
Petroleum (Amendment) Act, 1928
Petroleum (Consolidation) Act, 1928
Petroleum (Transfer of Licences) Act, 1936

PLANNING

Caravan Sites and Control of Development Act, 1960
Distribution of Industry Act, 1945
New Streets Act, 1951
New Towns Act, 1946 and 1965
Restriction of Ribbon Development Acts, 1935 and 1953
Town and Country Planning Acts, 1932, 1944, 1947, 1953, 1954, 1959, 1962 and 1963
Town and Country Planning (Amendment) Act, 1951
Town Development Act, 1952
Town Planning Act, 1925
Town and Country Planning Act, 1968

PRESERVATION OF AMENITIES AND APPEARANCES

Civic Amenities Act, 1967
Countryside Bill, 1967
Countryside (Scotland) Act, 1967
Forestry Acts, 1947 and 1951
Green Belt (London and the Home Counties) Act, 1938
National Parks and Access to the Countryside Act, 1949
National Trust Act, 1907

PUBLIC HEALTH AND SAFETY

Clean Air Act, 1956
Clean Rivers (Estuaries and Tidal Waters) Act, 1960
Coast Protection Act, 1949
Alkali, etc., Works Regulations Act, 1906
Dangerous Drugs Act, 1951
Explosives Acts, 1875 and 1923
Fire Services Act, 1947
Firearms Act, 1937
Fireworks Act, 1951
Food and Drugs Act, 1955
Litter Act, 1958
National Health Services Act, 1946
National Insurance (Industrial Injuries) Act, 1946
Noise Abatement Act, 1960
Pharmacy and Poison Act, 1933
Prescription Act, 1832

Prevention of Damage by Pests Act, 1949
Public Health Acts, 1875, 1925, 1936 and 1961
Public Health Amendment Act, 1890
Public Health Amendment Act, 1907
Public Health (Building in Streets) Act, 1887
Public Health (Drainage of Trade Premises) Act, 1937
Public Health (London) Act, 1936
Public Health (Smoke Abatement) Act, 1926
Rivers Pollution Prevention Act, 1876
Rivers (Prevention of Pollution) Act, 1951 and 1961
Street Offences Act, 1959

PUBLIC RECREATION AND ENTERTAINMENT

Betting and Gaming Act, 1960
Celluloid and Cinematograph Film Act, 1922
Cinematograph Acts, 1909 and 1952
Home Counties (Music and Dancing) Licencing Act, 1926
Licencing Acts, 1949, 1953, 1961 and 1964
Licencing (Consolidation) Act, 1910
Music and Dancing Licences (Middlesex) Act, 1894
Public Entertainments Act, 1875
Public Libraries and Museums Act, 1964
Theatres Act, 1843

RENTS, RATES AND TENANCIES

Housing Repairs and Rents Act, 1954
Landlord and Tenant Act, 1927
Rating and Valuation (Apportionment) Act, 1928
Rent Acts, 1957 and 1965

RIVERS AND WATERS GENERALLY

Clean Rivers (Estuaries and Tidal Waters) Act, 1960
Metropolis Water Act, 1902
Metropolis Water Board Act, 1932
River Boards Act, 1948
Rivers Pollution Prevention Act, 1876
Rivers (Prevention of Pollution) Acts, 1951 and 1961
Rural Water Supplies and Sewerage Acts, 1944, 1951, 1955 and 1965
Salmon and Freshwater Fisheries Act, 1923
Water Acts, 1945 and 1948
Water Resources Act, 1963

SERVICES

City of London Sewers Act, 1848
Electricity Acts, 1947 and 1957
Electricity Supply (Meters) Acts, 1936
Electric Lighting Act, 1882
Electric Lighting (Clauses) Act, 1899
Gas Act, 1948
Public Utilities Street Works Act, 1950
Rights of Lights Act, 1959
Post Offices Act, 1961
Telegraph Act, 1878
Thermal Insulation (Industrial Buildings) Act, 1957

TRANSPORT, TRAFFIC, ROADS AND HIGHWAYS

Airports Authority Act, 1965
Development and Road Improvement Funds Act, 1909
Harbours Acts, 1814 and 1964
Highways Act, 1959
Highways (Miscellaneous Provisions) Act, 1961
L.C.C. (Tramways and Improvements) Acts, 1902
London Passenger Transport Acts, 1933, 1934 and 1938
London Passenger Transport (Agreement) Amendment Act, 1935
Railways Act, 1921
Road and Rail Traffic Act, 1933
Road Traffic and Roads Improvement Act, 1960
Roads Improvements Act, 1925
Special Roads Act, 1949
Transport Acts, 1947 and 1953
Offices, Shops and Railway Premises Act, 1963

MISCELLANEOUS

Administration of Estates Act, 1925
Corporate Bodies' Contracts Act, 1960
Customs and Excise Act, 1952
Disorderly Houses Act, 1751
Education Acts, 1902, 1918, 1921 and 1936
House of Commons Disqualification Act, 1957
Law of Property Act, 1925
Nuclear Installations (Licencing and Insurance) Act, 1959
Occupier's Liability Act, 1957
Pipe-Lines Act, 1962
Radioactive Substances Acts, 1948 and 1960
Stamp Act, 1891
War Damage Act, 1943
Compensation (Defence) Act, 1939
Land Powers (Defence) Act, 1958

7 BRITISH STANDARDS, CODES OF PRACTICE, AND GOVERNMENT PUBLICATIONS

BRITISH STANDARDS—GENERAL SERIES

ADHESIVES

B.S. 745:1969 Animal glue for wood.

B.S. 1203:1963 Synthetic resin adhesives (phenolic and aminoplastic) for plywood.

B.S. 1204:—— Synthetic resin adhesives (phenolic and aminoplastic) for wood.
Part 1: 1964. Gap-filling adhesives. Amendments P.D. 5407, Dec. 1964; P.D. 5734, Jan. 1966.
Part 2: 1965. Close-contact adhesives. Amendment P.D. 5735, Jan. 1966.

B.S. 1444:1970 Cold-setting casein adhesive powders for wood.

B.S. 3046:1958 Paper-hanging pastes and powders.

B.S. 3357:1961 Glue size for decorators' use.

B.S. 3940:1965 Adhesives based on bitumen or coal tar.

B.S. 4071:1966 Polyvinyl acetate (P.V.A.) emulsion adhesives for wood.

AGGREGATES

B.S. 877:1967 Foamed or expanded blastfurnace slag lightweight aggregate for concrete.

B.S. 882, 1201:1965 Aggregates from natural sources for concrete (including granolithic).

B.S. 1047:1952 Air-cooled blastfurnace slag coarse aggregate for concrete.

B.S. 1162, 1410, 1418:1966 Mastic asphalt for building (natural rock asphalt aggregate).

B.S. 1165:1966 Clinker aggregate for concrete.

B.S. 1198–1200:1955 Building sands from natural sources (Confirmed 1966). Amendment P.D. 4835, March 1963.

B.S. 1621:1961 Bitumen macadam with crushed rock or slag aggregate.

B.S. 1984:1967 Gravel aggregates for surface treatment (including surface dressings) on roads.

B.S. 2040:1953 Bitumen macadam with gravel aggregate (Confirmed 1960).

B.S. 3797:1964 Lightweight aggregates for concrete.

B.S. 3892:1965 Pulverised fuel-ash for use in concrete.

BOARDS

B.S. 1142:1961 Fibre building boards. Amendment P.D. 6093, March 1967.

B.S. 1230:1955 Gypsum plasterboard. Amendments P.D. 4793, Feb. 1963; P.D. 5727, Jan. 1966; A.M.D. 121, Oct. 1968; A.M.D. 632, Nov. 1970.

B.S. 1811:—— Methods of test for wood chipboards and other particle boards.
Part 1: 1961. Imperial units. Amendments P.D. 4110, Apr. 1961; P.D. 5866, July 1966; P.D. 6105, March 1967; A.M.D. 338, Oct. 1969.
Part 2: 1969. Metric units.

B.S. 2572:1955 Phenolic laminated sheet. Amendments P.D. 3232, Dec. 1958; P.D. 4167, May 1961.

B.S. 2604:1963 Resin-bonded wood chipboard. Amendments P.D. 5375, Oct. 1964; P.D. 5867, July 1966; P.D. 6042, Feb. 1967; A.M.D. 124, Oct. 1968; A.M.D. 656, Dec. 1970.

B.S. 3290:1960 Toughened polystyrene extruded sheet.

B.S. 3444:1961 Blockboard and laminboard (A4 size). Amendment P.D. 6388, Apr. 1968.

B.S. 3536:1962 Asbestos insulating boards and asbestos wallboards.

B.S. 3583:1963 Information about blockboard and laminboard.

B.S. 3760:1966 Cast gypsum panels (with core).

B.S. 3837:1965 Expanded polystyrene board for thermal insulation purposes. Amendment P.D. 5552, July 1965.

B.S. 4022:1970 Prefabricated gypsum wallboard panels.

BRICKS, BLOCKS AND STONEWORK

B.S. 187:1967 Calcium silicate (sandlime and flintlime) bricks.

B.S. 1105:1963 Unreinforced woodwool slabs up to 3 in thick.

B.S. 1180:1944 Concrete bricks and fixing bricks. Amendments P.D. 774, May 1948; P.D. 4692, Nov. 1962.

B.S. 1207:1961 Hollow glass blocks.

B.S. 1217:1945 Cast stone.

B.S. 1758:1966 Fireclay refractories (bricks and shapes).

B.S. 2028, 1364:1968 Precast concrete blocks.

B.S. 2973:1961 Classification and methods of sampling and testing of insulating refractory bricks.

B.S. 3679:1963 Acid-resisting bricks and tiles.

B.S. 3921:—— Standard special bricks.
Part 1: 1965. Imperial units. Amendments P.D. 5991, Dec. 1966; A.M.D. 514, July 1970.
Part 2: 1969. Metric units.

B.S. 4046:1966 Compressed straw building slabs. Amendment P.D. 6200, July 1967.

BUILDERS' HARDWARE: GENERAL

B.S. 497:1967 Cast manhole covers, road gully gratings and frames, for drainage purposes. Amendment P.D. 6398, May 1968.

B.S. 1185:1963 Guards for underground stopvalves.

B.S. 1227:—— Hinges.
Part 1A: 1967. Hinges for general building purposes. Amendment P.D. 6260, Sept. 1967.

B.S. 1243:1964 Metal ties for cavity wall construction. Amendments P.D. 5692, Dec. 1965; P.D. 5974, Jan. 1967; P.D. 6284, Dec. 1967; A.M.D. 266, June 1969.

B.S. 1247:1955 Manhole step irons (malleable cast iron).

B.S. 1255:1953 Brackets and supports for lavatory basins and sinks (dimensions and workmanship). Amendment P.D. 1745, Nov. 1953.

B.S. 1291:1946 Ferrous traps for baths.

B.S. 1331:1954 Builders' hardware for housing. Amendments P.D. 2320, Oct. 1955; P.D. 2902, Oct. 1957.

B.S. 1968:1953 Floats for ballvalves (copper). Amendments P.D. 3220, Nov. 1958; P.D. 4667, Sept. 1962.

B.S. 2456:1954 Floats for ballvalves (plastics) for cold water. Amendments P.D. 2953, Jan. 1958; P.D. 3917, Sept. 1960; P.D. 6065, March 1967.

B.S. 3457:1962 Materials for water tap washers. Amendments P.D. 4543, Apr. 1962; P.D. 5525, May 1965.

B.S. 3827:—— Glossary of terms relating to builders' hardware.
Part 1: 1964. Locks (including locks and latches in one case).
Part 2: 1967. Latches.
Part 3: 1967. Catches.
Part 4: 1967. Door, drawer, cupboard and gate furniture.

COMPLETE STRUCTURES, STRUCTURAL COMPONENTS AND MATERIALS

B.S 4:—— Structural steel sections.
Part 1: 1962. Hot-rolled sections. Amendments P.D. 4611, July 1962; P.D. 5468, Feb. 1965.
P.D. 5032, Addendum No. 1, 1963 to B.S. 4: Part 1: 1962. Hot-rolled sections.
P.D. 5352, Addendum No. 2, 1964 to B.S. 4: Part 1: 1962. Hot-rolled sections.
Part 2: 1969. Hot-rolled hollow sections.

B.S. 449:1959 The use of structural steel in building (incorporating B.S. Code of Practice C.P. 113). Amendments P.D. 3857, July 1960; P.D. 4311, Nov. 1961; P.D. 4546, Apr. 1962; P.D. 5137, Jan. 1964; P.D. 5425, Feb. 1965; P.D. 5854, June 1966; P.D. 6126, Apr. 1967; A.M.D. 94, Sept. 1968.
Supplement 1: 1959 (P.D. 3343) recommendations for design.
Addendum 1: 1961 (P.D. 4064). The use of cold formed steel sections in building. Amendment P.D. 4390, Nov. 1961.

B.S. 476:—— Fire tests on building materials and structures.
Part 1: 1953. Fire tests on building materials and structures.

B.S. 1754:1961 Steel barns with curved roofs.

B.S. 1860:—— Structural timber. Measurement of characteristics affecting strength.
Part 1: 1959. Softwood.

B.S. 1991:—— Letter symbols, signs and abbreviations.
Part 4: 1961. Structures, materials, and soil mechanics.

B.S. 2053:1965 General-purpose farm buildings of framed construction. Amendment P.D. 6386, Apr. 1968.

B.S. 2539:1954 Preferred dimensions of reinforced concrete structural members.

B.S. 3830:1964 Vitreous enamelled steel building components. Amendment P.D. 5514, Apr. 1965.

B.S. 4169:1970 Glued-laminated timber structural members.

B.S. 4360:1968 Weldable structural steels. Amendment A.M.D. 303, Sept. 1969.
Part 2: 1969. Metric units.

DAMP-PROOF COURSES

B.S. 743:1970 Materials for damp-proof courses.

B.S. 2832:1957 Hot applied damp-resisting coatings for solums.

DOOR AND WINDOW FURNITURE

B.S. 455:1957 Schedule of sizes for locks and latches for doors in buildings.

B.S. 1228:1945 Iron, steel and non-ferrous door bolts. Amendment P.D. 443, Jan. 1946.

B.S. 2088:1954 Performance tests for locks. Amendment P.D. 3069, June 1958.

B.S. 2911:—— Letter plates.
Part 1: 1957. Manufacture. Amendment P.D. 3861, July 1960.
Part 2: 1960. Standard height and fixing recommendations.

B.S. 3621:1963 Thief-resistant locks for hinged doors. Amendments P.D. 5431, Jan. 1965; P.D. 5737, Jan. 1966.

B.S. 3827:—— Glossary of terms relating to builders' hardware.
Part 1: 1964. Locks (including locks and latches in one case).
Part 2: 1967. Latches.
Part 3: 1967. Catches.
Part 4: 1967. Door, drawer, cupboard and gate furniture.

DOORS

B.S. 459:—— Doors.
Part 1: 1954. Panelled and glazed wood doors. Amendments P.D. 2203, June 1955; P.D. 3062, May 1958; P.D. 4075, Feb. 1961; P.D. 5450, Feb. 1965; P.D. 6067, March 1967.
Part 2: 1962. Flush doors. Amendments P.D. 5454, Feb. 1965; P.D. 6161, May 1967; P.D. 6375, Apr. 1968.
Part 3: 1951. Plywood faced fire-check flush doors and wood and metal frames (half-hour and one-hour types). Amendments P.D. 1962, Sept. 1954; P.D. 2205, June 1955; P.D. 3567, Dec. 1959; P.D. 4298, Sept. 1961; P.D. 5455, Feb. 1965; A.M.D. 60, Aug. 1968.
Part 4: 1965. Matchboarded doors. Amendment P.D. 5506, March 1965.

B.S. 1245:1951 Metal door frames (steel). Amendments P.D. 2780, May 1957; P.D. 3077, May 1958.

B.S. 1285:1963 Wood surrounds for steel doors and windows. Amendments P.D. 5460, Feb. 1965; P.D. 6140, May 1967; P.D. 6399, May 1968.

B.S. 1567:1953 Wood door frames and linings (Confirmed 1960). Amendments P.D. 1666, July 1953; P.D. 1848, Apr. 1954; P.D. 2214, June 1955; P.D. 3051, May 1958; P.D. 3837, June 1960; P.D. 5464, Feb. 1965.

B.S. 2504:1954 Wood doors and frames for milking parlours. Amendment P.D. 2215, June 1955.

DUCTING

B.S. 3954:1965 Asbestos cement ducting.

B.S. 3973:1966 Asbestos-cement cable conduits and troughs.

B.S. 4108:1967 Pitch fibre conduit.

ELECTRICAL SERVICES

B.S. 31:1940 Steel conduit and fittings for electrical wiring. Amendments C.F. 9846, March 1942; P.D. 5663, Oct. 1965; P.D. 6129, Apr. 1967; A.M.D. 248, May 1969.

B.S. 372:1930 Two-pin side-entry wall plugs and sockets for special circuits. Amendments C.C. 9440, March 1933; C.E. 9577, Oct. 1938; C.G. 409, May 1942; A.M.D. 454, March 1970.

B.S. 546:1950 Two-pole and earthing-pin plugs, socket outlets and socket-outlet adaptors for circuits up to 250 volts. Amendments P.D. 1752, Dec. 1953; P.D. 4389, Nov. 1961; A.M.D. 251, May 1969.
P.D. 4007: Supplement No. 1: 1960. Plugs made of resilient material.

B.S. 816:1952 Requirements for electrical appliances and accessories. Amendments P.D. 4166, May 1961; P.D. 5118, Jan. 1964.
816 and 710: Supplement No. 1: 1958. Earthing and insulation of table lamps, floor standards and other portable or adjustable light fittings.

B.S. 2484:1961 Cable covers, concrete and earthenware. Amendment P.D. 6158, May 1967.

B.S. 2655:—— Lifts, escalators, passenger conveyors and paternosters.
Part 1: 1970. General requirements for electric, hydraulic and hand-powered lifts.
Part 3: 1965. Outline dimensions.

B.S. 2706:1956 Non-ferrous conduit and conduit fittings (aluminium and zinc alloy). Amendments P.D. 3253, Dec. 1958; A.M.D. 252, May 1969.

B.S. 6007:1969 Elastomer-insulated cables for electric power and lighting.

B.S. 6500:1969 Insulated flexible cords.

EXTERNAL WALLS, AND FINISHES

B.S. 690:1963 Asbestos-cement slates, corrugated sheets and semi-compressed flat sheets. Amendment P.D. 6302, Jan. 1968.

B.S. 1318:1955 Wood battens and counter-battens for slating and tiling (Confirmed 1966).

B.S. 3717:1964 Asbestos cement decking.

B.S. 3798:1964 Coping units (of clayware, unreinforced cast concrete, unreinforced cast stone, natural stone and slate).

B.S. 4049:1966 Glossary of terms applicable to internal plastering, external rendering and floor screeding.

B.S. 4131:1967 Terrazzo tiles.

FENCING AND GATES

B.S. 1485:1948 Galvanised wire netting.

B.S. 1722:—— Fences.
Part 1: 1963. Chain link fences. Amend-

ments P.D. 5318, Aug. 1964; P.D. 5579, July 1965; P.D. 6089, March 1967.

Part 2: 1963. Woven wire fences. Amendments P.D. 5000, Aug. 1963; P.D. 5319, Aug. 1964; P.D. 5581, July 1965; P.D. 6109, March 1967.

Part 3: 1963. Strained wire fences. Amendments P.D. 5001, Aug. 1963; P.D. 5580, July 1965; P.D. 6110, March 1967.

Part 4: 1963. Cleft chestnut pale fences. Amendments P.D. 5320, Aug. 1964; P.D. 5582, July 1965; P.D. 6113, March 1967.

Part 5: 1963. Close-boarded fences including oak pale fences. Amendments P.D. 5002, Aug. 1963; P.D. 5321, Aug. 1964; P.D. 5583, July 1965.

Part 6: 1963. Wooden palisade fences. Amendments P.D. 5003, Aug. 1963; P.D. 5584, July 1965.

Part 7: 1963. Wooden post and rail fences. Amendments P.D. 5322, Aug. 1964; P.D. 6114, March 1967; P.D. 6417, May 1968.

Part 8: 1966. Mild steel or wrought iron continuous bar fences.

Part 9: 1963. Mild steel or wrought iron un-climbable fences with round or square verticals and flat standards and horizontals.

Part 10: 1963. Anti-intruder chain link fences. Amendments P.D. 5356, Oct. 1964; P.D. 6115, March 1967; A.M.D. 644, Dec. 1970.

Part 11: 1965. Woven wood fences.

B.S. 3470:1962   Field gates and posts. Amendments P.D. 4682, Oct. 1962; P.D. 4931, May 1963; P.D. 5327, Sept. 1964.

B.S. 3854:1965   Farm stock fences. Amendment P.D. 6111, March 1967.

B.S. 4092:——   Domestic front entrance gates.

Part 1: 1966. Metal gates.

Part 2: 1966. Wooden gates.

B.S. 4102:1967   Steel wire for fences.

FIRE PROTECTION, RESISTANCE AND TESTING

B.S. 459:——   Doors.

Part 3: 1951. Plywood faced fire-check flush doors and wood and metal frames (half-hour and one hour types). Amendments P.D. 1962, Sept. 1954; P.D. 2205, June 1955; P.D. 3567, Dec. 1959; P.D. 4298, Sept. 1961; P.D. 5455, Feb. 1965; A.M.D. 60, Aug. 1968.

B.S. 476:——   Fire tests on building materials and structures.

Part 1: 1953. Fire tests on building materials and structures. Amendment A.M.D. 409, Jan. 1970.

Part 3: 1958. External fire exposure roof tests. Amendment P.D. 3276, Feb. 1959.

B.S. 1635:1970   Graphical symbols and abbreviations for fire protection drawings.

B.S. 2788:1956   Fireguards for solid fuel fires. Amendments P.D. 2884, Aug. 1957; P.D. 3615, Dec. 1959; P.D. 3801, May 1960.

B.S. 3140:1967   Nursery type fireguards suitable for use with solid fuel appliances. Amendment A.M.D. 27, July 1968; A.M.D. 271, June 1969.

B.S. 3248:1960   Spark guards for solid fuel fires. Amendment P.D. 4313, Sept. 1961.

B.S. 3980:1966   Boxes for foam inlets and dry risers. Amendment P.D. 6083, March 1967.

FIXINGS

B.S. 916:1953   Black bolts, screws and nuts. Amendments P.D. 1894, May 1954; P.D. 4164, May 1961; P.D. 4331, Oct. 1961; P.D. 5906, Aug. 1966.

B.S. 1202:——   Nails.

Part 1: 1966. Steel nails.

Part 2: 1966. Copper nails.

Part 3: 1962. Aluminium nails.

B.S. 1210:1963   Wood screws. Amendment P.D. 5467, Feb. 1965.

B.S. 1494:——   Fixing accessories for building purposes.

Part 1: 1964. Fixings for sheet, roof and wall coverings. Amendment P.D. 6192, June 1967.

Part 2: 1967. Sundry fixings.

B.S. 1579:1960   Connectors for timber.

B.S. 1768:1963   Unified precision hexagon bolts, screws and nuts (U.N.C. and U.N.F. threads). Normal series. Amendments P.D. 5706, Dec. 1965; P.D. 6223, July 1967.

B.S. 1769:1951   Unified black hexagon bolts, screws and nuts (U.N.C. and U.N.F. threads). Heavy series. Amendments P.D. 2141, March 1955; P.D. 2788, May 1957; P.D. 3620, Jan. 1960; P.D. 4334, Oct. 1961; P.D. 6002, Dec. 1966.

B.S. 3139:——   High-strength friction grip bolts for structural engineering.

Part 1: 1959. General grade bolts. Amendments P.D. 3657, Feb. 1960; P.D. 4195, June 1961; P.D. 5394, Nov. 1964; A.M.D. 87, Aug. 1968.

B.S. 3294:——   The use of high-strength friction grip bolts in structural steelwork.

Part 1: 1960. General grade bolts. Amendments P.D. 4429, Jan. 1962; P.D. 5262, June 1964; P.D. 5963, Dec. 1966; A.M.D. 183, Jan. 1969.

B.S. 3410:1961   Metal washers for general engineering purposes.

B.S. 3692:1967   I.S.O. metric precision hexagon bolts, screws and nuts.

B.S. 4190:1967   I.S.O. metric black hexagon bolts, screws and nuts.

B.S. 4219:1967   Slotted grub-screws—metric series.

B.S. 4320:1968   Specification for metal washers for general engineering purposes.

BRITISH STANDARDS

FLOOR FINISHES

B.S. 776:1963	Materials for magnesium oxychloride (magnesite) flooring.
B.S. 810:1966	Sheet linoleum (calendered types) cork carpet, and linoleum tiles.
B.S. 1187:1959	Wood blocks for floors. Amendment A.M.D. 21, June 1968.
B.S. 1197:1955	Concrete flooring tiles and fittings.
B.S. 1286:1945	Clay tiles for flooring (Confirmed 1956). Amendments P.D. 503, May 1946; P.D. 709, Oct. 1947; P.D. 3367, May 1959; P.D. 6052, March 1967.
B.S. 1324:1962	Asphalt tiles for paving and flooring (natural rock asphalt). Amendment P.D. 5811, March 1966.
B.S. 1450:1963	Black pitch mastic flooring.
B.S. 1711:1951	Solid rubber flooring (Confirmed 1961). Amendment P.D. 4138, Apr. 1961.
B.S. 1863:1952	Felt-backed linoleum.
B.S. 2592:1955	Thermoplastic flooring tiles, sometimes known as 'asphalt' tiles.
B.S. 3187:1959	Electrically conducting rubber flooring. Amendment P.D. 3705, March 1960.
B.S. 3260:1969	P.V.C. (vinyl) asbestos floor tiles.
B.S. 3261:1960	Flexible P.V.C. flooring. Amendments P.D. 3985, Nov. 1960; P.D. 4096, March 1961; P.D. 4353, Oct. 1961; P.D. 5152, Feb. 1964; P.D. 5238, May 1964.
B.S. 3398:1961	Anti-static rubber flooring.
B.S. 3672:1963	Coloured pitch mastic flooring.
B.S. 4049:1966	Glossary of terms applicable to internal plastering, external rendering and floor screeding.
B.S. 4050:1966	Wood mosaic flooring. Amendment P.D. 6401, May 1968.
B.S. 4131:1967	Terrazzo tiles.

FLOORING

B.S. 1297:1970	Grading and sizing of softwood flooring.
B.S. 3809:1964	Woodwool permanent formwork and infill units for reinforced concrete floor and roof slabs.

FLUES AND LININGS

B.S. 41:1964	Cast iron spigot and socket flue or smoke pipes and fittings.
B.S. 567:1968	Asbestos cement flue pipes and fittings (light quality).
B.S. 715:1970	Sheet metal flue pipes and accessories for gas-fired appliances.
B.S. 835:1967	Asbestos cement flue pipes and fittings, heavy quality.
B.S. 1181:1961	Clay flue linings and chimney pots (dimensions and workmanship only).
B.S. 1289:1945	Pre-cast concrete flue blocks for gas fires (of the domestic type) and ventilation.
B.S. 1294:1946	Soot doors for domestic buildings (Confirmed 1954). Amendment P.D. 489, March 1946.
B.S. 3572:1962	Access fittings for chimneys and other high structures in concrete or brickwork. Amendment P.D. 5589, July 1965.
B.S. 4076:1966	Steel chimneys.
B.S. 4207:1967	Monolithic linings for steel chimneys and flues.

HEATING AND VENTILATING

B.S. 493:1967	Airbricks and gratings for wall ventilation.
B.S. 758:——	Small domestic hot-water supply boilers using solid fuel.
	Part 1: 1955. Manually controlled boilers. Amendments P.D. 2418, Apr. 1956; P.D. 2698, May 1957; P.D. 4317, Oct. 1961; P.D. 4432, Feb. 1962.
	Part 2: 1960. Thermostat controlled boilers. Amendment P.D. 4139, Apr. 1961.
B.S. 779:1961	Cast iron boilers for central heating and hot water supply.
B.S. 799:——	Oil burning equipment.
	Part 1: 1962. Atomising burners and associated equipment.
	Part 2: 1964. Vaporising burners and associated equipment.
B.S. 853:——	Calorifiers for central heating and hot water supply.
	Part 1: 1960. Mild steel and cast iron.
	Part 2: 1960. Copper.
B.S. 855:1961	Welded steel boilers for central heating and hot water supply. Amendment P.D. 4627, Aug. 1962.
B.S. 1250:——	Domestic appliances burning town gas.
	Part 4: 1965. Space heating appliances.
B.S. 1251:1970	Open fireplace components.
	(1) Firebacks for 350 mm, 400 mm and 450 mm open fires.
	(2) Fireplace surrounds and hearths.
	(3) Adjustable chimney-throat restrictors (insertible).
	(4) Lintels for open fire assemblies.
B.S. 1289:1945	Pre-cast concrete flue blocks for gas fires (of the domestic type) and ventilation.
B.S. 1846:——	Glossary of terms relating to solid fuel burning equipment.
	Part 1: 1968. Domestic appliances.
	Part 2: 1968. Industrial water heating and steam raising installations.
B.S. 2767:1956	Valves and unions for radiators (low pressure hot water). Amendments P.D. 3065, May 1958; P.D. 4118, March 1961; P.D. 5551, July 1965.
B.S. 2845:——	Coke-burning inset open fires without boiler and without convection.
	Part 1: 1957. Dimensional and constructional requirements. Amendments P.D. 3517, Sept. 1959; P.D. 3981, Nov. 1960.
	Part 2: 1959. Performance and constructional requirements. Amendments P.D. 3668, Feb. 1960; P.D. 3982, Nov. 1960; P.D. 4848, March 1963.

B.S. 3128:1959 Constructional and performance requirements for inset open fires with boiler and without convection. Amendments P.D. 3667, Feb. 1960; P.D. 3980, Nov. 1960; P.D. 4100, March 1961; P.D. 4849, March 1963; P.D. 5517, Apr. 1965.

B.S. 3376:1961 Open fires with convection, with or without boiler.

B.S. 3377:1969 Back boilers for use with domestic solid fuel appliances.

B.S. 3378:1961 Domestic heating stoves using coke and other solid fuels.

B.S. 3456:—— The testing and approval of household electrical appliances.
Part A. Heating and cooking appliances.
Section A1: 1966. General requirements. Amendments P.D. 6250, Sept. 1967; A.M.D. 181, Jan. 1969.
Section A2: 1962. Electric room heaters. Amendments P.D. 4929, May 1963; P.D. 5054, Oct. 1963; P.D. 5203, Apr. 1964; A.M.D. 51, Aug. 1968; A.M.D. 281, July 1969; A.M.D. 538, June 1970.
Section A8: 1963. Electric immersion heaters. Amendment A.M.D. 154, Nov. 1968; A.M.D. 392, Dec. 1969.
Section A11: 1966. Thermal-storage room heaters. Amendment A.M.D. 61, Aug. 1968.
Section A13: 1964. Thermal-storage electric water-heaters. Amendment A.M.D. 156, Nov. 1968.
Part B. Motor-operated appliances.
Section B13: 1967. Ventilating fans.

B.S. 3528:1962 Convection-type space heaters operating on steam or hot water. Amendment P.D. 5099, Nov. 1963.

INTERNAL WALL FINISHES AND CEILING FINISHES

B.S. 584:1967 Wood trim (softwood).
B.S. 1053:1966 Water paint and distemper for interior use.
B.S. 1230:—— Gypsum plasterboard.
Part 1: 1955. Imperial units.
Part 2: 1970. Metric units.
B.S. 1246:1959 Metal skirtings, picture rails and beads. Amendments P.D. 5294, July 1964; P.D. 5740, Feb. 1966.
B.S. 1248:1954 Wallpapers. Amendments P.D. 4970, Aug. 1963; P.D. 6232, Aug. 1967.
B.S. 1281:1966 Glazed ceramic tiles and tile fittings for internal walls.
B.S. 1317:1946 Wood laths for plastering (Confirmed 1959).
B.S. 1369:1947 Metal lathing (steel) for plastering. Amendment P.D. 1198, June 1951.
B.S. 2552:1955 Polystyrene tiles for walls and ceilings.
B.S. 3760:1966 Cast gypsum panels (with core).
B.S. 3932:1965 Expanded polystyrene tiles and profiles for the building industry.

B.S. 4022:1970 Prefabricated gypsum wallboard panels.
B.S. 4049:1966 Glossary of terms applicable to internal plastering, external rendering and floor screeding.
B.S. 4131:1967 Terrazzo tiles.

JOINTS, JOINTING MATERIALS AND GASKETS

B.S. 217:1961 Red lead for paints and jointing compounds.
B.S. 219:1959 Soft solders. Amendments P.D. 4843, March 1963; P.D. 5087, Nov. 1963.
B.S. 544:1969 Linseed oil putty for use in wooden frames.
B.S. 1737:1951 Jointing materials and compounds for water, town gas and low-pressure steam installations. Amendment P.D. 1683, Aug. 1953.
B.S. 1878:1952 Corrugated copper jointing strip for expansion joints (for use in general building construction) (Confirmed 1961).
B.S. 2494:—— Rubber joint rings for gas mains, water mains and drainage purposes.
Part 1: 1955. Rubber joint rings for gas mains and water mains. Amendments P.D. 3756, May 1960; P.D. 4002, Dec. 1960; P.D. 4343, Oct. 1961; P.D. 6291, Dec. 1967; A.M.D. 39, July 1968.
Part 2: 1967. Rubber joint rings for drainage purposes. Amendment A.M.D. 40, July 1968.
B.S. 2499:1966 Hot-applied joint-sealing compounds for concrete pavements.
B.S. 2815:1957 Compressed asbestos fibre jointing.
B.S. 4243:1967 Cork/paper jointing.
B.S. 4249:1967 Paper jointing.
B.S. 4254:1967 Two-part polysulphide-based sealing compounds for the building industry.
B.S. 4255:—— Preformed rubber gaskets for weather exclusion from buildings.
Part 1: 1967. Non-cellular gaskets. Amendment A.M.D. 136, Nov. 1968.
B.S. 4315:—— Methods of test for resistance to air and water penetration.
Part 1: 1968. Windows and gasket-glazing systems.

KITCHEN EQUIPMENT AND FIXTURES

B.S. 1195:1948 Kitchen fitments and equipment. Amendments P.D. 1447, July 1952; P.D. 1474, Sept. 1952; P.D. 1958, Sept. 1954; P.D. 3189, Oct. 1958; P.D. 3224, Nov. 1958; P.D. 4099, March 1961.
B.S. 1206:1945 Fireclay sinks (dimensions and workmanship) (Confirmed 1954 and 1959). Amendments P.D. 330, Jan. 1952; P.D. 4644, Sept. 1962.
B.S. 1226:1945 Draining boards (Confirmed 1954). Amendments P.D. 404, Oct. 1945; P.D. 1305, Dec. 1951.
B.S. 1229:1945 Fireclay washtubs and tub and sink sets (dimensions and workmanship) (Con-

firmed 1957). Amendment P.D. 1361, Apr. 1952.

B.S. 1244:1956 Metal sinks for domestic purposes. Amendment P.D. 6361, March 1968.

B.S. 1250:—— Domestic appliances burning town gas.
Part 1: 1966. General requirements.
Part 2: 1963. Cooking appliances. Amendment P.D. 5391, Nov. 1964.
Part 3: 1963. Water-heating appliances. Amendment P.D. 5852, June 1966.
Part 5: 1963. Refrigerators. Amendments P.D. 5449, Jan. 1965; P.D. 5587, July 1965.
Part 6: 1965. Laundering appliances. Amendment P.D. 5805, March 1966.

B.S. 1252:1957 Domestic solid fuel cookers with integral boilers. Amendments P.D. 3383, May 1959; P.D. 4212, July 1961; P.D. 4822, Feb. 1963.

B.S. 3456:—— The testing and approval of household electrical appliances.
Part A. Heating and cooking appliances.
Section A1: 1966. General requirements. Amendment P.D. 6250, Sept. 1967; A.M.D. 181, Jan. 1969.
Section A7: 1963. Electric washboilers.

B.S. 3705:1964 Recommendations for provision of space for domestic kitchen equipment.

B.S. 4135:1967 Sinks for domestic purposes made from cast acrylic sheet.

LAYOUT, SHAPE, DIMENSIONS IN GENERAL

B.S. 1708:1951 Modular co-ordination.

B.S. 2900:1970 Recommendations for the co-ordination of dimensions in building. Glossary of terms.

B.S. 3626:1963 Recommendations for a system of tolerances and fits for building.

B.S. 3778:1964 Storey heights.

B.S. 4011:1966 Recommendations for the co-ordination of dimensions in building. Basic sizes for building components and assemblies.

B.S. 4176:1967 Floor to floor heights.

B.S. 4330:1968 Recommendations for the co-ordination of dimensions in building: Controlling dimensions.

LIGHTING

B.S. 3820:1964 Electric light fittings. Amendments P.D. 6376, Apr. 1968; A.M.D. 357, Oct. 1969.

MATERIALS: ASPHALTS AND BITUMINOUS MATERIALS

B.S. 988, 1097, 1076, 1451:1966. Mastic asphalt for building (limestone aggregate). Amendments P.D. 6154, May 1967; A.M.D. 419, Jan. 1970.

B.S. 1162, 1410, 1418:1966. Mastic asphalt for building (natural rock asphalt aggregate).

B.S. 1310:1965 Coal tar pitches for building purposes. Amendments P.D. 5745, Feb. 1966; P.D. 6256, Sept. 1967.

B.S. 1621:1961 Bitumen macadam with crushed rock or slag aggregate. Amendment P.D. 6415, May 1968.

B.S. 1690:1962 Cold asphalt. Amendment A.M.D. 5, May 1968.

MATERIALS: CEMENT, PLASTER, ETC.

B.S. 12:1958 Portland cement (ordinary and rapid-hardening). Amendments P.D. 3729, Apr. 1960; P.D. 4676, Nov. 1962; A.M.D. 198, Jan. 1969.

B.S. 146:1958 Portland-blastfurnace cement. Amendments P.D. 3733, Apr. 1960; P.D. 4699, Nov. 1962; P.D. 6092, March 1967.

B.S. 890:1966 Building limes.

B.S. 915:1947 High alumina cement. Amendments P.D. 995, Jan. 1950; P.D. 1074, Aug. 1950; P.D. 1457, Aug. 1952; P.D. 4677, Nov. 1962.

B.S. 1014:1961 Pigments for cement, magnesium oxychloride and concrete.

B.S. 1191:—— Gypsum building plasters.
Part 1: 1967. Excluding premixed lightweight plasters.
Part 2: 1967. Premixed lightweight plasters.

B.S. 1317:1946 Wood laths for plastering (Confirmed 1959).

B.S. 1369:1947 Metal lathing (steel) for plastering. Amendment P.D. 1198, June 1951.

B.S. 4027:1966 Sulphate-resisting Portland cement. Amendment A.M.D. 215, Feb. 1969.

MATERIALS: CONCRETE INCLUDING REINFORCING MATERIALS

B.S. 877:1967 Foamed or expanded blastfurnace slag lightweight aggregate for concrete.

B.S. 882, 1201:1965 Aggregates from natural sources for concrete (including granolithic).

B.S. 1047:1952 Air-cooled blastfurnace slag coarse aggregate for concrete.

B.S. 1165:1966 Clinker aggregate for concrete.

B.S. 1881:1970 Methods of testing concrete.

B.S. 1926:1962 Ready-mixed concrete.

B.S. 2539:1954 Preferred dimensions of reinforced concrete structural members.

B.S. 2691:1969 Steel wire for prestressed concrete.

B.S. 2787:1956 Glossary of terms for concrete and reinforced concrete. Amendment P.D. 3811, June 1960.

B.S. 3617:1963 Stress relieved 7-wire strand for prestressed concrete. Amendment P.D. 5513, Apr. 1965.

B.S. 3797:1964 Lightweight aggregates for concrete.

B.S. 3809:1964 Woodwool permanent formwork and in-fill units for reinforced concrete floor and roof slabs.

B.S. 3892:1965 Pulverised fuel-ash for use in concrete. Amendment A.M.D. 25, July 1968.

B.S. 4449:1969 Hot rolled steel bars for the reinforcement of concrete.

B.S. 4461:1969   Cold worked steel bars for the reinforcement of concrete. Amendment A.M.D. 442, Feb. 1970.

B.S. 4466:1969   Bending dimensions and scheduling of bars for the reinforcement of concrete. Amendment A.M.D. 440, Feb. 1970.

B.S. 4482:1969   Hard drawn mild steel wire for the reinforcement of concrete. Amendment A.M.D. 475, March 1970.

B.S. 4483:1969   Steel fabric for the reinforcement of concrete.

MATERIALS: GLASS

B.S. 952:1964   Classification of glass for glazing and terminology for work on glass. Amendment P.D. 5494, Apr. 1965.

B.S. 1207:1961   Hollow glass blocks.

MATERIALS: INSULATION

B.S. 1334:1969   The use of thermal insulating materials for central heating and hot and cold water supply installations.

B.S. 1588:1969   The use of thermal insulating materials in the temperature range 200°F to 450°F (95°C to 230°C).

B.S. 1758:1966   Fireclay refractories (bricks and shapes).

B.S. 2972:1961   Methods of test for thermal insulating materials. Amendments P.D. 4474, March 1962; P.D. 5315, Aug. 1964; P.D. 5892, July 1966.
Supplement No. 1: 1962. Methods of test for thermal insulating materials (P.D. 4642).

B.S. 2973:1961   Classification and methods of sampling and testing of insulating refractory bricks.

B.S. 3290:1960   Toughened polystyrene extruded sheet.

B.S. 3533:1962   Glossary of terms relating to thermal insulation.

B.S. 3536:1962   Asbestos insulating boards and asbestos wall-boards.

B.S. 3590:1970   Sprayed asbestos insulation.

B.S. 3837:1965   Expanded polystyrene board for thermal insulation purposes. Amendment P.D. 5552, July 1965.

B.S. 3869:1965   Rigid expanded polyvinyl chloride for thermal insulation purposes and building applications. Amendment P.D. 5778, Feb. 1966.

B.S. 3927:1965   Phenolic foam materials for thermal insulations and building applications. Amendment P.D. 6062, March 1967.

B.S. 3958:——   Thermal insulating materials.
Part 1: 1970. 85% magnesia preformed insulation.
Part 2: 1970. Calcium silicate preformed insulation.
Part 3: 1967. Metal mesh-faced mineral wool mats and mattresses.

B.S. 4021:1966   Flexible polyurethane foam sheeting for use in laminates.

MATERIALS: METALS

B.S. 405:1945   Expanded metal (steel) for general purposes.

B.S. 899:1961   Rolled copper sheet, strip and foil.

B.S. 1161:1951   Aluminium and aluminium alloy sections. Amendment P.D. 1770, Dec. 1953.
P.D. 1331: 1952. Addendum No. 1 to B.S. 1161: 1951, Notes on aluminium and aluminium alloy sections. Amendment P.D. 4398, Dec. 1961.

B.S. 1178:1969   Milled lead sheet and strip for building purposes.

B.S. 2569:——   Sprayed metal coatings.
Part 1: 1964. Protection of iron and steel by aluminium and zinc against atmospheric corrosion. Amendment A.M.D. 55, Aug. 1968.
Part 2: 1965. Protection of iron and steel against corrosion and oxidation at elevated temperatures.

B.S. 2855:1957   Corrugated aluminium sheets for general purposes. Amendment P.D. 4570, May 1962.

B.S. 2870:1968   Rolled copper and copper alloys. Sheet, strip and foil. Amendment A.M.D. 428, Feb. 1970.

B.S. 2994:1958   Cold rolled steel sections.

B.S. 3083:1959   Hot-dipped galvanised corrugated steel sheets for general purposes.

B.S. 3428:1961   Troughed aluminium building sheet.

B.S. 3987:1966   Anodised wrought aluminium for external architectural applications.

MATERIALS: RIGID SHEETS

B.S. 3757:1964   Rigid P.V.C. sheet.
Part 1: 1964. Pressed sheet.
Part 2: 1965. Calendered and extruded sheet.

B.S. 3794:1964   Decorative laminated plastics sheets.

B.S. 3835:1964   Rigid P.V.C. profiles for fitting sheet lining materials. Amendment P.D. 5909, Aug. 1966.

B.S. 4036:1966   Asbestos-cement fully compressed flat sheets.

B.S. 4154:1967   Corrugated plastics translucent sheets made from thermosetting polyester resins (glass fibre reinforced).

B.S. 4203:1967   Extruded rigid P.V.C. corrugated sheeting. Amendment A.M.D. 34, Aug. 1968.

MATERIALS: STONE

B.S. 2847:1957   Glossary of terms for stone used in building. Amendment P.D. 2900, Oct. 1957.

MATERIALS: TIMBER

B.S. 373:1957 Testing small clear specimens of timber.

B.S. 565:1963 Glossary of terms relating to timber and woodwork.

B.S. 881, 589:1955 Nomenclature of commercial timbers, including sources of supply.

B.S. 913:1954 Pressure creosoting of timber.

B.S. 1088, 4079:1966 Plywood for marine craft. Amendment P.D. 6127, Apr. 1967.

B.S. 1186:—— Quality of timber and workmanship in joinery.
Part 1: 1952. Quality of timber (Confirmed 1958). Amendments P.D. 2975, Feb. 1958; P.D. 5461, Feb. 1965; P.D. 5958, Dec. 1966; A.M.D. 167, Dec. 1968.
Part 2: 1955. Quality of workmanship. Amendments P.D. 5462, Feb. 1965; P.D. 5957, Dec. 1966; P.D. 6185, June 1967; P.D. 6397, Apr. 1968.

B.S. 1282:1959 Classification of wood preservatives and their methods of application. Amendment P.D. 4252, Aug. 1961.

B.S. 1336:1946 Knotting. Amendment P.D. 2497, June 1956.

B.S. 1455:1963 Plywood manufactured from tropical hardwoods.

B.S. 1860:—— Structural timber. Measurement of characteristics affecting strength.
Part 1: 1959. Softwood.

B.S. 3051:1958 Coal tar oil types of wood preservatives (other than creosote to B.S. 144). Amendment P.D. 4832, March 1963.

B.S. 3452:1962 Copper/chrome water-borne wood preservatives and their application.

B.S. 3453:1962 Fluoride/arsenate/chromate/dinitrophenol water-borne wood preservatives and their application.

B.S. 3493:1962 Information about plywood. Amendment P.D. 4686, Oct. 1962.

B.S. 3819:1964 Grading rules for sawn home grown softwood.

B.S. 3842:1965 Treatment of plywood with preservatives.

B.S. 4047:1966 Grading rules for sawn home grown hardwood.

B.S. 4072:1966 Wood preservation by means of waterborne copper/chrome/arsenic compositions.

B.S. 4169:1970 Glued-laminated timber structural members.

MATERIALS: GENERAL

B.S. 1982:1968 Methods of testing fungal resistance of manufactured building materials made of or containing materials of organic origin.

B.S. 3519:1962 Glossary of terms applicable to cork and cork products.

B.S. 3959:1965 Coir matting.

B.S. 4037:1966 Coir door mats.

B.S. 4060:1966 Compressed wool felts. Amendment P.D. 6082, March 1967.

MEMBRANES, BUILDING PAPERS, ETC.

B.S. 1521:1965 Waterproof building papers.

B.S. 1763:1967 Thin P.V.C. sheeting (flexible, unsupported). Amendment A.M.D. 98, Sept. 1968.

B.S. 2739:1967 Thick P.V.C. sheeting (flexible, unsupported). Amendment A.M.D. 99, Sept. 1968.

B.S. 3012:1970 Low and intermediate density polythene sheet for general purposes.

B.S. 4016:1966 Building papers (breather type).

PAINTS, STAINS AND PIGMENTS, INCLUDING PROTECTIVE COATINGS

B.S. 144:1954 Coal tar creosote for the preservation of timber. Amendment P.D. 4833, March 1963.

B.S. 217:1961 Red lead for paints and jointing compounds.

B.S. 277, 278:1936 Ready mixed paints (oil gloss) zinc oxide base. Amendment P.D. 1968, Sept. 1954; P.D. 4795, Feb. 1963.

B.S. 913:1954 Pressure creosoting of timber.

B.S. 1014:1961 Pigments for cement, magnesium oxychloride and concrete.

B.S. 1053:1966 Water paint and distemper for interior use.

B.S. 1070:1956 Black paint (tar base).

B.S. 1215:1945 Oil stains. Amendments P.D. 3850, July 1960; A.M.D. 581, Sept. 1970.

B.S. 1282:1959 Classification of wood preservatives and their methods of application. Amendment P.D. 4252, Aug. 1961.

B.S. 1358:1969 Colours for enamels on metal and ceramic bases.

B.S. 1448:1948 Nomenclature of decorative metallic finishes.

B.S. 2015:1965 Glossary of paint terms.

B.S. 2521 and 2523:1966 Lead-based priming paints. Amendment P.D. 6074, March 1967.

B.S. 2524:1966 Red-oxide linseed oil priming paint.

B.S. 2525–27:1969 Undercoating and finishing paints for protective purposes (white lead-based).

B.S. 2660:1955 Colours for building and decorative paints. Amendments P.D. 3091, June 1958; P.D. 5879, June 1966.
Individual colour panels to B.S. 2660.
Supplement No. 1: 1961. Table of colorimetric values of colours to B.S. 2660.

B.S. 3051:1958 Coal tar oil types of wood preservatives (other than creosote to B.S. 144). Amendment P.D. 4832, March 1963.

B.S. 3416:1961 Black bitumen coating solutions for cold application. Amendment P.D. 4905, May 1963.

B.S. 3452:1962 Copper/chrome water-borne wood preservatives and their application.

B.S. 3453:1962   Fluoride/arsenate/chromate/dinitrophenol water-borne wood preservatives and their application.

B.S. 3634:1963   Black bitumen oil varnish.

B.S. 3698:1964   Calcium plumbate priming paints.

B.S. 3761:1970   Non-flammable solvent-based paint removers.

B.S. 3826:1969   Silicone-based water repellents for masonry.

B.S. 3842:1965   Treatment of plywood with preservatives.

B.S. 4072:1966   Wood preservation by means of water-borne copper/chrome/arsenic compositions.

B.S. 4147:1967   Hot-applied bitumen-based coatings for ferrous products.

PAVING, ROADS, EXTERNAL WORKS AND FEATURES

B.S. 63:1951   Single-sized roadstone and chippings. Amendments P.D. 1587, March 1953; P.D. 2009, Oct. 1954; P.D. 3488, Aug. 1959; A.M.D. 6, May 1968.

B.S. 76:1964   Tars for road purposes.

B.S. 340:1963   Specification for precast concrete kerbs, channels, edgings and quadrants.

B.S. 368:1956   Precast concrete flags. Amendment P.D. 4896, Apr. 1963.

B.S. 435:1931   Granite and whinstone kerbs, channels, quadrants and setts. Amendment P.D. 3538, Nov. 1959.

B.S. 594:1961   Rolled asphalt (hot process). Amendments P.D. 4566, May 1962; A.M.D. 4, May 1968.

B.S. 706:1936   Sandstone kerbs, channels, quadrants and setts (Confirmed 1960). Amendment P.D. 3670, Feb. 1960.

B.S. 802:1967   Tarmacadam with crushed rock or slag aggregate. Amendment P.D. 6125, Apr. 1967.

B.S. 1241:1959   Tarmacadam and tar carpets (gravel aggregate).

B.S. 1242:1960   Tarmacadam 'tar paving' for footpaths, playgrounds and similar works. Amendment P.D. 6241, Aug. 1967.

B.S. 1324:1962   Asphalt tiles for paving and flooring (natural rock asphalt). Amendment P.D. 5811, March 1966.

B.S. 1373:1967   Clothes-line posts.

B.S. 1446:1962   Mastic asphalt (natural rock asphalt aggregate) for roads and footways. Amendment P.D. 5945, Nov. 1966.

B.S. 1447:1962   Mastic asphalt (limestone aggregate) for roads and footways. Amendment P.D. 5935, Nov. 1966.

B.S. 1716:1963   Cycle stands.

B.S. 1984:1967   Gravel aggregates for surface treatment (including surface dressings) on roads.

B.S. 2040:1953   Bitumen macadam with gravel aggregate (Confirmed 1960).

B.S. 2542:1960   Recommendations for the use of bitumen emulsion (anionic) for roads.

B.S. 3690:1970   Bitumens for road purposes.

B.S. 3969:1965   Recommendations for turf for general landscape purposes.

B.S. 3975:——   Glossary for landscape work. Part 4: 1966. Plant description.

B.S. 4008:1966   Cattle grids on private roads.

PIPES AND FITTINGS: DRAINAGE

B.S. 65 and 540:1966 Clay drain and sewer pipes including surface water pipes and fittings. Amendment P.D. 6410, May 1968.

B.S. 437:——   Cast iron spigot and socket drain pipes and fittings. Part 1: 1970. Pipes, bends, branches and access fittings.

B.S. 497:1967   Cast manhole covers, road gully gratings and frames for drainage purposes. Amendments P.D. 6398, May 1968; A.M.D. 554, Aug. 1970.

B.S. 539:1968   Specification of dimensions of fittings for use with clay drain and sewer pipes.

B.S. 556:1966   Concrete cylindrical pipes and fittings including manholes, inspection chambers and street gullies.

B.S. 1130:1943   Schedule of cast iron drain fittings, spigot and socket type, for use with drain pipes to B.S. 437: 1933.

B.S. 1182:1955   Cast brass thimbles (spigot and socket) and tailpieces (for drainage connections).

B.S. 1185:1963   Guards for underground stopvalves.

B.S. 1194:1969   Concrete porous pipes for under-drainage.

B.S. 1196:1944   Clayware field drain pipes (Confirmed 1959). Amendment P.D. 2069, Dec. 1954.

B.S. 2760:——   Pitch-impregnated fibre pipes, and fittings, for drainage below and above ground. Part 1: 1966. Pipes and couplings. Part 2: 1967. Fittings.

B.S. 3656:1963   Asbestos cement pipes and fittings for sewerage and drainage. Amendment P.D. 6055, March 1967; A.M.D. 322, Oct. 1969.

B.S. 4101:1967   Concrete unreinforced tubes and fittings with ogee joints for surface water drainage.

PIPES AND FITTINGS: PLUMBING

B.S. 416:1967   Cast iron spigot and socket soil, waste and ventilating pipes (sand cast and spun) and fittings.

B.S. 504:1961   Drawn lead traps. Amendment P.D. 4448, Jan. 1962.

B.S. 582:1965   Asbestos cement soil, waste and ventilating pipes and fittings. (Withdrawn.)

B.S. 1010:1959   Draw-off taps and stop valves for water services (screwdown pattern). Amendments P.D. 3493, Sept. 1959; P.D. 3739, Apr. 1960; P.D. 4367, Nov. 1961; P.D. 4767, Jan. 1963; P.D. 4867, March 1963; P.D. 5225, May 1964; P.D. 5432, Jan. 1965; P.D. 5433, Jan. 1965; P.D. 5501, March 1965; P.D. 5888, Aug. 1966; P.D. 6051, March 1967; P.D. 6121, Apr. 1967; A.M.D. 260, June 1969.

B.S. 1212:1953   Ballvalves (Portsmouth type) excluding floats. Amendments P.D. 1932, Aug. 1954; P.D. 2333, Nov. 1955; P.D. 2460, Apr. 1956; P.D. 3237, Jan. 1959; P.D. 3545, Nov. 1959; P.D. 5116, Jan. 1964; P.D. 5424, Jan. 1965; P.D. 5829, May 1966; P.D. 5933, Nov. 1966.

B.S. 1291:1946   Ferrous traps for baths.

B.S. 1415:1955   Mixing valves (manually operated) for ablutionary and domestic purposes. Amendment P.D. 5235, May 1964.

B.S. 1968:1953   Floats for ballvalves (copper). Amendment P.D. 3220, Nov. 1958; P.D. 4667, Sept. 1962.

B.S. 1972:1967   Polythene pipe (type 32) for cold water services. Amendments A.M.D. 190, Jan. 1969; A.M.D. 369, Nov. 1969.

B.S. 2580:1955   Underground plug cocks for cold water services (Scottish type).

B.S. 2879:1957   Draining taps (screw-down pattern). Amendment P.D. 3841, July 1960.

B.S. 3284:1967   Polythene pipe (type 50) for cold water services.

B.S. 3380:——   Wastes for sanitary appliances and overflows for baths.
Part 1: 1961. Wastes (excluding skeleton sink wastes) and bath overflows. Amendment P.D. 5634, Aug. 1965.
Part 2: 1962. Skeleton sink wastes.

B.S. 3505:1968   Unplasticised P.V.C. pipe (type 1420) for cold water services.

B.S. 3868:1965   Prefabricated drainage stack units: galvanised steel.

B.S. 3943:1965   Plastics waste traps. Amendment A.M.D. 32, Aug. 1968.

PIPES AND FITTINGS: GENERAL

B.S. 61:——   Copper tubes (heavy gauge) for general purposes.
Part 1: 1947. Copper tubes (heavy gauge). Amendment P.D. 4542, Apr. 1962.
Part 2: 1969. Threads for light gauge copper tubes and fittings.

B.S. 66:1970   Cast copper alloy pipe fittings for use with screwed copper tubes.

B.S. 78:——   Cast iron spigot and socket pipes (vertically cast) and spigot and socket fittings.
Part 1: 1961. Pipes.
Part 2: 1965. Fittings. Amendment P.D. 5731, Jan. 1966.

B.S. 99:1922   Copper-alloy pipe fittings screwed for low- and medium-pressure B.S. copper tubes.

B.S. 143 and 1256:1968   Malleable cast iron and cast copper alloy screwed pipe fittings for steam, air, water, gas and oil. Amendment A.M.D. 139, Nov. 1968.

B.S. 486:1966   Asbestos cement pressure pipes. Amendments P.D. 6128, Apr. 1967; P.D. 6301, Jan. 1968.

B.S. 534:1966   Steel pipes, fittings and specials for water, gas and sewage.

B.S. 602, 1085:1956   Lead pipes for other than chemical purposes. Amendment P.D. 5862, June 1966.

B.S. 659:1967   Light gauge copper tubes (light drawn).

B.S. 864:1953   Capillary and compression fittings of copper and copper alloy for use with copper tube complying with B.S. 659, B.S. 1386 and B.S. 3931. Amendments P.D. 2915, Dec. 1957; P.D. 3925, Sept. 1960; P.D. 5754, Feb. 1966; P.D. 6411, May 1968.

B.S. 1143:1955   Salt-glazed ware pipes with chemically resistant properties. Amendment P.D. 2869, Aug. 1957.

B.S. 1184:1961   Copper and copper alloy traps. Amendment A.M.D. 201, Feb. 1969.

B.S. 1211:1958   Centrifugally cast (spun) iron pressure pipes for water, gas and sewage.

B.S. 1256:1952   Malleable cast iron (whiteheart process) and cast copper alloy pipe fittings for steam, air, water, gas and oil. Screwed B.S.P. taper male thread and parallel female thread.

B.S. 1386:1957   Copper tubes to be buried underground. Amendments P.D. 4449, March 1962; P.D. 5290, July 1964; A.M.D. 113, Oct. 1968.

B.S. 1710:1960   Identification of pipelines. Amendment P.D. 5564, July 1965.

B.S. 1740:1965   Wrought pipe fittings, iron and steel (screwed B.S.P. thread). Amendment P.D. 6408, May 1968.

B.S. 1775:1964   Steel tubes for mechanical, structural and general engineering purposes. Amendments P.D. 6050, Feb. 1967; P.D. 6170, May 1967.

B.S. 1952:1964   Copper alloy gate valves for general purposes. Amendments P.D. 5717, Jan. 1966; P.D. 6037, Feb. 1967.

B.S. 2017:1963   Copper tubes for general purposes.

B.S. 2035:1966   Cast iron flanged pipes and flanged fittings.

B.S. 3063:1965   Dimensions of gaskets for pipe flanges.

B.S. 3601:1962   Steel pipes and tubes for pressure purposes. Carbon steel: ordinary duty. Amendments P.D. 5022, Sept. 1963; P.D. 5171, Feb. 1964; P.D. 5288, July 1964; P.D. 5713, Dec. 1965; P.D. 6381, Apr. 1968.

B.S. 3867:1969   Outside diameters and pressure ratings of pipes of plastics materials.

B.S. 3931:1965   Hard-drawn thin wall copper tubes. Amendment A.M.D. 311, Aug. 1969.

B.S. 3952:1965   Cast iron butterfly valves for general purposes. Amendments P.D. 5813, Apr. 1966; P.D. 5964, Jan. 1967; P.D. 6414, May 1968.

B.S. 3961:1965   Cast iron screw-down stop valves and stop and check valves for general purposes. Amendments P.D. 5869, July 1966; P.D. 5970, Jan. 1967; P.D. 6180, June 1967.

B.S. 4090:1966   Cast iron check valves for general purposes.

B.S. 4133:1967   Flanged steel parallel slide valves for general purposes.

B.S. 4159:1967   Colour marking of plastics pipes to indicate pressure ratings.

RAINWATER GOODS

B.S. 460:1964   Cast iron rainwater goods.

B.S. 569:1967   Asbestos cement rainwater goods.

B.S. 1091:1963   Pressed steel gutters, rainwater pipes, fittings and accessories.

B.S. 1431:1960   Wrought copper and wrought zinc rainwater goods.

B.S. 2908:1957   Precast concrete eaves gutters.

B.S. 2997:1958   Aluminium rainwater goods. Amendment P.D. 6403, May 1968.

REFUSE DISPOSAL

B.S. 792:1947   Mild steel dustbins (Confirmed 1957). Amendments P.D. 787, May 1948; P.D. 2817, June 1957; P.D. 3492, Aug. 1959; P.D. 5605, July 1965.

B.S. 1136:1956   Mild steel refuse storage containers. Amendments P.D. 3571, Nov. 1959; P.D. 4841, March 1963.

B.S. 1577:1949   Mild steel refuse or food waste containers.

B.S. 1703:——   Refuse chutes.
Part 1: 1967. Hoppers.
Part 2: 1968. Chutes.

B.S. 3495:1962   Aluminium refuse storage containers.

B.S. 3654:1963   Galvanised steel dustbins for dustless emptying.

B.S. 3735:1964   Rubber components for steel dustbins. Amendment A.M.D. 62, Aug. 1968.

ROOFING

B.S. 402:1945   Clay plain roofing tiles and fittings (Confirmed 1954).

B.S. 473, 550:1967   Concrete roofing tiles and fittings.

B.S. 476:——   Fire tests on building materials and structures.
Part 3: 1958. External fire exposure roof tests. Amendment P.D. 3276, Feb. 1959.

B.S. 680:1944   Roofing slates.

B.S. 690:1963   Asbestos cement slates, corrugated sheets and semi-compressed flat sheets. Amendment P.D. 6302, Jan. 1968.

B.S. 747:1968   Roofing felts. Amendment A.M.D. 69, Aug. 1968.

B.S. 849:1939   Plain sheet zinc roofing. Amendment C.F. 2877, June 1939.

B.S. 1318:1955   Wood battens and counter-battens for slating and tiling (Confirmed 1966).

B.S. 1424:1948   Clay single-lap roofing tiles and fittings (dimensions and workmanship only). Amendment P.D. 849, Nov. 1948.

B.S. 1569:1965   Copper sheet and strip for roofing and other building purposes.

B.S. 2717:1956   Glossary of terms applicable to roof coverings.

B.S. 3717:1964   Asbestos cement decking.

B.S. 3809:1964   Woodwool permanent formwork and infill units for reinforced concrete floor and roof slabs.

SANITARY FIXTURES AND BATHROOM EQUIPMENT

B.S. 1125:1969   W.C. flushing cisterns (including dual flush cisterns) and flush pipes.

B.S. 1188:1965   Ceramic wash basins and pedestals.

B.S. 1189:1961   Cast iron baths for domestic purposes. Amendment P.D. 4534, Apr. 1962.

B.S. 1213:1945   Ceramic washdown W.C. pans (dimensions and workmanship) (Confirmed 1957). Amendments P.D. 769, Apr. 1948; P.D. 1750, Nov. 1953; P.D. 4462, Feb. 1962; P.D. 5509, Apr. 1965; A.M.D. 134, Nov. 1968.

B.S. 1254:1945   W.C. seats (plastics). Amendments P.D. 1415, June 1952; P.D. 5250, May 1964; P.D. 6000, Jan. 1967.

B.S. 1255:1953   Brackets and supports for lavatory basins and sinks (dimensions and workmanship). Amendment P.D. 1745, Nov. 1953.

B.S. 1329:1956   Metal lavatory basins for domestic purposes. Amendment P.D. 5367, Oct. 1964.

B.S. 1390:1947   Sheet steel baths for domestic purposes (Confirmed 1954).

B.S. 1876:1952   Automatic flushing cisterns for urinals (Confirmed 1959). Amendment P.D. 3150, Aug. 1958.

B.S. 2081:1954   Portable closets for use with chemicals.

B.S. 2089:1954   W.C. seats (wooden) (Confirmed 1966). Amendments P.D. 1887, May 1954; P.D. 5822, Apr. 1966.

B.S. 3402:1969   Quality of vitreous china sanitary appliances.

B.S. 4118:1967   Glossary of sanitation terms. Amendment A.M.D. 356, Nov. 1969.

B.S. 4305:1968   Baths for domestic purposes made from cast acrylic sheet.

STAIRS, RAMPS AND LADDERS

B.S. 585:1956   Wood stairs.

B.S. 1247:1955   Manhole step irons (malleable cast iron).

B.S. 2037:1964   Aluminium ladders, steps and trestles for the building and civil engineering industries.

B.S. 4211:1967   Steel ladders for permanent access.

STORAGE FITMENTS AND EQUIPMENT

B.S. 826:1955   Adjustable steel shelving (angle post type). Amendment P.D. 2986, March 1958.

B.S. 1292:1945   Storage fitments for living rooms and bedrooms. Amendment P.D. 1437, July 1952.

B.S. 1765:1951   Hospital bedside lockers.

STREET FURNITURE

B.S. 1308:1957   Concrete street lighting columns. Amendment P.D. 3577, Dec. 1959.

B.S. 1788:1964   Street-lighting lanterns for use with electric lamps. Amendments P.D. 6276, Nov. 1967; A.M.D. 241, Apr. 1969.

BRITISH STANDARDS

B.S. 1840:1960   Steel columns for street lighting.
B.S. 3989:1966   Aluminium street lighting columns.

TANKS AND CYLINDERS

B.S. 417:1964   Galvanised mild steel cisterns and covers, tanks and cylinders.
B.S. 699:1966   Copper cylinders for domestic purposes.
B.S. 1563:1949   Cast-iron sectional tanks (rectangular) (Confirmed 1964). Amendment P.D. 5030, Sept. 1963.
B.S. 1564:1949   Pressed steel sectional tanks (rectangular). Amendments P.D. 5792, March 1966; P.D. 6053, March 1967.
B.S. 1565:1949   Galvanised mild steel indirect cylinders, annular or saddle-back type.
B.S. 1566:——   Copper indirect cylinders for domestic purposes.
Part 1: 1966. Double feed indirect cylinders.
B.S. 1966:1967   Domed ends for tanks and pressure vessels.
B.S. 2777:1963   Asbestoscement cisterns.
B.S. 3198:1960   Combination hot water storage units (copper) for domestic purposes. Amendment P.D. 6395, Apr. 1968; A.M.D. 224, March 1969.
B.S. 4213:1967   Polyolefin or olefin copolymer moulded cold water storage cisterns. Amendment A.M.D. 189, Jan. 1969.

WINDOWS

B.S. 644:——   Wood windows.
Part 1: 1951. Wood casement windows. Amendments P.D. 1233, July 1951; P.D. 1270, Sept. 1951; P.D. 1352, Feb. 1952; P.D. 1464, Aug. 1952; P.D. 1849, Apr. 1954; P.D. 1961, Sept. 1954; P.D. 2082, Jan. 1955; P.D. 2730, Feb. 1957; P.D. 3510, Oct. 1959; P.D. 4827, March 1963; P.D. 5169, March 1964; P.D. 5447, Jan. 1965.
Part 2: 1958. Wood double-hung sash windows. Amendments P.D. 3295, Feb. 1959; P.D. 4828, March 1963; P.D. 5458, Feb. 1965.
Part 3: 1951. Wood double-hung sash and case windows—Scottish type. Amendments P.D. 2210, June 1955; P.D. 4829, March 1963; P.D. 5459, Feb. 1965.
B.S. 990:1967   Steel windows generally for domestic and similar buildings.
B.S. 1239 and 1240:1956   Lintels.
1239. Cast concrete lintels.
1240. Natural stone lintels.
B.S. 1285:1963   Wood surrounds for steel windows and doors. Amendments P.D. 5460, Feb. 1965; P.D. 6140, May 1967; P.D. 6399, May 1968.
B.S. 1422:1956   Steel subframes, sills and window boards for metal windows. Amendments P.D. 4973, July 1963; P.D. 6139, May 1967.

B.S. 1612:1950   Timber dutch lights. Amendments P.D. 1165, March 1951.
B.S. 1787:1951   Steel windows for industrial buildings. Amendment P.D. 5898, Aug. 1966.
B.S. 2503:1954   Steel windows for agricultural use (Confirmed 1966).
B.S. 2903:1954   Timber dutch light structures.
B.S. 4315:——   Part 1: 1968. Windows and gasket glazing systems. Resistance to air and water penetration.
B.S. 4374:1968   Sills of clayware, cast concrete, cast stone, slate and natural stone.

GENERAL

B.S. 381C:1964   Colours for specific purposes. Amendment P.D. 5846, Oct. 1966.
P.D. 5824: 1966. Supplement No. 1 to B.S. 381C. Table of colorimetric values of colours to B.S. 381C.
B.S. 648:1964   Schedule of weights of building materials.
B.S. 661:1969   Glossary of acoustical terms.
B.S. 685:1951   Sequence of trade headings and specification items for building work (Confirmed 1960). Amendment P.D. 5100, Nov. 1963.
B.S. 1192:1969   Building drawing practice.
B.S. 2929:1957   Safety colours for use in industry. Amendments P.D. 3021, May 1958; P.D. 3261, Jan. 1959; P.D. 3760, May 1960; P.D. 5788, March 1966.
B.S. 3589:1963   Glossary of general building terms.

BRITISH STANDARD CODES OF PRACTICE
(Ajr)

BRICKS, BLOCKS AND STONEWORK

C.P. 121.101:1951   Brickwork. Amendments P.D. 1534, Nov. 1952; P.D. 2624, Nov. 1956.
C.P. 121.201:1951   Masonry walls ashlared with natural stone or with cast stone (Confirmed 1963).
C.P. 121.202:1951   Masonry. Rubble walls (Confirmed 1963).
C.P. 122:1952   Walls and partitions of blocks and slabs. Amendments P.D. 1769; Dec. 1953; P.D. 2531, July 1956; P.D. 6102, March 1967.
Part 1: 1966. Hollow glass blocks.

COMPLETE STRUCTURES, STRUCTURAL COMPONENTS AND MATERIALS

C.P. 11:1965   Farm dairy buildings.
C.P. 2007:1960   Design and construction of reinforced and prestressed concrete structures for the storage of water and other aqueous liquids. Amendments P.D. 5420, Dec. 1964; A.M.D. 628, Nov. 1970.

DOORS

C.P. 151:—— Doors and windows including frames and linings.
Part 1. Wooden doors. Amendment P.D. 5567, July 1965.

DUCTING

C.P. 413:1951 Design and construction of ducts for services. Amendment P.D. 1392, Apr. 1952.

EXTERNAL WALLS AND FINISHES

C.P. 111:1964 Structural recommendations for loadbearing walls. Amendments P.D. 5804, March 1966; P.D. 6156, May 1967; A.M.D. 547, July 1970.

C.P. 123.101:1951 Dense concrete walls. Amendments P.D. 1301, Nov. 1951; P.D. 1404, June 1952.

C.P. 143:—— Sheet roof and wall coverings.
Part 1: 1958. Aluminium, corrugated and troughed. Amendment P.D. 4346, Oct. 1961.
Part 2: 1961. Galvanised corrugated steel.
Part 3: 1960. Lead. Amendment P.D. 4347, Oct. 1961; A.M.D. 615, Oct. 1970.
Part 4: 1960. Copper. Amendments P.D. 4348, Oct. 1961; A.M.D. 556, Aug. 1970.
Part 5: 1964. Zinc.
Part 6: 1962. Corrugated asbestoscement.
Part 7: 1965. Aluminium.

C.P. 212:—— Wall tiling.
Part 2: 1966. External ceramic wall tiling and mosaics.

C.P. 221:1960 External rendered finishes.

FIRE PROTECTION, RESISTANCE AND TESTING

C.P. 3:—— Code of basic data for the design of buildings.
Chapter IV: 1948. Precautions against fire.
Part 1: 1962. Fire precautions in flats and maisonettes over 80 ft in height.
Part 2: 1968. Shops and departmental stores.
Part 3: 1968. Office buildings. Amendment P.D. 6407, May 1968.

FLOORING

C.P. 201:1951 Timber flooring. Amendment P.D. 6136, May 1967.

C.P. 201:—— Flooring of wood and wood products.
Part 1: 1967. Wood flooring (board, strip, block and mosaic).

C.P. 202:1959 Tile flooring and slab flooring.

C.P. 203:1969 Sheet and tile flooring (cork, linoleum, plastics and rubber).

C.P. 204:1965 In-situ floor finishes.

C.P. 209:—— Care and maintenance of floor surfaces.
Part 1: 1963. Wooden flooring.

FLUES AND LININGS

C.P. 131.101:1951 Flues for domestic appliances burning solid fuel. Amendment P.D. 1445, July 1952.

C.P. 337:1963 Flues for gas appliances up to 150 000 Btu/h rating. Amendment P.D. 5607, Aug. 1965.

FOUNDATIONS AND SITE

C.P. 101:1963 Foundations and sub-structures for non-industrial buildings of not more than four storeys.

C.P. 2001:1957 Site investigations.

C.P. 2003:1959 Earthworks.

HEATING AND VENTILATING

C.P. 3:—— Code of basic data for the design of buildings.
Chapter I(C): 1950. Ventilation.
Chapter VIII: 1949. Heating and thermal insulation.

C.P. 324.202:1951 Provision of domestic electric water-heating installations.

C.P. 332:—— Selection and installation of town gas space heating.
Part 1: 1961. Independent domestic appliances. Amendment P.D. 5611, Aug. 1965.
Part 2: 1964. Central heating boilers for domestic premises. Amendments P.D. 5612, Aug. 1965; A.M.D. 529, June 1970.
Part 4: 1966. Ducted warm air systems. Amendment A.M.D. 355, Nov. 1969.

C.P. 338:1957 Domestic propane-gas-burning installations in permanent dwellings. Amendments P.D. 2965, Jan. 1958; P.D. 4809, Feb. 1963.

C.P. 341.300–307:1956 Central heating by low-pressure hot water.

C.P. 342:—— Centralised hot water supply.
Part 1: 1970. Individual dwellings.

C.P. 352:1958 Mechanical ventilation and air conditioning in buildings.

C.P. 403:1952 Open fires, heating stoves and cookers burning solid fuel.

C.P. 403.101:1952 Small boiler systems using solid fuel.

INSULATION

C.P. 3:—— Code of basic data for the design of buildings.
Chapter III: 1960. Sound insulation and noise reduction.
Chapter VIII: 1949. Heating and thermal insulation.

C.P. 299:1970 Sprayed asbestos insulation. Metric units.

CODES OF PRACTICE

INTERNAL WALL FINISHES AND CEILING FINISHES

C.P. 211:1966 Internal plastering.
C.P. 212:—— Wall tiling.
    Part 1: 1963. Internal ceramic wall tiling in normal conditions.

LIGHTING

C.P. 3:—— Code of basic data for the design of buildings. Chapter I, Lighting: Part 1: 1964. Daylighting.
    Chapter I(B): 1945. Sunlight (houses, flats and schools only).
    Chapter VII(F): 1945. Provision of artificial light (houses, flats and schools only).
C.P. 1004:—— Street lighting.
    Parts 1 and 2: 1963.
    Part 1. General principles.
    Part 2. Lighting for traffic routes. Amendments P.D. 5405, Dec. 1964; A.M.D. 230, Apr. 1969.

LOADING

C.P. 3:—— Code of basic data for the design of buildings. Chapter V: 1952. Wind loads. Amendments P.D. 2966, Feb. 1958; P.D. 5516, Apr. 1965; P.D. 6285, Dec. 1967.
    Chapter V: Part 1: 1967. Dead and imposed loads (metric). Amendments A.M.D. 141, Nov. 1968; A.M.D. 587, Sept. 1970.

MATERIALS: CONCRETE, INCLUDING REINFORCEMENT

C.P. 114:1957 Structural use of reinforced concrete in buildings. Amendments P.D. 5463, Feb. 1965; P.D. 6151, May 1967.
C.P. 115:1959 The structural use of prestressed concrete in buildings.
C.P. 116:1965 The structural use of precast concrete. Amendments P.D. 6152, May 1967; A.M.D. 218, Feb. 1969.
C.P. 117:—— Composite construction in structural steel and concrete.
    Part 1: 1965. Simply-supported beams in building.
C.P. 123.101:1951 Dense concrete walls. Amendments P.D. 1301, Nov. 1951; P.D. 1404, June 1952.

MATERIALS: GLASS

C.P. 122:1952 Walls and partitions of blocks and slabs. Amendments P.D. 1769, Dec. 1953; P.D. 2531, July 1956; P.D. 6102, March 1967. Part 1: 1966. Hollow glass blocks.

MATERIALS: METALS

C.P. 117:—— Composite construction in structural steel and concrete.
    Part 1: 1965. Simply-supported beams in building. Amendment A.M.D. 218, Feb. 1969.
C.P. 143:—— Sheet roof and wall coverings.
    Part 1: 1958. Aluminium, corrugated and troughed. Amendment P.D. 4346, Oct. 1961.
    Part 2: 1961. Galvanised corrugated steel.
    Part 3: 1960. Lead. Amendments P.D. 4347, Oct. 1961; A.M.D. 615, Oct. 1970.
    Part 4: 1960. Copper. Amendments P.D. 4348, Oct. 1961; A.M.D. 556, Aug. 1970.
    Part 5: 1964. Zinc.
    Part 7: 1965. Aluminium.
C.P. 2008:1966 Protection of iron and steel structures from corrosion.

MATERIALS: TIMBER

C.P. 98:1964 Preservative treatment for constructional timber.
C.P. 112:1967 The structural use of timber.

MATERIALS: GENERAL

C.P. 143:—— Part 6: 1962. Corrugated asbestos-cement.

PAINTS, STAINS, PIGMENTS, PROTECTIVE COATINGS

C.P. 98:1964 Preservative treatment for constructional timber.
C.P. 99:1965 Frost precautions for water services. Amendment P.D. 6416, May 1968.
C.P. 102:1963 Protection of buildings against water from the ground.
C.P. 231:1966 Painting of buildings.
C.P. 2008:1966 Protection of iron and steel structures from corrosion.

PIPES AND FITTINGS: DRAINAGE

C.P. 301:1950 Building drainage. Amendment P.D. 1829, March 1954.
C.P. 302.100:1956 Small domestic sewage treatment works.
C.P. 302.200:1949 Cesspools (Confirmed 1963). Amendment P.D. 2943, Nov. 1957.
C.P. 303:1952 Surface water and subsoil drainage.
C.P. 304:1968 Sanitary pipework above ground. Amendment A.M.D. 187, Jan 1969.

PIPES AND FITTINGS: GENERAL

C.P. 2010:—— Pipelines.
    Part 1: 1966. Installation of pipelines in land.

REFUSE DISPOSAL

C.P. 306:1960   The storage and collection of refuse from residential buildings.

ROOFING

C.P. 142:1968   Slating and tiling.
C.P. 143:——   Sheet roof and wall coverings.
Part 1: 1958. Aluminium, corrugated and troughed. Amendment P.D. 4346, Oct. 1961.
Part 2: 1961. Galvanised corrugated steel.
Part 3: 1960. Lead. Amendments P.D. 4347, Oct. 1961; A.M.D. 615, Oct. 1970.
Part 4: 1960. Copper. Amendments P.D. 4348, Oct. 1961; A.M.D. 556, Aug. 1970.
Part 5: 1964. Zinc.
Part 6: 1962. Corrugated asbestos-cement.
Part 7: 1965. Aluminium.
C.P. 144:——   Roof coverings.
Part 1: 1968. Built-up bitumen felt.
Part 2: 1966. Mastic asphalt. Amendments P.D. 6103, March 1967; A.M.D. 657, Nov. 1970.
C.P. 199:——   Roof deckings.
Part 1: 1968. Asbestos cement.

SANITARY FIXTURES AND BATHROOM EQUIPMENT

C.P. 305:1952   Sanitary appliances. Amendment P.D. 1847, Apr. 1954.

SERVICES

C.P. 3:——   Code of basic data for the design of buildings.
Chapter VII: 1950. Engineering and utility services. Amendments P.D. 1468, Aug. 1952; P.D. 5362, Oct. 1964.
C.P. 99:1965   Frost precautions for water services. Amendment P.D. 6416, May 1968.
C.P. 310:1965   Water supply.
C.P. 321:1965   Electrical installations (withdrawn).
C.P. 331:——   Installation of pipes and meters for town gas.
Part 1: 1957. Service pipes. Amendments P.D. 3115, July 1958; P.D. 5606, Aug. 1965.
Part 3: 1965. Installation pipes.
C.P. 332:——   Selection and installation of town gas space heating.
Part 1: 1961. Independent domestic appliances. Amendment P.D. 5611, Aug. 1965.
Part 2: 1964. Central heating boilers for domestic premises. Amendments P.D. 5612, Aug. 1965; A.M.D. 529, June 1970.
Part 4: 1966. Ducted warm air systems. Amendment A.M.D. 355, Nov. 1969.

C.P. 333:——   Selection and installation of town gas hot water supplies.
Part 1: 1964. Domestic premises. Amendment P.D. 5608, Aug. 1965.
Part 2: 1948. Schools. Amendment P.D. 5609, Aug. 1965.

STREET FURNITURE

C.P. 1004:——   Street lighting.
Parts 1 and 2: 1963.
Part 1. General principles.
Part 2. Lighting for traffic routes.

WINDOWS

C.P. 145:——   Glazing systems.
Part 1: 1969. Patent glazing.
C.P. 151:——   Doors and windows including frames and linings.
C.P. 152:1966   Glazing and fixing of glass for buildings. Amendment P.D. 6107, March 1967.

GENERAL

C.P. 3:——   Code of basic data for the design of buildings.
Chapter IX: 1950. Durability.
Chapter X: 1950. Precautions against vermin and dirt.
C.P. 96:——   Access for the disabled to buildings.
Part 1: 1967. General recommendations.
C.P. 97:——   Metal scaffolding.
Part 1: 1967. Common scaffolds in steel.
C.P. 117:——   Composite construction in structural steel and concrete.
Part 2: 1967. Beams of bridges.
C.P. 326:1965   The protection of structures against lightning.

SELECTION OF GOVERNMENT PUBLICATIONS—

(These publications are available from any branch of H.M.S.O.)

POST-WAR BUILDING STUDIES (Ajv)

6. Gas installations (1944).
11. Electrical installations (1944), reprinted (1952).
19. Heating and ventilation of dwellings (1945).
20. Fire grading of buildings. Part 1. General principles and structural precautions (1946), reprinted (1957).
22. Farm buildings for Scotland (1945), reprinted (1958).
23. House construction (1945) (out of print).
24. School furniture and equipment (1946).
27. Heating and ventilating of schools (1947) (out of print).
33. Basic design temperatures for space heating (1956).

NATIONAL BUILDING STUDIES (Ajv)

BULLETINS

3. Concreting and bricklaying in cold weather (1948).
4. Sand-lime and concrete bricks (1948) (new edition in preparation).
7. Sands for plasters, mortars and external renderings (1950).
9. Some common defects in brickwork (1950).
10. External rendered finishes for walls (1951) (out of print).

SPECIAL REPORTS

1. Structural requirements for houses (1948) (out of print).
3. Sand-lime bricks (1948) (out of print).
12. Mining subsidence: Effects on small houses (1951).
19. The assessment of vibration intensity and its application to the study of building vibrations (1953) (out of print).
22. Fire hazard of internal linings (1954).
24. A note on the history of reinforced concrete in buildings (1957).
25. The durability of reinforced concrete in buildings (1957).
26. Simplified daylight tables (1958), reprinted (1966).
27. A short history of the structural fire protection of buildings (1958).
28. Incentives for the building industry (1959).
29. Organisation of building sites (1959).
30. Study of alternative methods of house construction (1959).
31. Mobile tower cranes for two and three-storey buildings (1940).
32. Simplified tables of external loads in buried pipelines (1962) (being reprinted).
33. A qualitative study of some buildings in the London area (1963).
34. Multi-storey flats, design, building methods and costs (1963).
35. Pipe laying principles. Notes on construction methods for underground pipelines designed by the computed load method (1964).
36. Prefabrication—A history of its development in Great Britain (1965).
37. Loading charts for the design of rigid buried pipelines (1966).
38. High-strength beddings for unreinforced concrete and clayware pipes (1967).
39. Qualitative studies of buildings (1965).

RESEARCH PAPERS

8. The analysis of concretes (1950).
10. An economic design of rigid steel frames for multi-storey buildings (1951).
13. Studies in composite construction. Part I. The composite action of brick panel walls supported on reinforced concrete beams (1952).
19. Dynamic stresses in cast iron girder bridges (1954).
20. Reactions between aggregates and cement. Part IV. Alkali-aggregate interaction (1958).

22. Studies in composite construction. Part II. The interaction of floors and beams in multi-storey buildings (1955).
23. Condensation in sheeted roofs (1958).
25. Reactions between aggregates and cement. Parts V and VI (1958).
27. Noise in three groups of flats with different floor insulations (1958).
28. Studies in composite construction. Part III (1960).
29. Temperatures and humidities in pig houses (1960).
31. Studies in bridge-deck systems. Part II. Bending moments in a plate and girder system (1960).
32. The forces applied to the floor by foot in walking. Part I. Walking on a level surface (1951). Part II. Walking on a slope. Part III. Walking on stairs (1966).
33. Field measurements of sound insulations between dwellings (1960).
34. A study of space and water heating in local authority flats, 1956–59 (1961).
35. Effect of impact loading on prestressed and ordinary reinforced concrete beams (1961).
36. Effect of embedding aluminium and aluminium alloys in building materials (1963).
37. Studies on bridge-deck systems. Part III. Tests on model slab and girder bridge deck systems (1963).
38. The strength of encased stanchions (1965).
39. Childrens play on housing estates (1966).
40. Heat transfer and condensation in domestic boiler chimneys (1965).
41. Modern offices—A user survey (1966).

BUILDING RESEARCH STATION (Ajt)

DIGESTS: FIRST SERIES

3. House foundations on shrinkable clays (February 1949).
4. Pattern staining in buildings (March 1949).
6. The avoidance of cracking in masonry construction of concrete or sand-lime bricks (revised January 1957).
7. The lifting of clay and concrete floor tiles (June 1949).
8. The use of copper and galvanised steel in the same hot water system (July 1949).
9. Building on made-up ground or filling (August 1949).
11. Damp-proof courses in parapet walls (revised, February 1963).
12. The design of flat concrete roofs in relation to thermal effects (November 1949).
14. Plastering on metal lathing (January 1950).
16. Domestic heating by solid fuel (March 1950).
18. Smoky chimneys (revised, October 1955).
20. The weathering, preservation and maintenance of natural stone masonry, Part I (July 1950).
21. The weathering, preservation and maintenance of natural stone masonry, Part II (new edition in preparation).
23. Condensation problems in buildings (October 1950).
24. Granolithic concrete floors (November 1950).
26. Blowing, popping or pitting of internal plaster (January 1951).
31. Concrete in sulphate-bearing clays and groundwaters (June 1951).
33. The causes of dampness in buildings (August 1951).

34. The principles of natural ventilation of buildings (September 1951).
35. Heat loss from dwellings (October 1951).
36. Sound absorbent treatments (revised, September 1954).
38. Painting asbestos cement (May 1966).
41. The treatment of damp walls (April 1952).
42. The short-bored pile foundation (May 1952).
46. Building limes (revised, April 1966).
47. The control of lichens, moulds and similar growths on building materials (August 1963).
53. Perforated clay bricks (April 1953).
58. Wall and ceiling surfaces, and condensation (September 1953).
60. Condensation in domestic chimneys (superseding Digest No. 5) (November 1953).
73. Corrosion-resistant floors. Part I. Design considerations (January 1955).
74. Corrosion-resistant floors. Part II. Materials for finishes (February 1955).
78. Vibrations in buildings (June 1955).
81. Artificial lighting of building interiors: lamps and fittings (September 1955).
82. Building mastics: bonding new concrete to old (November 1955).
88. Sound insulation of dwellings. Part I (May 1956).
89. Sound insulation of dwellings. Part II (revised, January 1963).
90. Colourless waterproofing treatment for damp walls. Analysis of water encountered in construction (July 1956).
92. Pulverised fuel ash in building materials (September 1956).
94. Domestic heating—Estimation of seasonal heat requirements and fuel consumption in houses (November 1956).
98. Light cladding. Part I. General principles of design (May 1957).
99. Light cladding. Part I (continued June 1957).
100. Taking stock (with Index to Digests Nos. 1–100) (July 1957).
101. B.S. 2660. Range of colours (August 1957).
105. Lime blazing in brickwork: soil-pipe branch joints (December 1957).
106. Fire, materials and structures (January 1958).
108. Sand for concrete (March 1958).
109. Building economics, cost planning (April 1958).
110. Corrosion of non-ferrous metals, Part 1 (May 1958).
111. Corrosion of non-ferrous metals. Part 2 (June 1958).
113. Costs of mechanical plant (August 1958).
114. Questions and answers (September 1958).
116. Roof drainage (November 1958).
117. Condensation and the design of factory roofs (December 1958).
118. Reducing laboratory vibrations, spray traps (January 1959).
119. Questions and answers (February 1959).
121. Packed bricks (April 1959).
122. Wind effects on roofs (May 1959).
123. Sulphate attack on brickwork (June 1959).
124. Small underground drains and sewers: Part 1 (July 1959).
125. Small underground drains and sewers: Part 2 (August, 1959).
128. Stone preservatives and jointing plasterboard (November 1959).

129. Cranes for building (December 1959).
130. Supersulphate cement. Cracking of asbestos-cement sheets (January 1960) (being reprinted).
132. Condensation in dwellings (March 1960).
133. Domestic heating and thermal insulation (April 1960).

DIGESTS: SECOND SERIES

3. Working in winter or bad weather (August 1960).
4. Repairing brickwork (September 1960).
5. Materials for concrete (December 1960).
6. Drainage for housing (January 1961).
7. Noise in the home (February 1961).
8. Built-up felt roofs (March 1961).
9. Dry-lined interior to dwellings (April 1961).
10. Lifting equipment for cranes (May 1961).
12. Structural design in architecture (July 1961).
13. Concrete mix proportioning and control. Part 1 (August 1961).
14. Concrete mix proportioning and control. Part 2 (September 1961).
15. Pipes and fittings for domestic water supply (October 1961).
16. Aerated concrete. Part 1. Manufacture and properties (November 1961).
18. Design of timber floors to prevent dry rot (January 1962).
19. Lighting of drawing offices (February 1962).
20. Layout and equipment for drawing offices (March 1962).
21. New types of paint (revised, January 1960).
22. Socket outlet wiring for houses (May 1962).
23. An index of exposure to driving rain (June 1962).
25. Lightweight aggregate concretes. Part 1. Materials and properties (August 1962).
26. Lightweight aggregate concretes. Part 2. Uses (August 1962).
27. Rising damp in walls (October 1962) (with corrections, 1966).
28. Factory building studies (November 1962).
29. Aluminium in building. Part 1. Properties and uses (November 1962).
30. Aluminium in building. Part 2. Finishes (January 1963).
31. Lightweight aggregate concretes—Structural application (February 1963).
32. Simplified plumbing for housing (March 1963).
33. Sheet and tile flooring made from thermoplastic binders (April 1963).
34. Design of gutters and rainwater pipes (May 1963).
35. Shrinkage of natural aggregates in concrete (June 1963).
36. Jointing with mastics and gaskets. Part 1 (July 1963).
37. Jointing with mastics and gaskets. Part 2 (August 1963).
38. Noise and buildings (September 1963).
39. Cellular plastics for buildings (October 1963).
40. Refuse disposal in blocks of flats (November 1963).
41. Estimated daylight in buildings. Part 1 (December 1963).
42. Estimated daylight in buildings. Part 2 (January 1964).
43. Safety in domestic buildings. Part 1 (February 1964).
44. Safety in domestic buildings. Part 2 (March 1964).
45. Design and appearance. Part 1 (May 1964).
46. Design and appearance. Part 2 (May 1964).
47. Granolithic concrete, concrete tiles and terrazzo flooring (includes Addendum to Digest 89 (first series) (June 1964).

GOVERNMENT PUBLICATIONS

48. Multi-storey flats—design, building methods and costs (July 1964).
49. Choosing specifications for plastering (August 1964).
50. Index to B.R.S. Digests 3–135 (first series) and 1–49 (second series) (September 1964).
51. Developments in roofing (October 1964).
52. Space and water heating in local authority flats (November 1964).
53. C.P.M. explained (December 1964).
54. Damp proofing solid floors (January 1965).
55. Painting walls, Part 1 (February 1965).
56. Painting walls, Part 2 (March 1965).
57. Painting walls, Part 3 (April 1965).
58. Mortars for jointing (May 1965).
59. Protection against corrosion of reinforcing steel in concrete (June 1965).
60. Chimney design for domestic boilers (July 1965).
61. Strength of brickwork, block work and concrete walls (August 1965).
62. Index to B.R.S. Digests. Index to Digests 3–135 (first series) and 1–61 (second series) (September 1965).
63. Soils and foundations, Part 1 (October 1965).
64. Soils and foundations, Part 2 (November 1965).
65. The selection of clay building bricks, Part 1 (December 1965).
66. The selection of clay building bricks, Part 2 (January 1966).
67. Soils and foundations, Part 3 (February 1966).
68. Window design and solar heat gain (March 1966).
69. Application and durability of plastics (April 1966).
70. Painting metals in buildings, Part 1 (May 1966).
71. Painting metals in buildings, Part 2 (June 1966).
72. Home grown softwoods for building (July 1966).
73. Prevention of decay in window joinery (August 1966).
75. Cracking in buildings (October 1966).
76. Integrated daylight and artificial light in buildings (November 1966).
77. Damp-proof courses (December 1966).
78. Ventilation of internal bathrooms and w.c.'s in dwellings (January 1967).
79. Clay tile flooring (February 1967).
80. Soil and waste pipe systems for housing (March 1967).
81. Hospital sanitary services; some design and maintenance problems (April 1967).
82. Improving room acoustics (May 1967).
83. Plumbing with stainless steel (June 1967).
84. Accuracy in building: where, when, how much? (July 1967).
85. Joints between concrete wall panels: open drained joints (August 1967).
86. Index to B.R.S. Digests 3–133 (first series) and 3–85 (second series) (September 1967).
87. Electrical supplies for construction sites (October 1967).
88. Electrical supplies for construction sites, Part 2 (November 1967).
89. Sulphate attack in brickwork (January 1968).
90. Concrete in sulphate-bearing soils and groundwaters (February 1968).
91. Prevention of condensation (March 1968).
92. Building overseas in warm climates (April 1968).
93. Cellular plastics for building, Part 1 (May 1968).
94. Cellular plastics for building, Part 2 (June 1968).
95. Choosing a type of pile (July 1968).

98. Durability of metals in natural waters (October 1968).
99. Wind loading on building, Part 1 (November 1968).

OTHER PUBLICATIONS

Building Science Abstracts (published monthly).
Principles of modern building. Vol. 1. Walls, partitions and chimneys. Vol. 2. Floor and roofs.
Domestic heating in America (1946) (out of print).
Analysis of symmetric cylindrical shells.
Thermal insulation of buildings. G. D. Nash, J. Comrie and H. R. Broughton (1955).
Drainage pipework in dwellings. A. F. E. Wise (1958).

FACTORY BUILDING STUDIES

1. Modern multi-storey factories. W. A. Allen (1959).
2. The lighting of factories. M. J. Keyte and H. L. Gloag (1959).
3. Floor finishes for factories. F. C. Harper and P. A. Stone (1959).
4. Structural loading in factories. H. V. Apcar (1959).
5. Sites and foundations. A. D. M. Penman (1960).
6. Noise in factories (1960).
7. Structural framework for single-storey factory buildings (1960).
8. Colouring in factories. H. L. Gloag (1960).
9. Fire protection in factories. G. J. Langdon-Thomas (1960).
10. Electricity supply and distribution. A. G. Aldessey-Millhouse (1961).
11. Thermal insulation of factory buildings. D. G. Nash (1961).
12. The economics of factory buildings (1962).

TROPICAL BUILDING STUDIES (NEW SERIES)

1. Density in housing areas. P. H. M. Stevens.
2. Buildings for the storage of crops, in warm climates (1960).
3. Solar radiation: thermal effects on building materials (1962).
5. Soil stabilisation. A review of principles and practice (1963).

TECHNICAL PAPERS (OLD SERIES)

28. Protractors for the computation of daylight factors. A. F. Dufton (1946). (Daylight factor protractors referred to in Technical Paper No. 28).
30. The applications of electro-osmosis to practical problems in foundations and earthworks. L. Casaorande (1947) (out of print).

DEPARTMENT OF EDUCATION AND SCIENCE
(Ajv)

BULLETINS

1. New primary schools (1955) (reprinted 1967).
3. Village schools (1961).
4. Cost study (1957) (new edition in preparation).
7. Fire and the design of schools (1961).
8. Development projects: Wokingham School (1955).
9. Colour in school buildings (1962).
13. Fuel consumption in schools (1955) (reprinted 1967). Supplement: test with oil-fired warm air system (1957). Supplement: tests with coal-fired automatic stoker warm air system (1960).
16. Development projects: junior schools, Amersham (1958).
17. Development projects: secondary school, Arnold (1960).
18. Schools in the U.S.A. (1961).
19. The story of C.L.A.S.P. (1961).
20. Youth service buildings: general mixed clubs (1961).
21. Remodelling old schools (1963).
22. Development projects: youth club, Withywood, Bristol (1963).
23. Primary school plans. A second selection (1964).

BUILDING BULLETINS (NEW SERIES)

24. Controlling dimensions for educational building (1964).
25. Secondary school design, sixth form and staff (1965).
26. Secondary school design: physical education (1965).
27. Boarding schools for maladjusted children (1965).
28. Playing fields and hard surface areas (1966).
29. Harris College, Preston (1966).
30. Secondary school design, drama and music (1966).
31. Secondary school design. Workshop crafts (1966).
32. New problems in secondary school design. Additions for the fifth form (1966).
33. Lighting in schools (1967).
34. Secondary school design. Designing for arts and crafts (1967).
35. New problems in school design. Middle schools (1966).
36. Eveline Lowe Primary School, London (1967).
37. University building notes. Student residence (1967).
38. School furniture dimensions (1967).
39. Designing for science: Oxford School development problems in school design (1968).
40. Comprehensive schools from existing buildings. New problems in school design (1968)
41. Rosebery County School for Girls, Epsom, Surrey (1968).
42. Co-ordination of components for educational building (1968).

PAMPHLETS

33. Story of post-war school building (1957).

MISCELLANEOUS

The standards for schools premises regulations (1959).

MINISTRY OF HOUSING AND LOCAL GOVERNMENT

DESIGN BULLETINS

1. Some aspects of designing for old people (1962) (metric edition 1968).
2. Grouped flatlets for old people (1962).
3. Service cores in high flats: Part 1. Sanitary plumbing (1962). Part 2. Selection and planning of passenger lifts (1962) (reprinted 1967). Part 3. Mechanical ventilation of inner rooms (1963). Part 4. G.P.O. telephone installations. Part 5. Aerial installations for sound and television reception (1964). Part 6. Service cores in high flats. Cold water services (1965). Part 7. Service cores in high flats. Protection against lightning (1967).
4. Swimming pools (1962).
5. Landscaping for flats. The treatment of ground space on high-density housing estates (1967).
6. Space in the home (metric edition) (1968).
7. Housing cost yardstick for schemes at medium and high densities (out of print).
8. Dimensions and components for housing with special reference to industrialised building (out of print).
9. Swimming bath costs with some notes on design (1965).
10. Cars in housing. Part 1. Some medium-density layouts (1966) (reprinted 1967).
11. Old peoples' flatlets at Stevenage. An account of the project with an appraisal (1966).
12. Cars in housing. Part 2. I. Dimensions. II. Multi-storey parking garages (1967).
13. Safety in the home (1967).
14. House planning (1968).
16. Co-ordination of components in housing: metric dimensional framework (1968).

Flatlets for old people (1958) (out of print).
More flatlets for old people (1960).
Flats and houses (1958): design and economy (1958).
Sunlight indicator standard diagrams from 'flats and houses' 21 January to 22 November.
Housing manual (1949) (out of print).
Housing manual (1949)—technical appendices (1951) (out of print).
Housing for special purposes (1961) (out of print). Supplement to Housing Manual.
Houses (1952). Supplement to Housing Manual (out of print).
Houses (1953). Supplement to Housing Manual (out of print).
Houses that save softwood (1953) (out of print).
Model Byelaws—Series IV. Buildings (1953). Amendment.

PLANNING BULLETINS

1. Town centres. Approach to renewal.
2. Residential areas. Higher densities.
3. Town centres. Cost and control of redevelopment.
4. Town centres—current practice.
5. Planning for daylight and sunlight (1964).
6. Town and Country Planning Act (1962). Development plan maps. Part 1. Continuous revision. Part 2. The addition of colour (1964).
7. Parking in town centres (1965).

Quicker completion of house interiors (1953).

CENTRAL HOUSING AND ADVISORY COMMITTEE (Ajv)

REPORTS OF SUB-COMMITTEES

Conversion of existing houses (1945).
Homes for today and tomorrow (1961).
Care and maintenance of fittings and equipment in the modern house (1950).
Councils and their houses, management of estates (1959).

MINISTRY OF PUBLIC BUILDING AND WORKS (Aju)

Assessment of new building projects (agreement) (1965).
Building regulations advisory committee. First report.
Building regulations, 1965. Technical memoranda: fire–stairs–space. General index (1966).
Building research and development advisory council on second report (1953) (out of print).
Building research and information services.
Building apprenticeship and training council. First to fourth report (out of print).
Building and civil engineering (1959) (reprinted 1967).
D.C. 8. Recommended dimensions of space allocated and assemblies used in education, health, housing and office buildings (1968).
Directorate of building management, research and development.
R. and D. Building Management Handbooks:
  1. Preparing to build.
  2. Selective tendering for local authorities. Guide to procedure.
  3. Network analysis in construction design.
  5. Professional collaboration in designing buildings, including a training exercise.
National Brick Advisory Council papers:
  1. The getting of clay with special reference to labour requirements (reprinted 1956) (out of print).
  4. Firing of common bricks (March 1951) (reprinted 1956).
  5. Clay building bricks of the United Kingdom (out of print).
  6. Clay brick making in Great Britain (February 1950) (out of print).
A National Building Agency (reprinted 1966).
Production of building components in shipyards.
Programme and progress (January 1965).
Standards in building: Retention of moneys on building and civil engineering contracts (out of print).
  Schedule of rates for building works.
    Part 1 (1965).
    Part 2 (1965) Amendment No. 1.
Survey of problems before the construction industries (1952).
United Kingdom housing mission to Canada (June 1963).

ADVISORY LEAFLETS

1. Painting new plaster and cement.
2. Plasters used in building: gypsum and anhydrite.
3. Lagging hot and cold water systems in houses.
5. Laying screeds as an underlay for floor coverings.
6. Limes for mortar.
7. Concreting in cold weather.
8. Bricklaying in cold weather.
9. Plaster mixes for inside work.
10. Dry rot.
11. Painting metalwork.
12. Fixing, pointing and glazing metal windows.
13. Site costing for builders.
14. Programming and progressing for builders.
15. Sands for plasters, mortars and renderings.
16. Mortars for brickwork.
17. Fixing fibre board wall linings.
18. Powered hand tools—electric tools for woodworking.
19. Powered hand tools—pneumatic and electric tools.
20. Powered hand tools—maintenance and safety precautions.
21. Plastering on building boards.
22. Care of small plant and hand tools.
23. Damp-proof courses.
24. Laying drain pipes.
25. Painting woodwork.
26. Making concrete.
27. Rendering outside walls.
28. Painting asbestos cement.
29. Care in the use of timber.
30. Installing solid fuel.
31. Installing solid fuel appliances, No. 2. Heating stoves, independent boilers and cookers.
32. Handling concrete on housing sites.
33. Care of builders' machines.
34. House insulation. Simple aids to warmer homes.
35. Prestressed concrete.
36. Metal scaffolding.
37. Emulsion paint.
38. Lightweight concrete.
39. Special cements other than ordinary Portland cement.
40. Weather and the builder.
41. Frost precautions in household water supply.
42. Woodworm.
43. Testing concrete.
44. Smoky chimneys.
45. Warmth without waste.
46. Lead burning.
47. Dampness in buildings.
48. Setting out on site.
49. Simple concrete lintels.
50. Chimneys for domestic boilers.
51. Watertight basements, Part 1.
52. Watertight basements, Part 2.
53. Making fixings to hard materials.
54. Woodworking machinery for builders.
55. Timber sizes for small buildings, Part 1.
56. Timber sizes for small buildings, Part 2.
57. Newer types of paint and their uses.
58. Inserting a damp-proof course in an existing building.
59. Electricity on building sites.
60. Ready-mixed concrete.
61. Condensation.
62. Maintaining exposed woodwork.
63. Fire risks on building sites.
64. Plasterboard dry linings.
65. Calcium silicate bricks and how to use them.

66. Laying flexible drain and sewer pipes such as pitch-fibre and P.V.C.
67. Building without accidents.
68. Timber connectors.
69. Reducing noise in buildings.

TECHNICAL NOTES

1. Simplified plumbing.
2. Polythene tubes for cold water services.
3. Importance of thermal insulation in building.
4. Ring circuit electrical installations for housing.
5. Vibrated concrete in building.
6. Mix design for vibrated concrete.
7. Prestressed concrete.

See also publications from the following, reported in H.M.S.O. sections list *Building*.

Ministry of Labour.
Ministry of Health.
National Physical Laboratory.
Forest Products Research Publications.
Road Research Publications.
Fire Research Station.

LIST OF HANDBOOKS AND SPECIAL ISSUES BY B.S.I. APPLICABLE TO THE BUILDING INDUSTRY

B.S. Handbook No. 3: 1955. Building materials and components. (2 volumes) Loose-leaf.
B.S.I. Yearbook.
P.D. 420:1953   Methods of protection against corrosion for light gauge steel used in building.
P.D. 4845:1968   The British Standards Institution—its activities and organisation.
P.D. 5686:1969   The use of S.I. units.
P.D. 6030:1967   Programme for the change to the metric system in the construction industry.
P.D. 6031:1968   Use of the metric system in the construction industry (A4 size).
P.D. 6112:1967   Guide to the preparation of specifications.
P.D. 6245:1967   Going metric—first stages. (Single copies free.)
P.D. 6249:1967   Dimensional co-ordination in building. Estimate of timing for B.S.I. work (A4 size).
P.D. 6286:1969   Metric standards published and in progress (complete to 31 July 1969).
P.D. 6421:1968   The change to metric in the construction industry.

8 DIRECTORY

GENERAL

BRITISH COLOUR COUNCIL
10a, Chandos Street, Cavendish Square, London, W.1.
(Tel: 01–580 8946)

BRITISH MUSEUM
Bloomsbury, London, W.C.1. (Tel: 01–636 1555)

CENTRAL COUNCIL FOR THE DISABLED
34, Eccleston Square, London, S.W.1. (Tel: 01–222 7487)

CHURCH COMMISSIONERS
1, Millbank, London, S.W.1. (Tel: 01–930 5444)

CONSUMERS' ASSOCIATION
14, Buckingham Street, London, W.C.2.
(Tel: 01–930 9921)

COUNTY COUNCIL ASSOCIATION
Eaton House, 66a, Eaton Square, Westminster,
London, S.W.1. (Tel: 01–235 5173)

HOUSING CENTRE TRUST
13, Suffolk Street, Haymarket, London, S.W.1.
(Tel: 01–930 2881)

INDUSTRIAL SOCIETY
48, Bryanston Square, London, W.1. (Tel: 01–262 2401)

INSTITUTE OF CONTEMPORARY ARTS
17–18, Dover Street, London, W.1. (Tel: 01–499 6186)

NATIONAL PLAYING FIELDS ASSOCIATION
Playfield House, 57b, Catherine Place, London, S.W.1.
(Tel: 01–834 9274/5)

NATIONAL SOCIETY FOR CLEAN AIR
Field House, Breams Buildings, London, E.C.4.
(Tel: 01–242 5038)

NOISE ABATEMENT SOCIETY
6–8, Old Bond Street, London, W.1. (Tel: 01–493 5877)

ROYAL SOCIETY
6, Carlton House Terrace, London, S.W.1.
(Tel: 01–839 5561)

ROYAL SOCIETY OF ARTS
John Adam Street, London, W.C.2.
(Tel: 01–839 2366)

ROYAL SOCIETY OF HEALTH
90, Buckingham Palace Road, London, S.W.1.
(Tel: 01–730 5134)

ROYAL SOCIETY FOR THE PREVENTION OF ACCIDENTS
52, Grosvenor Gardens, London, S.W.1.
(Tel: 01–730 2246)

RURAL INDUSTRIES BUREAU
35, Camp Road, London, S.W.19 (Tel: 01–946 5101)

GOVERNMENT DEPARTMENTS AND OFFICES, INCLUDING NATIONALISED INDUSTRIES C.I./SfB (Akm)
(Indexed under official title and main subject)

AGREEMENT BOARD
Lord Alexander House, Waterhouse Street, Hemel
Hempstead, Herts. (Tel: Hemel Hempstead 3701)

ARTS COUNCIL OF GREAT BRITAIN
4, St. James Square, London, S.W.1. (Tel: 01–930 9737)

BOARD OF TRADE
1, Victoria Street, London S.W.1. (Tel: 01–222 7577)

BRITISH COUNCIL
65, Davies Street, London, W.1. (Tel: 01–499 8011)

BRITISH IRON AND STEEL RESEARCH ASSOCIATION
24, Buckingham Gate, London, S.W.1. (Tel: 01–828 7931)

BUILDING RESEARCH STATION
Bucknalls Lane, Garston, nr Watford, Herts.
(Tel: Garston 4040)

BRITISH STEEL CORPORATION
33, Grosvenor Place, London, S.W.1. (Tel: 01–235 1212)

CENTRAL ELECTRICITY GENERATING BOARD
Sudbury House, 15, Newgate Street, London, E.C.1.
(Tel: 01–248 1202)

CENTRAL OFFICE OF INFORMATION
Hercules House, Hercules Road, Westminster Bridge Road,
London, S.E.1. (Tel: 01–928 2345)

COAL UTILISATION COUNCIL
19, Rochester Row, London, S.W.1. (Tel: 01–834 2337)

COMMISSION FOR THE NEW TOWNS
Glen House, Stag Place, London, S.W.1.
(Tel: 01–834 8034)

COMMISSIONERS FOR CROWN LANDS, OFFICE OF
55, Whitehall, London, S.W.1. (Tel: 01–839 2211)

COMMONWEALTH INSTITUTE
Kensington High Street, London, W.8. (Tel: 01–937 8252)

CONSTRUCTION INDUSTRY TRAINING BOARD
Radnor House, London Road, Norbury, London, S.W. 16.
(Tel: 01–764 5060)

DEPARTMENT FOR AGRICULTURE FOR SCOTLAND
St. Andrew's House, Edinburgh 1. (Tel: Waverley 8404)

DEPARTMENT OF ECONOMIC AFFAIRS
Storeys Gate, London, S.W.1. (Tel: 01–839 7848)

DEPARTMENT FOR EDUCATION AND SCIENCE
Curzon Street House, Curzon Street, London, W.1.
(Tel: 01–493 7070)

DESIGN COUNCIL
28, Haymarket, London, S.W.1. (Tel: 01–839 8000)
ELECTRICITY COUNCIL
Trafalgar Buildings, 1, Charing Cross, London, S.W.1.
(Tel: 01–930 6757)
FOREST PRODUCTS RESEARCH LABORATORY
Princes Risborough, Aylesbury, Bucks
(Tel: Princes Risborough 101)
FORESTRY COMMISSION
25, Savile Row, London, W.1. (Tel: 01–734 0221)
GAS COUNCIL
4–5, Grosvenor Place, London, S.W.1. (Tel: 01–235 4321)
GEOLOGICAL SURVEY OF GREAT BRITAIN AND
MUSEUM OF PRACTICAL GEOLOGY
Exhibition Road, South Kensington, London, S.W.7.
(Tel: 01–589 9441)
H.M. LAND REGISTRY
32, Lincoln's Inn Fields, London, W.C.2.
(Tel: 01–405 3488)
H.M. STATIONERY OFFICE
Publications Sale Office, 49, High Holborn, London, W.C.1.
(Tel: 01–928 6977, ext 423) and
423, Oxford Street, London, W.1. (01–629 3492)
HOME OFFICE
Whitehall, London, S.W.1. (Tel: 01–930 8100)
HOUSING CORPORATION
Sloane Square House, London, S.W.1. (Tel: 01–730 9991)
INLAND REVENUE, OFFICE OF CHIEF VALUER
Somerset House, London, W.C.2. (Tel 01–836 2407)
LAND COMMISSION
Government Buildings, Kenton Bar, Newcastle-upon-Tyne
(Tel: Newcastle-upon-Tyne 869811)
LOCATION OF OFFICES BUREAU
Lonsdale Chambers, 27, Chancery Lane, London, W.C.2.
(Tel: 01–405 2921)
METEOROLOGICAL OFFICE
London Road, Bracknell, Berks. (Tel: Bracknell 20242)
MINISTRY OF AGRICULTURE, FISHERIES AND FOOD
Great Westminster House, Horseferry Road, London, S.W.1.
(Tel: 01–834 8511)
MINISTRY OF HEALTH
Alexander Fleming House, Elephant and Castle,
London, S.E.1. (Tel: 01–407 5522)
MINISTRY OF HOUSING AND LOCAL GOVERNMENT
Whitehall, London, S.W.1. (Tel: 01–930 4300)
MINISTRY OF LABOUR
8, St. James Square, London, S.W.1. (Tel: 01–930 6200)
MINISTRY OF LAND AND NATURAL RESOURCES
Gwydyr House, Whitehall, London, S.W.1.
(Tel: 01–930 7844)
MINISTRY OF POWER
Thames House, Millbank, London, S.W.1.
(Tel: 01–222 7000)
MINISTRY OF PUBLIC BUILDINGS AND WORKS
Lambeth Bridge House, Albert Embankment,
London, S.E.1. (Tel: 01–735 7611)
MINISTRY OF SOCIAL SECURITY
10, John Adam Street, London, W.C.2. (Tel: 01–930 9066)
MINISTRY OF TECHNOLOGY
Millbank Tower, Millbank, London, S.W.1.
(Tel: 01–834 2255)
MINISTRY OF TRANSPORT
St. Christopher House, Southwark, London, S.E.1.

(Tel: 01–928 7999)
MINISTRY OF WORKS (SCOTTISH BRANCH HEADQUARTERS)
122, George Street, Edinburgh 2.
(Tel: Caledonian 2533)
NATIONAL BUILDING AGENCY
N.B.A. House, Arundel Street, London, W.C.2.
(Tel: 01–836 4488)
NATIONAL COAL BOARD
Hobart House, Grosvenor Place, London, S.W.1.
(Tel: 01–235 2020)
NATIONAL ELECTRONICS COUNCIL
Abell House, John Islip Street, London, S.W.1.
(Tel: 01–834 4422)
NATIONAL HEALTH SERVICE
London Area: 40, Eastbourne Terrace, London, W.2.
NATIONAL PHYSICAL LABORATORY
Queens Road, Teddington, Middlesex (Tel: 01–977 3222)
ORDNANCE SURVEY
Romsey Road, Southampton (Tel: Southampton 75555)
PUBLIC RECORD OFFICE
Chancery Lane, London, W.C.2. (Tel: 01–405 0741)
ROAD RESEARCH LABORATORY
Crowthorne, Berks. (Tel: Crowthorne 3131)
ROYAL FINE ART COMMISSION
2, Carlton Gardens, London, S.W.1. (Tel: 01–930 3935)
SCIENCE RESEARCH COUNCIL
State House, High Holborn, London, W.C.1.
(Tel: 01–242 1262)
SCOTTISH EDUCATION DEPARTMENT
St. Andrews House, Edinburgh 1. (Tel: Waverley 6591)
SCOTTISH HOME AND HEALTH DEPARTMENT
St. Andrews House, Edinburgh 1. (Tel: Waverley 2501)
SCOTTISH LAND COURT
1, Grosvenor Crescent, Edinburgh 12.
(Tel: Caledonian 3595)
SCOTTISH OFFICE
Dover House, Whitehall, London, S.W.1.
(Tel: 01–930 6151)
TITHE REDEMPTION COMMISSION
Finsbury Square House, 33/37, Finsbury Square,
London, E.C.2. (Tel: 01–606 2052)
WAR DAMAGE COMMISSION
Eagle House, 90, Cannon Street, London, E.C.4.
(Tel: 01–623 2000)
WATER POLLUTION RESEARCH LABORATORY
Elder Way, London Road, Stevenage, Herts.
(Tel: Stevenage 820)
WELSH BOARD OF HEALTH
Cathays Park, Cardiff. (Tel: Cardiff 28066)
WELSH OFFICE
47, Parliament Street, London, S.W.1. (Tel: 01–930 3151)
and Cathays Park, Cardiff (Tel: Cardiff 28066)

LIBRARIES, BUILDING CENTRES,
INFORMATION SOURCES IN GENERAL
C.I./SfB (Agm) (Indexed under name)

ADVISORY SERVICE FOR THE BUILDING INDUSTRY
39, Devonshire Street, London, W.1. (Tel: 01–580 6244/5/6)

AGRICULTURAL LAND SERVICE
Ministry of Agriculture, Fisheries and Food,
Great Westminster House, Horseferry Road, London, S.W.1.
(Tel: 01–834 8511)
ASSOCIATION OF SPECIAL LIBRARIES AND INFORMATION BUREAUX
3, Belgrave Square, London, S.W.1. (Tel: 01–235 5050)
ATLAS COMPUTING SERVICE
44, Gordon Square, London, W.C.1. (Tel: 01–387 3421)
BARBOUR INDEX LTD
10, Porchester Gardens, London, W.2. (Tel: 01–727 8044)
BRITISH STANDARDS INSTITUTION
2, Park Street, London, W.1. (Tel: 01–629 9000)
BUILDING CENTRE (BIRMINGHAM)
The Engineering and Building Centre, Broad Street,
Birmingham 1. (Tel: Midland 1914)
BUILDING CENTRE (IRELAND)
17, Lower Baggot Street, Dublin (Tel: Dublin 62745)
BUILDING CENTRE (LIVERPOOL)
Liverpool Building and Design Centre, Hope Street,
Liverpool 1. (Tel: Royal 8566)
BUILDING CENTRE (LONDON)
26, Store Street, London, W.C.1. (Tel: 01–636 5400)
BUILDING CENTRE (MANCHESTER)
Manchester Building and Design Centre Ltd,
115, Portland Street, Manchester 1. (Tel: Central 9802)
BUILDING CENTRE (NORTHERN IRELAND)
4, Arthur Place, Belfast, Northern Ireland
(Tel: Belfast 21601)
BUILDING CENTRE (NOTTINGHAM)
Midland Building and Design Centre, Mansfield Road,
Nottingham (Tel: Nottingham 45651)
BUILDING CENTRE (SCOTLAND)
Building Centre of Scotland Ltd, 425, Sauchiehall Street,
Glasgow, C.2. (Tel: Glasgow, Douglas 5911)
BUILDING CENTRE (SOUTHERN COUNTIES)
Grosvenor House, Cumberland Place,
Southampton SO1 2BD (Tel: Southampton 27350)
BUILDING AND DESIGN CENTRE (BRISTOL)
Stonebridge House, Colston Avenue, The Centre, Bristol 1.
(Tel: Bristol 27002)
BUILDING INFORMATION CENTRE (CAMBRIDGE)
The Building Information Centre (Cambridge),
16, Trumpington Street, Cambridge (Tel: Cambridge 59625)
BUILDING INFORMATION CENTRE (COVENTRY)
Coventry Building Information Centre, Department of
Architecture and Planning, Earl Street, Coventry CV1 5RT,
Warwickshire (Tel: Coventry 25555, ext 2512)
BUILDING INFORMATION CENTRE (STOKE-ON-TRENT)
College Road, Stoke-on-Trent, Staffordshire
(Tel: Stoke-on-Trent 23214)
BUILDING LIBRARY AND INFORMATION SERVICES
10, St. George's Street, Hanover Square, London, W.1.
(Tel: 01–734 3691)
CENTRAL OFFICE OF INFORMATION
Hercules Road, Westminster Bridge Road, London, S.E.1
(Tel: 01–928 2345)
CONSTRUCTION INDUSTRY INFORMATION GROUP
c/o Royal Institute of British Architects, 66, Portland Place,
London, W.1. (Tel: 01–580 5533)
CONSTRUCTION INDUSTRY RESEARCH AND INFORMATION
ASSOCIATION
6, Storey's Gate, London, S.W.1. (Tel: 01–839 6881)
COUNCIL OF INDUSTRIAL DESIGN

The Design Centre, 28, Haymarket, London, S.W.1.
(Tel: 01–839 8000)
DESIGN AND BUILDING CENTRE (MIDLAND) LTD
See BUILDING CENTRE (NOTTINGHAM)
DESIGN CENTRE (LONDON)
See DESIGN COUNCIL
DESIGN CENTRE (SCOTLAND)
46, West George Street, Glasgow C.2.
(Tel: Glasgow, Douglas 3914)
FARM BUILDINGS CENTRE
c/o National Agricultural Centre, Kenilworth CU8 2CG,
Warwickshire (Tel: Coventry 22345)
LIBRARY ASSOCIATION
Ridgemount Street, London, W.C.1. (Tel: 01–636 7543)
NATIONAL BUILDING AGENCY
N.B.A. House, Arundel Street, London, W.C.2.
(Tel: 01-835 4488)
NATIONAL COMPUTING CENTRE
Quay House, Quay Street, Manchester 3.
(Tel: Deansgate 19731)
NATIONAL LENDING LIBRARY FOR SCIENCE AND TECHNOLOGY
Boston Spa, Yorkshire

NATIONAL LIBRARIES
Bodleian Library, Oxford
British Museum, London
National Central Library, London
National Library of Scotland, Edinburgh
National Library of Wales, Aberystwyth
Scottish Central Library, Edinburgh
Trinity College, Dublin
University Library, Cambridge

JOURNALS AND PUBLISHERS
C.I./SfB (Abd)

Architect and Building News (Fortnightly)
Building and Contract Journals Ltd,
32, Southwark Bridge Road, London, S.E.1.
Architect and Surveyor (Alternate months)
Incorporated Association of Architects and Surveyors,
29, Belgrave Square, London, S.W.1.
The Architects' Journal (Weekly)
Architectural Press Ltd, 9–13 Queen Anne's Gate,
London, S.W.1.
Architectural Design (Monthly)
Standard Catalogue Co Ltd, 26, Bloomsbury Way,
London, W.C.1.
Architectural Review (Monthly)
Architectural Press Ltd, 9–13, Queen Anne's Gate,
London, S.W.1.
Architecture 71 (Monthly)
Appletron Press Ltd, 117, Charter House Street,
London, E.C.1.
Architecture East Midlands (Alternate months)
Corinthian Press Ltd, 258, Gray's Inn Road, London, W.C.1.
Architecture North West (Alternate months)
North West Publishers Ltd, Rossfield Road,
Ellesmere Port, Cheshire
Architecture Wales (Alternate months)
Corinthian Press Ltd, 258, Gray's Inn Road, London, W.C.1.

Arena (Quarterly)
Architectural Association, 34–6, Bedford Square,
London, W.C.1.
Board Manufacture (Monthly)
Pressmedia Ltd, Ivy Hatch, Sevenoaks, Kent
British Clayworker (Monthly)
Clay and Brick Publications Ltd, 4, Catherine Street,
Aldwych, London, W.C.2.
Build (Monthly)
Creation Ltd, Creation House, Grafton Street, Dublin 2.
Builder's Merchants Journal (Monthly)
Morgan Bros (Publishers) Ltd, 28, Essex Street, Strand,
London, W.C.2.
Building (Weekly)
The Builder Ltd, 4, Catherine Street, Aldwych,
London, W.C.2.
Building Equipment News (Monthly)
Building and Contract Journals Ltd,
32, Southwark Bridge Road, London, S.E.1.
Building Industries and Scottish Architect (Monthly)
Jack and Carrick, 19, Queen Street, Glasgow, C.1.
Building Maintenance (Monthly)
Factory Publication Ltd, Hermes House,
89, Blackfriars Road, London, S.E.1.
Building Materials (Monthly)
Grampian Press Ltd, The Tower, 229–243, Shepherd's
Bush Road, Hammersmith, London, W.6.
Building Science (Quarterly)
Pergamon Publications Ltd, Headington Hill Hall, Heading-
ton, Oxford
Building Science Abstracts (Monthly)
H.M.S.O. for Building Research Station,
Atlantic House, Holborn Viaduct, London, E.C.1.
Building Technology and Management (Alternate months)
Pergamon Press Ltd, Headington Hill Hall, Oxford
Building with Steel (Quarterly)
C. H. W. Roles and Associates Ltd for B.C.S.A.,
70, Goswell Road, London, E.C.1.
Cement and Lime Manufacturer (Alternate months)
Concrete Publications Ltd, 60, Buckingham Gate,
London, S.W.1.
Chartered Surveyor (Monthly)
Royal Institute of Chartered Surveyors,
12, Great George Street, Parliament Square, London, S.W.1.
Claycraft (Monthly)
London and Sheffield Publishing Co Ltd,
7, Chesterfield Gardens, Curzon Street, London, W.1.
Commercial Decor and Contract Furnishing Digest (Monthly)
Westbourne Publishing Group Ltd,
Crown House, London Road, Morden, Surrey
Concrete Building and Concrete Products (Monthly)
Concrete Publications Ltd, 60, Buckingham Gate,
London, S.W.1.
Concrete Quarterly (Quarterly)
Cement and Concrete Association,
52, Grosvenor Gardens, London, S.W.1.
Construction News (Weekly)
Construction Publications Ltd, Elm House,
10–16, Elm Street, London, W.C.1.
Construction Technology (Monthly)
Forth Publishing Co Ltd, Atholl Crescent, Edinburgh 3.
Contract Journal (Weekly)
Building and Contract Journals Ltd,

32, Southwark Bridge Road, London, S.E.1.
Contractor (Monthly) (includes *Contractor's Record* and
Municipal Engineering, Supply and Demand, Site and Plant)
John Morris Publicity Ltd, Publicity House,
Streatham Hill, London, S.W.2.
Design (Monthly)
H.M.S.O. for Co.I.D., Atlantic House, Holborn Viaduct,
London, E.C.1.
Flooring (Monthly) (incorporating *Flooring and Finishes News*)
Metcalfe Publications Ltd, 50, Gray's Inn Road,
London, W.C.1.
The House Builder and Estate Developer (Monthly)
82, New Cavendish Street, London, W.1.
Housing (Alternate months)
Institute of Housing Managers, 5th Floor,
Victoria House, Southampton Row, London, W.C.1.
Housing and Planning Review (Alternate months)
National Housing and Town Planning Council,
Reg Lawson and Co, Green Dragon House, High Street,
Croydon, Surrey
Housing Review (Alternate months)
The Housing Centre Trust, 13, Suffolk Street,
London, S.W.1.
The Illustrated Carpenter and Builder (Weekly)
Construction Publications Ltd, Elm House, Elm Street,
London, W.C.1.
Industrial Architecture (Monthly)
Fountain Press Ltd, 46, Chancery Lane, London, W.C.2.
Industrial Daily News (Daily)
Industrial Publications Ltd, Pear Tree Court,
London, E.C.1.
Industrialised Building Systems and Components (Monthly)
Building and Contract Journals Ltd,
32, Southwark Bridge Road, London, S.E.1.
Insulation (Monthly)
Lomax Erskine Publications Ltd, 8, Buckingham Street,
London, W.C.2.
Interior Design and Contract Furnishing (Monthly)
National Trade Press Business Journals Ltd,
33–39, Bowling Green Lane, London, E.C.1.
Irish Builder and Engineer (Fortnightly)
Sackville Press Ltd, 11–13, Findlater Place, Dublin 1.
Irish Contracts Weekly (Weekly)
Eccles Place, Dublin 1.
The Ironmonger, Builder's Merchant and Hardwareman (Weekly)
Morgan Bros (Publishers) Ltd, 28, Essex Street, Strand,
London, W.C.2.
Journal of the Royal Institute of British Architects (Monthly)
Royal Institute of British Architects,
66, Portland Place, London, W.1.
Journal of the Town Planning Institute (Monthly)
Town Planning Institute, 26, Portland Place, London, W.1.
Keystone (Quarterly)
Association of Building Technicians,
22, London Bridge Road, London, S.E.1.
The Master Builder's Journal (Monthly)
Trade Press (F.M.B.) Ltd, 33, John Street, London, W.C.1.
Monthly List of New Materials (Monthly)
The Building Centre, 26, Store Street, London, W.C.1.
Municipal Journal, Public Works Engineer and *Contractors'
Guide* (Weekly)
Municipal Journal Ltd, 3, Clements Inn, London, W.C.2.
National Builder (Monthly)

The Federated Employers Press Ltd,
02, New Cavendish Street, London, W.1.
New Building (Monthly)
New Property Press Ltd, Bleak House,
5, St. Peter's Street, London, N.1.
Northern Architect (Alternate months)
Oriell Press Ltd, 27, Ridley Place, Newcastle-upon-Tyne 1.
Official Architecture and Planning (Monthly) (now
incorporating *The Modular Quarterly*)
Architecture and Planning Publications Ltd,
4, Catherine Street, Aldwych, London, W.C.2.
Portico (Quarterly)
Faculty of Architects and Surveyors, 68, Gloucester Place,
London, W.1.
Southern Building News (Monthly)
Mailwork Services Ltd, 37–39, Oxford Street,
Southampton
Stone Industries (Alternate months)
Stone Industrial Publications Ltd,
54–55, Wilton Road, London, S.W.1.
Structural Engineer (Monthly)
John Morris Publicity Ltd, Publicity House,
41, Streatham Hill, London, S.W.2.
System Building and Design (Monthly)
Products Journal Ltd, Summit House, Glebe Way,
West Wickham, Kent
Town and Country Planning (Monthly)
Town and Country Planning Association,
28, King Street, London, W.C.2.

TRADE ASSOCIATIONS AND THOSE DEALING WITH SPECIFIC MATERIALS C.I./SfB (Akp)

ABRASIVE INDUSTRIES ASSOCIATION
42, Abbey House, Victoria Street, London, S.W.1.
(Tel: 01–222 3868)
ADHESIVES MANUFACTURERS ASSOCIATION
21, Tothill Street, London, S.W.1. (Tel: 01–930 6711)
THE ALUMINIUM FEDERATION
Portland House, Stag Place, London, S.W.1.
(Tel: 01–828 3941)
ARCHITECTURAL METALWORK CRAFTSMEN'S ASSOCIATION
2, Caxton Street, London, S.W.1. (Tel: 01–222 4813)
ASBESTOS CEMENT MANUFACTURERS ASSOCIATION
15, Tooks Court, London, E.C.4. (Tel: 01–242 7161)
ASPHALT ROADS ASSOCIATION
14, Howick Place, London, S.W.1. (Tel: 01–834 2529)
ASSOCIATED LEAD MANUFACTURERS LTD
Clements House, 14, Gresham Street, London, E.C.2.
(Tel: 01–606 4400)
ASSOCIATED TANK MANUFACTURERS
Wortley Road, Rotherham, Yorks. (Tel: Rotherham 4201)
ASSOCIATION OF BRITISH PLYWOOD AND VENEER MANUFACTURERS
Epworth House, 25, City Road, London, E.C.1.
(Tel: 01–628 5801)
ASSOCIATION OF BRITISH ROOFING FELT MANUFACTURERS
69, Cannon Street, London, E.C.4. (Tel: 01–248 4444)
ASSOCIATION OF BRITISH WOODWOOL MANUFACTURERS
c/o Federation of British Industries, 21, Tothill Street,
London, S.W.1. (Tel: 01–930 6711)

ASSOCIATION OF BRONZE AND BRASS FOUNDERS
67, Harborne Road, Birmingham 15. (Tel: Edgbaston 4141)
ASSOCIATION OF FLOORING CONTRACTORS
14, Bryanston Street, London, W.1. (Tel: 01–935 1781)
ASSOCIATION OF INDUSTRIALISED BUILDING COMPONENTS
MANUFACTURERS LTD
26, Store Street, London, W.C.1. (Tel: 01–636 5400)
BRICK DEVELOPMENT ASSOCIATION
Hanover House, 73–78, High Holborn, London, W.C.1.
(Tel: 01–405 5434)
BRITISH CARPET CENTRE
Dorland House, 14–16, Lower Regent Street,
London, S.W.1. (Tel: 01–930 8711)
BRITISH CAST CONCRETE FEDERATION
60, Buckingham Gate, London, S.W.1. (Tel: 01–828 8746)
BRITISH CERAMIC TILE COUNCIL
Federation House, Station Road, Stoke-on-Trent, Staffs.
(Tel: Stoke-on-Trent 45147)
BRITISH CONSTRUCTIONAL STEELWORK ASSOCIATION
Hancock House, 87, Vincent Square, London, S.W.1.
(Tel: 01–834 1713)
BRITISH GRANITE AND WHINSTONE FEDERATION
16, Berkeley Street, London, W.1. (Tel: 01–493 3392)
BRITISH INDUSTRIAL FLOOR MACHINE ASSOCIATION
15, Tooks Court, Cursitor Street, London, E.C.4.
(Tel: 01–242 7161)
BRITISH IRON FOUNDERS ASSOCIATION
30, St. James Square, London, S.W.1. (Tel: 01–930 6866)
BRITISH LIGHTING COUNCIL
Brettenham House, 16–18, Lancaster Place, Strand,
London, W.C.2. (Tel: 01–836 7337)
BRITISH PLASTICS FEDERATION
47–48, Piccadilly, London, W.1. (Tel: 01–734 2041/5)
BRITISH PRECAST CONCRETE FEDERATION
9, Catherine Place, London, S.W.1. (Tel: 01–828 8746)
BRITISH READY MIXED CONCRETE ASSOCIATION
19, The Crescent, Ilford, Essex (Tel: 01–554 4133)
BRITISH ROAD FEDERATION
26, Manchester Square, London, W.1. (Tel: 01–935 0221)
BRITISH ROAD TAR ASSOCIATION
9, Harley Street, London, W.1. (Tel: 01–636 3833)
BRITISH SLAG FEDERATION
69–73, Theobalds Road, London, W.C.1.
(Tel: 01–242 2950)
BRITISH STONE FEDERATION
Alderman House, 37, Soho Square, London, W.1.
(Tel: 01–437 7107)
BRITISH WOODWORK MANUFACTURERS ASSOCIATION
Carrington House, 130, Regent Street, London, W.1.
(Tel: 01–734 4448)
BRITISH WOOD PRESERVING ASSOCIATION
6, Southampton Place, London, W.C.1. (Tel: 01–242 4347)
BUILDING AND ALLIED TRADES ENQUIRY BUREAU
3, Berners Street, London, W.1. (Tel: (01–636 5474)
BUILDING BOARD MANUFACTURERS' ASSOCIATION OF
GREAT BRITAIN
Plough Place, Fetter Lane, London, E.C.4.
(Tel: 01–583 0686)
CAST IRON HEATING BOILER AND RADIATOR MANUFACTURERS'
ASSOCIATION
69, Cannon Street, London, E.C.4. (Tel: 01–248 4444)
CATERING EQUIPMENT MANUFACTURERS' ASSOCIATION
21, Tothill Street, London, S.W.1. (Tel: 01–930 6711)

CEMENT AND CONCRETE ASSOCIATION
52, Grosvenor Gardens, London, S.W.1. (Tel: 01–235 6661)

CEMENT MAKERS' FEDERATION
Terminal House, 52, Grosvenor Gardens, London, S.W.1.
(Tel: 01–730 2148)

CLAY PRODUCTS TECHNICAL BUREAU
Drayton House, 30, Gordon Street, London, W.1.
(Tel: 01–387 2338)

COAL UTILISATION COUNCIL
19, Rochester Row, London, S.W.1. (Tel: 01–834 2339)

CONFEDERATION OF PAINTING AND DECORATING TRADE
EMPLOYERS
6, Haywra Street, Harrogate, Yorks. (Tel: Harrogate 67292)

CONTRACTORS' PLANT ASSOCIATION
Orchard House, Great Smith Street, London, S.W.1.
(Tel: 01–222 4114)

COPPER DEVELOPMENT ASSOCIATION
55, South Audley Street, London, W.1.
(Tel: 01–499 8811)

DECORATIVE LIGHTING MANUFACTURERS' ASSOCIATION
69, Cannon Street, London, E.C.4. (Tel: 01–248 4444)

DESIGN AND INDUSTRIES ASSOCIATION
13, Suffolk Street, London, S.W.1. (Tel: 01–930 0540)

ELECTRIC LIGHT FITTINGS ASSOCIATION
8, Leicester Square, London, W.C.2. (Tel: 01–437 0678)

ELECTRICAL CONTRACTORS' ASSOCIATION
2nd Floor, 145, Charing Cross Road, London, W.C.2.
(Tel: 01–734 7161)

ELECTRICAL CONTRACTORS' ASSOCIATION OF SCOTLAND
23, Heriot Row, Edinburgh 3. (Tel: Caledonian 7221)

ELECTRICAL DEVELOPMENT ASSOCIATION
Trafalgar Buildings, 1, Charing Cross, London, W.1.
(Tel: 01–930 6757)

ELECTRICITY COUNCIL
30, Millbank, London, S.W.1. (Tel: 01–834 2333)

ENGINEERING EQUIPMENT USERS ASSOCIATION
20, Grosvenor Gardens, London, S.W.1.
(Tel: 01–730 9958/9)

FARM BUILDINGS ASSOCIATION
35, Belgrave Square, London, S.W.1. (Tel: 01–235 5323)

FEDERATION OF ASSOCIATIONS OF SPECIALISTS AND
SUB-CONTRACTORS
14, Bryanston Street, London, W.1. (Tel: 01–935 1781)

FEDERATION OF BUILDING BLOCK MANUFACTURERS
5, Elm Road, Beckenham, Kent (Tel: 01-650 4505)

FEDERATION OF CIVIL ENGINEERING CONTRACTORS
Romney House, Tufton Street, Westminster, London, S.W.1.
(Tel: 01–222 2544–6)

FEDERATION OF MANUFACTURERS OF CONSTRUCTION EQUIPMENT
8, St. Bride Street, London, E.C.4. (Tel: 01–353 3020)

FEDERATION OF MASTER BUILDERS
33, John Street, Holborn, London, W.C.1.
(Tel: 01–242 7583)

FEDERATION OF PAINTING CONTRACTORS
St. Stephen's House, Victoria Embankment, Westminster,
London, S.W.1. (Tel: 01–930 3902)

FEDERATION OF PILING SPECIALISTS
Dickens House, 15, Tooks Court, London, E.C.4.
(Tel: 01–242 7161)

FEDERATION OF REGISTERED HOUSE-BUILDERS
82, New Cavendish Street, London, W.1.
(Tel: 01–580 4041)

FELT ROOFING CONTRACTORS ADVISORY BOARD

Victoria House, Southampton Row, London, W.C.1.
(Tel: 01–405 0670)

FIBRE BUILDING BOARD DEVELOPMENT ORGANISATION LTD
Buckingham House, 6–7, Buckingham Street,
London, W.C.2. (Tel: 01–839 1122)

FINNISH PLYWOOD DEVELOPMENT ASSOCIATION
Finland House, 56, Haymarket, London, S.W.1.
(Tel: 01–930 3282)

FIRE PROTECTION ASSOCIATION
Aldermary House, Queen Street, London, E.C.4.
(Tel: 01–248 5222)

GAS COUNCIL
4–5 Grosvenor Place, London, S.W.1. (Tel: 01–235 4321)

GLASS MANUFACTURERS FEDERATION
19, Portland Place, London, W.1. (Tel: 01–580 6952)

GLAZED AND FLOOR TILE ASSOCIATION
Federation House, Station Road, Stoke-on-Trent, Staffs.
(Tel: Stoke-on-Trent 45747)

GUILD OF ARCHITECTURAL IRONMONGERS
52–54, High Holborn, London, W.C.1. (Tel: 01–242 7772)

GYPSUM PLASTERBOARD DEVELOPMENT ASSOCIATION
Ferguson House, 15–17, Marylebone Road, London, N.W.1.
(Tel: 01–486 4011)

HEATING AND VENTILATING CONTRACTORS' ASSOCIATION
Coastal Chambers, 172, Buckingham Palace Road,
London, S.W.1. (Tel: 01–730 8245)

HEATING CENTRE, THE
34, Mortimer Street, London, W.1. (Tel: 01–580 3238)

INSULATING GLAZING ASSOCIATION
6, Mount Row, London, W.1. (Tel: 01–629 8334)

INVISIBLE PANEL WARMING ASSOCIATION
Grand Buildings, Trafalgar Square, London, W.C.2.
(Tel: 01–930 4060)

LEAD DEVELOPMENT ASSOCIATION
34, Berkeley Square, London, W.1. (Tel: 01–499 8422)

LINOLEUM AND FELT BASE EMPLOYERS' FEDERATION
69, North End, Croydon, CR0 1TG (Tel: 01–686 2134)

LINOLEUM MANUFACTURERS' ASSOCIATION, THE
Vernon House, Bloomsbury Square, London, W.C.1.
(Tel: 01–405 8511)

MASTIC ASPHALT ADVISORY COUNCIL
c/o Peat Mitchell and Co, Glen House, Stag Place,
London, S.W.1. (Tel: 01–834 8866)

METAL FIXING ASSOCIATION FOR BUILDING INSULATION
32, Queen Anne Street, London, W.1. (Tel: 01–580 7616)

METAL WINDOW ASSOCIATION LTD
Burwood House, 16, Caxton Street, London, S.W.1.
(Tel: 01–222 5051)

NATIONAL ASSOCIATION OF MASTER ASPHALTERS
22, Upper Brook Street, London, W.1. (Tel: 01–499 5333)

NATIONAL BRASSFOUNDRY ASSOCIATION
5, Greenfield Crescent, Edgbaston, Birmingham 15.
(Tel: Edgbaston 2177/8)

NATIONAL CLAYWARE FEDERATION
7, Castle Street, Bridgwater, Somerset (Tel: Bridgwater 8251)

NATIONAL COUNCIL OF BUILDING MATERIALS PRODUCERS
Suite 18, Chantrey House, Eccleston Street, London, S.W.1.
(Tel: 01–730 9233/4)

NATIONAL ELECTRICAL CONTRACTORS AND TRADERS
ASSOCIATION
2nd Floor, 145, Charing Cross Road, London, W.C.2.
(Tel: 01–734 7161)

NATIONAL FEDERATED ELECTRICAL ASSOCIATION
2nd Floor, 145, Charing Cross Road, London, W.C.2.
(Tel: 01–734 7161)

NATIONAL FEDERATION OF BUILDERS AND PLUMBERS MERCHANTS
High Holborn House, 52–54, High Holborn,
London, W.C.1. (Tel: 01–242 7772)

NATIONAL FEDERATION OF BUILDING TRADES EMPLOYERS
82, New Cavendish Street, London, W.1.
(Tel: 01–580 4041)

NATIONAL FEDERATION OF CLAY INDUSTRIES
Drayton House, Gordon Street, London, W.C.1.
(Tel: 01–387 2568)

NATIONAL FEDERATION OF DEMOLITION CONTRACTORS
Ramillies Buildings, 1/9, Hills Place, Oxford Street,
London, W.1. (Tel: 01–437 2584/5/6)

NATIONAL FEDERATION OF MASTER PAINTERS AND DECORATORS
OF ENGLAND AND WALES
6, Haywra Street, Harrogate, Yorks. (Tel: Harrogate 67292)

NATIONAL FEDERATION OF MASTER STEEPLEJACKS AND
LIGHTNING CONDUCTOR ENGINEERS
Ramillies Buildings, 1/9, Hills Place, Oxford Street,
London, W.1. (Tel: 01–437 2584/5/6)

NATIONAL FEDERATION OF PLASTERING CONTRACTORS
82, New Cavendish Street, London, W.1.
(Tel: 01–580 4041)

NATIONAL FEDERATION OF PLUMBERS AND DOMESTIC
HEATING ENGINEERS
6, Gate Street, London, W.C.2. (Tel: 01–405 2678)

NATIONAL FEDERATION OF ROOFING CONTRACTORS
West Bar Chambers, 38, Boar Lane, Leeds, 1.
(Tel: Leeds 3–3361/2)

NATIONAL FEDERATION OF TERRAZZO/MOSAIC SPECIALISTS
2nd Floor, 19–20, Leicester Square, London, W.C.2.
(Tel: 01–839 6508/9)

NATURAL ASPHALT MINE-OWNERS AND MANUFACTURERS
COUNCIL
14, Howick Place, London, S.W.1. (Tel: 01–834 1600)

PAINTMAKERS ASSOCIATION OF GREAT BRITAIN
Prudential House, Wellesley House, Croydon CR9 2ET
(Tel: 01–686 3111/2/3)

PITCH FIBRE PIPE ASSOCIATION OF GREAT BRITAIN LTD
35, New Bridge Street, London, E.C.4.
(Tel: 01–248 5271)

PLATE GLASS ASSOCIATION
Mount Row, London, W.1. (Tel: 01–625 8334)

PLYWOOD MANUFACTURERS OF BRITISH COLUMBIA
Templar House, 81, High Holborn, London, W.C.1.
(Tel: 01–405 1105)

REINFORCED CONCRETE ASSOCIATION
14, Howick Place, London, S.W.1. (Tel: 01–828 9346)

SAND AND GRAVEL ASSOCIATION OF GREAT BRITAIN
48, Park Street, London, W.1. (Tel: 01–499 8967/8/9)

SAND-LIME BRICK MANUFACTURERS' ASSOCIATION
Hanover House, 73–78, High Holborn, London, W.C.1.
(Tel: 01–405 5434)

SCANDINAVIAN LIGHTING ASSOCIATION
Vernon Yard, 119, Portobello Road, London, W.11.
(Tel: 01–229 9961)

SHEET STEEL INFORMATION AND DEVELOPMENT ASSOCIATION
Albany House, Petty France, London, S.W.1.
(Tel: 01–799 1616)

SOLID SMOKELESS FUELS FEDERATION
York House, Empire Way, Wembley, Middlesex

(Tel: 01–902 5405)

STAINLESS STEEL DEVELOPMENT ASSOCIATION
7, Old Park Lane, London, W.1. (Tel: 01–629 7676)

STAINLESS STEEL FABRICATORS ASSOCIATION OF GREAT BRITAIN
Chamber of Commerce House, P.O. Box 360,
75, Harborne Road, Birmingham 15. (Tel: Edgbaston 6171)

STEEL WINDOW ASSOCIATION
Burwood House, Caxton Street, London, S.W.1.
(Tel: 01–222 5051)

STRUCTURAL INSULATION ASSOCIATION
32, Queen Anne Street, London, W.1. (Tel: 01–580 7616)

TIMBER BUILDING MANUFACTURERS ASSOCIATION OF
GREAT BRITAIN
4, High Street, Epsom, Surrey (Tel: Epsom 24481)

TIMBER RESEARCH AND DEVELOPMENT ASSOCIATION
The Building Centre, 26, Store Street, London, W.C.1.
(Tel: 01–636 8761/3)

TIMBER TRADE FEDERATION OF THE UNITED KINGDOM
Clareville House, Whitcomb Street, London, W.C.2.
(Tel: 01–839 1891)

VITREOUS ENAMEL DEVELOPMENT COUNCIL
28, Welbeck Street, London, W.1. (Tel: 01–486 2237)

ZINC DEVELOPMENT ASSOCIATION
34, Berkeley Square, London, W.1. (Tel: 01–499 6636)

PROFESSIONAL INSTITUTIONS AND ASSOCIATIONS C.I./SfB (Akp)

AGRICULTURAL ENGINEERS' ASSOCIATION
6, Buckingham Gate, London, S.W.1. (Tel: 01–828 7973)

ARCHITECTS' BENEVOLENT SOCIETY
66, Portland Place, London, W.1. (Tel: 01–580 5533)

ARCHITECTS' REGISTRATION COUNCIL OF THE UNITED KINGDOM
63, Hallam Street, London, W.1. (Tel: 01–580 5861)

ARCHITECTURAL ASSOCIATION
34–36, Bedford Square, London, W.C.1. (Tel: 01–636 0974)

ASSOCIATED MASTER PLUMBERS AND DOMESTIC ENGINEERS
81, Gower Street, London, W.C.1. (Tel: 01–580 7008)

ASSOCIATION OF BUILDING CENTRES
26, Store Street, London, W.C.1. (Tel: 01–636 5400)

ASSOCIATION OF BUILDING TECHNICIANS
156, Waterloo Road, London, S.E.1. (Tel: 01–928 5427)

ASSOCIATION OF CONSULTING ENGINEERS
Abbey House, 2, Victoria Street, London, S.W.1.
(Tel: 01–222 6557–8)

ASSOCIATION OF METROPOLITAN BOROUGH ENGINEERS AND
SURVEYORS
Town Hall, Haverstock Hill, London, N.W.3.
(Tel: 01–435 7171)

ASSOCIATION OF OFFICIAL ARCHITECTS
c/o Royal Institute of British Architects, 66, Portland Place,
London, W.1. (Tel: 01–580 5533)

ASSOCIATION OF PUBLIC HEALTH INSPECTORS
19, Grosvenor Place, London, S.W.1. (Tel: 01–235 5158)

BOARD OF BUILDING EDUCATION
48, Bedford Square, London, W.C.1. (Tel: 01–636 9924)

BOARD OF ARCHITECTURAL EDUCATION (R.I.B.A.)
66, Portland Place, London, W.1. (Tel: 01–580 5533)

BRITISH ARCHITECTURAL STUDENTS' ASSOCIATION
11, Manchester Square, London, W.1. (Tel: 01–486 1951)

BRITISH INSTITUTE OF MANAGEMENT
80, Fetter Lane, London, E.C.4. (Tel: 01–405 3456)

THE BUILDING SOCIETIES ASSOCIATION
10, Park Street, London, W.1. (Tel: 01–499 6549)

BUILDING SURVEYORS' INSTITUTE
189–93, Temple Chambers, Temple Avenue, London, E.C.4.
(Tel: 01–353 6405/6)

CENTRE FOR ADVANCED STUDIES IN ENVIRONMENT—
ARCHITECTURAL ASSOCIATION
36, Bedford Square, London, W.C.1. (Tel: 01–636 0974)

CHARTERED AUCTIONEERS' AND ESTATE AGENTS' INSTITUTE
29, Lincoln's Inn Fields, London, W.C.2.
(Tel: 01–242 6451)

CITY AND BOROUGH ARCHITECTS' SOCIETY
Town Hall, High Holborn, London, W.C.1.
(Tel: 01–405 3411)

CITY AND GUILDS OF LONDON INSTITUTE
76, Portland Place, London, W.1. (Tel: 01–580 3050)

COLLEGE OF ESTATE MANAGEMENT
St. Albans Grove, London, W.8. (Tel: 01–937 1546)

CONFEDERATION OF BRITISH INDUSTRY
21, Tothill Street, London, S.W.1. (Tel: 01–930 6711)

THE COUNTY ARCHITECTS' SOCIETY
The Hon Secretary, County Architects' Society, The Castle,
Winchester, Hants. (Tel: Winchester 4411, ext 209)

COUNTY PLANNING OFFICERS' SOCIETY
c/o County Planning Department, Oxfordshire County
Council, Park End Street Offices, Oxford (Tel: Oxford 49871)

COUNTY SURVEYORS' SOCIETY
c/o Hon Secretary, County Surveyor's Department,
5th Floor, Kennet House, 80–82, Kings Road, Reading,
Berks. (Tel: Reading 55981, ext 42)

FACULTY OF ARCHITECTS AND SURVEYORS
68, Gloucester Place, London, W.1. (Tel: 01–935 9966)

FEDERATION OF REGISTERED HOUSE BUILDERS
82, New Cavendish Street, London, W.1.
(Tel: 01–580 4041)

ILLUMINATING ENGINEERING SOCIETY
York House, Westminster Bridge Road, London, S.E.1.
(Tel: 01–928 7110)

INCORPORATED ASSOCIATION OF ARCHITECTS AND SURVEYORS
29, Belgrave Square, London, S.W.1. (Tel: 01–235 3755)

INCORPORATED INSTITUTE OF BRITISH DECORATORS AND
INTERIOR DESIGNERS
Alderman House, 37, Soho Square, London, W.1.
(Tel: 01–437 5056)

INSTITUTE OF ADVANCED ARCHITECTURAL STUDIES
Micklegate, York (Tel: York 24919)

INSTITUTE OF BUILDING
48, Bedford Square, London, W.C.1. (Tel: 01–636 9924)

INSTITUTE OF BUILDING ESTIMATORS LTD
10, Cromwell Place, London, S.W.7. (Tel: 01–589 3885)

INSTITUTE OF BUILDING SITE MANAGEMENT
21, Panton Street, London, S.W.1. (Tel: 01–930 5645)

INSTITUTE OF BUILDING SURVEYORS
186–7, Temple Chambers, Temple Avenue, London, E.C.4.
(Tel: 01–353 6405)

INSTITUTE OF CLERKS OF WORKS
52, Lincoln's Inn Fields, London, W.C.2.
(Tel: 01–405 9292)

INSTITUTE OF FUEL
18, Devonshire Street, Portland Place, London, W.1.
(Tel: 01–580 7124)

INSTITUTE OF LANDSCAPE ARCHITECTS
38, Russell Square, London, W.C.1. (Tel: 01–636 3473)

INSTITUTE OF PLUMBING
81, Gower Street, London, W.C.1. (Tel: 01–580 7008)

INSTITUTE OF QUANTITY SURVEYORS
98, Gloucester Place, London, W.1. (Tel: 01–935 1895)

INSTITUTE OF QUARRYING
62–64, Baker Street, London, W.1. (Tel: 01–486 2547/8/9)

INSTITUTE OF TRANSPORT
80, Portland Place, London, W.1. (Tel: 01–580 5216)

INSTITUTE OF REGISTERED ARCHITECTS
68, Gloucester Place, London, W.1. (Tel: 01–486 1945)

INSTITUTION OF BRITISH ENGINEERS
Windsor House, 46, Victoria Street, London, S.W.1.
(Tel: 01–799 5585)

INSTITUTION OF CIVIL ENGINEERS
1–7, Great George Street, London, S.W.1.
(Tel: 01–930 4577)

INSTITUTION OF ELECTRICAL ENGINEERS
Savoy Place, London, W.C.2. (Tel: 01–246 1871)

INSTITUTION OF FIRE ENGINEERS
148, New Walk, Leicester (Tel: Leicester 59171)

INSTITUTION OF GAS ENGINEERS
17, Grosvenor Crescent, London, S.W.1.
(Tel: 01–235 8266)

INSTITUTION OF HEATING AND VENTILATING ENGINEERS
49, Cadogan Square, London, S.W.1. (Tel: 01–235 7671)

INSTITUTION OF HIGHWAY ENGINEERS
14, Queen Anne's Gate, London, S.W.1.
(Tel: 01–839 3582)

INSTITUTION OF HOSPITAL ENGINEERS
45, Great Russell Street, London, W.C.1.
(Tel: 01–636 0131)

INSTITUTION OF MECHANICAL ENGINEERS
1, Birdcage Walk, London, S.W.1. (Tel: 01–930 7476)

INSTITUTION OF MUNICIPAL ENGINEERS
25, Eccleston Square, London, S.W.1. (Tel: 01–834 5083)

INSTITUTION OF PLANT ENGINEERS
2, Grosvenor Gardens, London, S.W.1. (Tel: 01–730 0469)

INSTITUTION OF PUBLIC HEALTH ENGINEERS
32, Eccleston Square, London, S.W.1. (Tel: 01–834 3017)

INSTITUTION OF STRUCTURAL ENGINEERS
11, Upper Belgrave Street, London, S.W.1.
(Tel: 01–235 4335)

INSTITUTION OF WATER ENGINEERS
11, Pall Mall, London, S.W.1. (Tel: 01–930 6641)

IRON AND STEEL INSTITUTE
4, Grosvenor Gardens, London, S.W.1. (Tel: 01–730 0061)

JOINT BUILDING GROUP
57, Russell Square, London, W.C.1. (Tel: 01–636 5871)

LONDON ASSOCIATION OF MASTER DECORATORS
37, Soho Square, London, W.1. (Tel: 01–437 5056)

LONDON MASTER BUILDERS' ASSOCIATION
47, Bedford Square, London, W.C.1. (Tel: 01–636 3891)

LONDON MASTER PLASTERERS' ASSOCIATION
47, Bedford Square, London, W.C.1. (Tel: 01–636 3891)

MODULAR SOCIETY
22, Buckingham Street, Strand, London, W.C.2.
(Tel: 01–839 4567)

NATIONAL ASSOCIATION OF EXHIBITION CONTRACTORS
10, Cromwell Place, London, S.W.7 (Tel: 01–589 3885)

NATIONAL ASSOCIATION OF REGISTERED HOUSE BUILDERS
82, New Cavendish Street, London, W.1.
(Tel: 01–580 4041)

NATIONAL ASSOCIATION OF SHOPFITTERS

2, Caxton Street, London, S.W.1. (Tel: 01–222 4813)
NATIONAL FEDERATION OF HOUSING SOCIETIES
86, Strand, London, W.C.2. (Tel: 01–836 2741)
NATIONAL HOUSE BUILDERS' REGISTRATION COUNCIL
58, Portland Place, London, W.1. (Tel: 01–580 0064)
NATIONAL JOINT COUNCIL FOR THE BUILDING INDUSTRY
11, Weymouth Street, London, W.1.
(Tel: 01–580 1740 and 2785)
PLASTICS INSTITUTE
11, Hobart Place, London, S.W.1. (Tel: 01–245 9555)
REGISTERED PLUMBERS' ASSOCIATION
Scottish Mutual House, North Street, Hornchurch, Essex
(Tel: Hornchurch 51236)
REINFORCED CONCRETE ASSOCIATION
14, Howick Place, London, S.W.1. (Tel: 01–834 9349)
ROYAL INSTITUTE OF BRITISH ARCHITECTS
66, Portland Place, London, W.1. (Tel: 01–580 5533)
ROYAL INSTITUTION OF CHARTERED SURVEYORS
12, Great George Street, London, S.W.1.
(Tel: 01–930 5322)
ROYAL INSTITUTE OF PUBLIC HEALTH AND HYGIENE
28, Portland Place, London, W.1. (Tel: 01–580 2731)
SOCIETY OF ARCHITECTURAL AND ASSOCIATED TECHNICIANS
42–46, Weymouth Street, London, W.1.
(Tel: 01–935 0118)
SOCIETY OF ENGINEERS
Abbey House, Victoria Street, London, S.W.1.
(Tel: 01–222 7244)
SOCIETY OF INDUSTRIAL ARTISTS AND DESIGNERS
7, Woburn Square, London, W.C.1. (Tel: 01–580 1984)
TOWN AND COUNTRY PLANNING ASSOCIATION
28, King Street, Covent Garden, London, W.C.2.
(Tel: 01–836 5006/7)
TOWN PLANNING INSTITUTE
26, Portland Place, London, W.1. (Tel: 01–636 9107)
VALUERS INSTITUTION
3, Cadogan Gate, London, S.W.1. (Tel: 01–235 2282)

RESEARCH ASSOCIATIONS C.I./SfB (Akp)

AGRICULTURAL RESEARCH COUNCIL
Cunard Building, 15, Regent Street, London, S.W.1.
(Tel: 01–839 4380)
BRICK DEVELOPMENT ASSOCIATION
Hanover House, 73–78, High Holborn, London, W.C.1.
(Tel: 01–405 5434)
BRITISH CAST IRON RESEARCH ASSOCIATION
Bordesley, Alvechurch, Birmingham (Tel: Redditch 2715)
BRITISH CERAMIC RESEARCH ASSOCIATION
Queens Road, Penkhull, Stoke-on-Trent, Staffs.
(Tel: Stoke-on-Trent 44045)
BRITISH COAL UTILISATION RESEARCH ASSOCIATION
Randalls Road, Leatherhead, Surrey
(Tel: Leatherhead 4411)
BRITISH COKE RESEARCH ASSOCIATION
Mill Lane, Wingerworth, Chesterfield, Derbyshire
(Tel: Chesterfield 76821)
BRITISH GLASS INDUSTRY RESEARCH ASSOCIATION
Northumberland Road, Sheffield 10.
(Tel: Sheffield 66001/4)
BRITISH IRON AND STEEL RESEARCH ASSOCIATION
24, Buckingham Gate, London, S.W.1. (Tel: 01–828 7931)

BRITISH NON-FERROUS METALS RESEARCH ASSOCIATION
81, Euston Street, London, N.W.1 (Tel: 01–387 6411)
BRITISH WELDING RESEARCH ASSOCIATION
19, Fitzroy Square, London, W.1. (Tel: 01–387 9595)
BUILDING RESEARCH STATION
Bucknalls Lane, Garston, Watford, Herts.
(Tel: Garston 4040)
CEMENT AND CONCRETE ASSOCIATION
Research Station, Training Centre, Fulmer, Bucks.
(Tel: Fulmer 2727)
CENTRE FOR URBAN STUDIES
University College, London, Flaxman House, Flaxman
Terrace, London W.C.1. (Tel: 01–387 0371)
COAL TAR RESEARCH ASSOCIATION
Oxford Road, Gomersal, Leeds (Tel: Cleckheaton 4251)
COMPUTER APPLICATIONS GROUP — ARCHITECTURAL
ASSOCIATION
34–36, Bedford Square, London, W.C.1.
(Tel: 01–636 0974)
CONSTRUCTION INDUSTRY RESEARCH AND INFORMATION
ASSOCIATION
6, Storeys Gate, London, S.W.1. (Tel: 01–839 6881)
ELECTRICAL RESEARCH ASSOCIATION
Cleeve Road, Leatherhead, Surrey (Tel: Leatherhead 4151)
ELLIS RESEARCH AND TESTING LABORATORIES LTD
Albury Laboratories, Albury, Guildford, Surrey
(Tel: Shere 2041/2/3)
FOREST PRODUCTS RESEARCH LABORATORY
Princes Risborough, Bucks. (Tel: Princes Risborough 101)
FURNITURE INDUSTRY RESEARCH ASSOCIATION
Maxwell House, Stevenage, Herts. (Tel: Stevenage 3433)
HEATING AND VENTILATING RESEARCH ASSOCIATION
Old Bracknell Lane, Bracknell, Berks. (Tel: Bracknell 5071)
JOINT FIRE RESEARCH ORGANISATION
Fire Research Station, Melrose Avenue, Boreham Wood,
Herts. (Tel: 01–953 6177)
NATIONAL RESEARCH DEVELOPMENT CORPORATION
Kingsgate House, Victoria Street, London, S.W.1.
(Tel: 01–828 3400)
NATIONAL INDUSTRIAL FUEL EFFICIENCY SERVICE
71, Grosvenor Street, London, W.1. (Tel: 01–493 9706)
NATIONAL PHYSICAL LABORATORY
Teddington, Middlesex (Tel: 01–977 3222)
NATURAL RUBBER PRODUCERS' RESEARCH ASSOCIATION
19, Buckingham Street, Adelphi, London, W.C.2.
(Tel: 01–930 9314/8)
RESEARCH ASSOCIATION OF BRITISH PAINT, COLOUR AND
VARNISH MANUFACTURERS
The Paint Research Association, 8, Waldegrave Road,
Teddington, Middlesex (Tel: 01–977 4427/8/9)
ROAD RESEARCH LABORATORY
Ministry of Transport, Crowthorne, Berks.
(Tel: Crowthorne 3131)
RUBBER AND PLASTICS RESEARCH ASSOCIATION OF
GREAT BRITAIN (R.A.P.R.A.)
Shawbury, Shrewsbury, Shropshire (Tel: Shawbury 383)
SCIENCE RESEARCH COUNCIL
State House, High Holborn, London, W.C.1.
(Tel: 01–242 1262)
R. H. HARRY STANGER LABORATORIES
The Laboratories, Summerfield House, Barnet Lane,
Elstree, Herts. (Tel: 01–953 1306)
TIMBER RESEARCH AND DEVELOPMENT ASSOCIATION

St. Johns Road, Tylers Green, Hughenden Valley,
High Wycombe, Bucks. (Tel. Naphill 3091)
TIN RESEARCH INSTITUTE
Fraser Road, Perivale, Greenford, Middlesex
(Tel: 01–997 4254)
WATER POLLUTION RESEARCH LABORATORY
Elder Way, London Road, Stevenage, Herts.
(Tel: Stevenage 820)
WELWYN HALL RESEARCH ASSOCIATION
The Hall, Church Street, Welwyn, Herts.
(Tel: Welwyn 5201/4)

PRESERVATION SOCIETIES C.I./SfB (Akp)

ANCIENT MONUMENTS BOARD FOR ENGLAND AND WALES
c/o Ministry of Public Buildings and Works, Sanctuary
Buildings, Great Smith Street, London, S.W.1.
(Tel: 01–222 7790)
ANCIENT MONUMENTS BOARD FOR SCOTLAND
c/o Ministry of Public Buildings and Works, 122, George
Street, Edinburgh 2. (Tel: Caledonian 2533)
ANCIENT MONUMENTS BOARD FOR WALES
Government Buildings, St. Agnes Road, Gabalfa, Cardiff
(Tel: Cardiff 62131)
ANCIENT MONUMENTS SOCIETY
12, Edwardes Square, London, W.8. (Tel: 01–937 1414)
ASSOCIATION FOR THE PRESERVATION OF RURAL SCOTLAND
39, Castle Street, Edinburgh 2. (Tel: Caledonian 8391)
CAMBRIDGE PRESERVATION SOCIETY
21, Northampton Street, Cambridge (Tel: Cambridge 56850)
CATHEDRALS ADVISORY COMMITTEE
83, London Wall, London, E.C.2. (Tel: 01–588 3842)
CIVIC TRUST
Walter House, Bedford Street, Strand, London, W.C.2.
(Tel: 01–836 5202)
CIVIC TRUST FOR THE NORTH EAST
26, Sutton Street, Durham (Tel: Durham 61182)
CIVIC TRUST FOR THE NORTH WEST
Century House, St. Peter's Square, Manchester 2.
(Tel: Manchester Central 0333)
CIVIC TRUST FOR SCOTLAND
183, West George Street, Glasgow, C.2.
(Tel: Glasgow Central 3689)
COMMONS, OPEN SPACES AND FOOTPATHS PRESERVATION
SOCIETY
166, Shaftesbury Avenue, London, W.C.2.
(Tel: 01–836 7220)
COUNCIL FOR THE CARE OF CHURCHES
83, London Wall, London, E.C.2. (Tel: 01–588 3842)
COUNCIL FOR THE PRESERVATION OF RURAL ENGLAND
4, Hobart Place, London, S.W.1. (Tel: 01–235 4771)
COUNCIL FOR THE PRESERVATION OF RURAL WALES
Meifod, Montgomeryshire, Wales (Tel: Meifod 383)
FRIENDS OF FRIENDLESS CHURCHES
12, Edwardes Square, London, W.8. (Tel: 01–937 1414)
THE GEORGIAN GROUP
2, Chester Street, London, S.W.1. (Tel: 01–235 3081)
HISTORICAL BUILDINGS COUNCILS
ENGLAND: Sanctuary Building, Great Smith Street,
                London, S.W.1. (Tel: 01–222 7790)
SCOTLAND: Argyll House, 3, Lady Dawson Street,
                Edinburgh, EH3 9SF

WALES: Welsh Office, Summit House, Windsor Place,
            Cardiff, CF 3BQ (Tel: Cardiff 42331)
NATIONAL MONUMENTS RECORD
Fielden House, 10, Great College Street, Westminster,
London, S.W.1. (Tel: 01–930 6554)
NATIONAL PARKS COMMISSION
1, Cambridge Gate, Regents Park, London, N.W.1.
(Tel: 01–935 0366)
NATIONAL TRUST FOR PLACES OF HISTORICAL INTEREST OR
NATURAL BEAUTY
42, Queen Anne's Gate, London, S.W.1.
(Tel: 01–930 1211/2/3)
NATIONAL TRUST FOR SCOTLAND
5, Charlotte Square, Edinburgh 2. (Tel: Caledonian 2184)
NATURE CONSERVANCY
19, Belgrave Square, London, S.W.1. (Tel: 01–235 3241)
PILGRIM TRUST
Millbank House, 2, Great Peter Street, London, S.W.1.
(Tel: 01–222 4231)
ROYAL COMMISSION ON ANCIENT AND HISTORICAL
MONUMENTS IN SCOTLAND
52–54, Melville Street, Edinburgh 3. (Tel: Caledonian 5994)
ROYAL COMMISSION ON ANCIENT MONUMENTS IN WALES AND
MONMOUTHSHIRE
Edleston House, Queens Road, Aberystwyth, Cardiganshire
(Tel: Aberystwyth 2256)
ROYAL COMMISSION ON HISTORICAL MONUMENTS IN ENGLAND
10, Great College Street, London, S.W.1.
(Tel: 01–930 9652)
SALTIRE SOCIETY
Gladstone's Land, 483, Lawnmarket, Edinburgh 1.
(Tel: Caledonian 7780)
SOCIETY FOR THE PROTECTION OF ANCIENT BUILDINGS
55, Great Ormond Street, London, W.C.1.
(Tel: 01–405 2646)
TOWN AND COUNTRY PLANNING ASSOCIATION
28, King Street, London, W.C.1. (Tel: 01–836 5006)
THE VICTORIAN SOCIETY
12, Magnolia Wharf, Strand-on-the-Green, London, W.4.
(Tel: 01–994 1510)

COUNTY COUNCILS—ENGLAND AND WALES C.I./SfB (Aks) (Indexed under name)

ANGLESEY
Shire Hall, Llangefni, Anglesey (Tel: Anglesey 3262)
BEDFORDSHIRE
Shire Hall Bedford (Tel: Bedford 67444)
Planning Department: 3, High Street, Bedford
(Tel: Bedford 67221)
BERKSHIRE
Wilton House, Parkside Road, Reading
(Tel: Reading 50891)
Planning Department: 49, Friar Street, Reading
(Tel: Reading 55981)
BRECONSHIRE
Rhyd Offices, Brecon, South Wales (Tel: Brecon 2286)
Planning Offices: 6, Glamorgan Street, Brecon, South
Wales (Tel: Brecon 3378)
BUCKINGHAMSHIRE
County Offices, Aylesbury (Tel: Aylesbury 5000)

CAERNARVONSHIRE
County Offices, Caernarvon (Tel: Caernarvon 2341)
CAMBRIDGESHIRE and ISLE OF ELY
Shire Hall, Castle Hill, Cambridge (Tel: Cambridge 58811)
CARDIGANSHIRE
County Hall, Aberaeron (Tel: Aberaeron 382)
CARMARTHENSHIRE
County Hall, Carmarthen (Tel: Carmarthen 6641)
CHESHIRE
County Hall, Chester (Tel: Chester 24678)
CORNWALL
County Hall, Truro, Cornwall (Tel: Truro 4282)
CUMBERLAND
15, Portland Square, Carlisle (Tel: Carlisle 23456)
DENBIGHSHIRE
Grove Park, Wrexham (Tel: Wrexham 3526/7)
Planning Department: County Planning Department,
Station Road, Ruthin (Tel: Ruthin 2201)
DERBYSHIRE
County Offices, Matlock (Tel: Matlock 3411)
DEVONSHIRE
County Hall, Exeter (Tel: Exeter 77977)
DORSET
County Hall, Dorchester (Tel: Dorchester 1000)
DURHAM
County Hall, Durham (Tel: Durham 4411)
ESSEX
County Hall, Chelmsford, Essex (Tel: Chelmsford 53233)
FLINTSHIRE
Llwynegrin, Mold (Tel: Mold 106)
Planning Department: County Buildings, Mold
(Tel: Mold 106)
GLAMORGANSHIRE
County Offices, Greyfriars Road, Cardiff
(Tel: Cardiff 28033)
GLOUCESTERSHIRE
Shire Hall, Gloucester (Tel: Gloucester 21444)
GREATER LONDON COUNCIL AND INNER LONDON EDUCATION
AUTHORITY
County Hall, London, S.E.1. (Tel: 01–928 5000)
HAMPSHIRE
The Castle, Winchester (Tel: Winchester 4411)
HEREFORDSHIRE
County Offices, Bath Street, Hereford (Tel: Hereford 6401)
HERTFORDSHIRE
County Hall, Hertford (Tel: Hertford 4242)
HOLLAND
See LINCOLNSHIRE (HOLLAND)
HUNTINGDON AND PETERBOROUGH
Hinchingbrooke Cottage, Brampton Road, Huntingdon
(Tel: Huntingdon 4651)
Planning Department: County Offices, Bridge Street,
Peterborough (Tel: Peterborough 68451)
ISLE OF ELY
See CAMBRIDGESHIRE and ISLE OF ELY
ISLE OF WIGHT
County Hall, Newport, Isle of Wight (Tel: Newport 2261)
KENT
Springfield, Maidstone (Tel: Maidstone 54371)
Planning Department: County Hall, Maidstone
(Tel: Maidstone 54321)
KESTEVEN
See LINCOLNSHIRE (KESTEVEN)

LANCASHIRE
County Hall, Preston (Tel: Preston 54868)
Planning Department: East Cliff County Offices, Preston
(Tel: Preston 54868)
LEICESTERSHIRE
123, London Road, Leicester (Tel: Leicester 29911)
Planning Department: Phoenix Building, Berridge Street,
Leicester (Tel: Leicester 20451)
LINCOLNSHIRE (HOLLAND)
County Hall, Boston (Tel: Boston 2281)
LINCOLNSHIRE (KESTEVEN)
County Offices, Sleaford (Tel: Sleaford 241/6)
LINCOLNSHIRE (LINDSEY).
County Offices, Lincoln (Tel: Lincoln 25282)
LINDSEY
See LINCOLNSHIRE (LINDSEY)
LONDON
See GREATER LONDON
MERIONETHSHIRE
County Offices, Lombard Street, Dolgellau
(Tel: Dolgellau 341)
MIDDLESEX
No longer in existence, see GREATER LONDON
MONMOUTHSHIRE
County Hall, Newport (Tel: Newport 65431)
Planning Department: Cambria House, Caerleon,
Newport (Tel: Newport 65431)
MONTGOMERYSHIRE
County Offices, Welshpool (Tel: Welshpool 3311)
NORFOLK
27, Thorpe Road, Norwich (Tel: Norwich 22288)
NORTHAMPTONSHIRE
Bolton House, Wooton Hall Park, Mere Way,
Northampton (Tel: Northampton 62246)
NORTHUMBERLAND
30–32, Great North Road, Newcastle-upon-Tyne
(Tel: Newcastle-upon-Tyne 28126)
Planning Department: County Hall, Newcastle-upon-Tyne
(Tel: Newcastle-upon-Tyne 26613)
NOTTINGHAMSHIRE
County Hall, West Bridgford, Nottingham
(Tel: West Bridgford 83366)
OXFORDSHIRE
Park End Street Offices, Oxford (Tel: Oxford 49871)
PEMBROKESHIRE
County Offices, Haverfordwest (Tel: Haverfordwest 3131)
RADNORSHIRE
County Hall, Llandrindod Wells
(Tel: Llandrindod Wells 2262)
RUTLAND
County Offices, Oakham (Tel: Oakham 2544)
SHROPSHIRE (SALOP)
The Shire Hall, Abbey Foregate, Shrewsbury
(Tel: Shrewsbury 52211)
SOKE OF PETERBOROUGH
See HUNTINGDON AND PETERBOROUGH
SOMERSET
County Architect's Department, County Hall, Taunton
(Tel: Taunton 3451)
Planning Department: Rodwell House, Park Street,
Taunton (Tel: Taunton 3451)
STAFFORDSHIRE
Green Hall, Lichfield Road, Stafford (Tel: Stafford 52251)

Planning Department: County Buildings, Martin Street, Stafford (Tel: Stafford 3121)
SUFFOLK (EAST)
County Hall, Ipswich (Tel: Ipswich 55801)
SUFFOLK (WEST)
Shire Hall, Bury St. Edmunds, Suffolk
(Tel: Bury St. Edmunds 2281)
Planning Department: Manor House, Bury St. Edmunds
(Tel: Bury St. Edmunds 2281)
SURREY
County Hall, Kingston-upon-Thames
(Tel: Kingston-upon-Thames 1050)
SUSSEX (EAST)
St. Anne's Crescent, Lewes (Tel: Lewes 4405)
Planning Department: County Hall, Lewes
(Tel: Lewes 5400)
SUSSEX (WEST)
County Hall, Chichester (Tel: Chichester 85100)
WARWICKSHIRE
Shire Hall, Warwick (Tel: Warwick 43431)
Planning Department: Northgate, Warwick
(Tel: Warwick 43431)
WESTMORLAND
County Hall, Kendal (Tel: Kendal 1000)
WILTSHIRE
County Hall, Trowbridge (Tel: Trowbridge 3641)
WORCESTERSHIRE
14, Castle Street, Worcester (Tel: Worcester 23400)
Planning Department: County Buildings, Worcester
(Tel: Worcester 23400)
YORKSHIRE (EAST RIDING)
County Hall, Beverley (Tel: Beverley 81281)
YORKSHIRE (NORTH RIDING)
County Hall, Northallerton (Tel: Northallerton 3123)
YORKSHIRE (WEST RIDING)
Bishopgarth, Westfield Road, Wakefield
(Tel: Wakefield 4761)
Planning Department: Northgate, Wakefield
(Tel: Wakefield 4734)

COUNTY COUNCILS—SCOTLAND
C.I./SfB (Aks) (Indexed under county)

ABERDEENSHIRE
55, Queen's Road, Aberdeen (Tel: Aberdeen 33293)
ANGUS
County Buildings, Forfar (Tel: Forfar 671)
ARGYLLSHIRE
County Offices, Dunoon (Tel: Dunoon 662)
Planning Department: Lochgilphead
(Tel: Lochgilphead 379)
AYRSHIRE
County Buildings, Ayr (Tel: Ayr 66922)
BANFFSHIRE
13, Cluny Square, Buckie (Tel: Buckie 3092)
BERWICKSHIRE
24, Newton Street, Duns (Tel: Duns 3235)
BUTE
County Offices, Rothesay (Tel: Rothesay 631)
CAITHNESS
County Offices, Wick (Tel: Wick 344)

CLACKMANNANSHIRE
County Buildings, Drysdale Street, Alloa (Tel: Alloa 2160)
DUMFRIESSHIRE
County Buildings, Dumfries (Tel: Dumfries 3141)
DUNBARTONSHIRE
County Council Offices, Crosslet, Dunbarton
(Tel: Dunbarton 2351)
EAST LOTHIAN
County Buildings, Haddington, East Lothian
(Tel: Haddington 2441)
FIFE
County Buildings, Cupar (Tel: Cupar 2081)
INVERNESS-SHIRE
County Buildings, Ardross Street, Inverness
(Tel: Inverness 34121)
KINCARDINESHIRE
Westfield House, Arduthie Road, Stonehaven
(Tel: Stonehaven 2066)
KINROSS-SHIRE
County Buildings, Kinross (Tel: Kinross 2105)
KIRKCUDBRIGHT (STEWARTRY OF)
County Offices, Kirkcudbright (Tel: Kirkcudbright 291)
LANARKSHIRE
County Buildings, Hamilton (Tel: Hamilton 21100)
MIDLOTHIAN
32, Palmerston Place, Edinburgh (Tel: Caledonian 2562)
MORAYSHIRE
County Buildings, Elgin (Tel: Elgin 2603)
NAIRNSHIRE Shared with MORAYSHIRE
ORKNEY
County Architect's Offices, Kirkwall (Tel: Kirkwall 529)
PEEBLESSHIRE
County Buildings, Peebles (Tel: Peebles 2153)
Planning Department: Jointly with MIDLOTHIAN,
32, Palmerston Place, Edinburgh (Tel: Caledonian 2562)
PERTHSHIRE
County Offices, York Place, Perth (Tel: Perth 21222)
Planning Department: Commercial Bank Buildings,
Princes Street, Perth (Tel: Perth 22247)
RENFREWSHIRE
16, Back Sneddon Street, Paisley (Tel: Paisley 5454)
ROSS AND CROMARTY
Tulloch Street, Dingwall (Tel: Dingwall 3381)
Planning Department: Old Academy Buildings,
Tulloch Street, Dingwall (Tel: Dingwall 2243)
ROXBURGHSHIRE
County Offices, Newtown, St. Boswells
(Tel: St. Boswells 2201)
SELKIRKSHIRE
County Surveyors Office, 12, Ettrick Terrace, Selkirk
(Tel: Selkirk 2372)
STIRLINGSHIRE
County Offices, Spittal Street, Stirling (Tel: Stirling 3111)
SUTHERLAND
County Offices, Dornoch (Tel: Dornoch 331)
WEST LOTHIAN
County Buildings, Linlithgow (Tel: Linlithgow 250)
Planning Department: Commercial Bank House,
53, High Street, Linlithgow (Tel: Linlithgow 250)
WIGTOWNSHIRE
23, Lewis Street, Stranraer (Tel: Stranraer 2151)
ZETLAND
92, St. Olaf Street, Lerwick (Tel: Lerwick 450)

DIRECTORY

TRADE UNIONS C.I./SfB (Akp)
(Indexed under name and initials)

A.S.T.R.O.S. — AMALGAMATED SLATERS, TILERS AND ROOFING
OPERATIVES SOCIETY
430, Holderness Road, Hull, Yorks. (Tel: Hull 78638)

A.S.P.D. — AMALGAMATED SOCIETY OF PAINTERS AND
DECORATORS
55, South Side, Clapham Common, London, S.W.4.
(Tel: 01–622 0021)

A.S.W. — AMALGAMATED SOCIETY OF WOODWORKERS
9–11, Macaulay Road, Clapham Common, London, S.W.4.
(Tel: 01–622 2362)

A.U.A.W. — AMALGAMATED UNION OF ASPHALT WORKERS
Jenkin House, 173A, Queens Road, Peckham,
London, S.E.15 (Tel: 01–639 1669)

A.U.B.T.W. — AMALGAMATED UNION OF BUILDING TRADE
WORKERS
'The Builders', Crescent Lane, Clapham Common,
London, S.W.4. (Tel: 01–622 2442)

A.B.T. — ASSOCIATION OF BUILDING TECHNICIANS
22, London Bridge Street, London, S.E.1.
(Tel: 01–407 7567)

A.S.S.E.T. — ASSOCIATION OF SUPERVISORY STAFFS, EXECUTIVES
AND TECHNICIANS
Sutton House, 2–4, Homerton High Street, London, E.9.
(Tel: 01–985 4792/4)

C.E.U. — CONSTRUCTION ENGINEERING UNION
140, Lower Marsh, Waterloo, London, S.E.1.
(Tel: 01–928 5781)

D.A.T.A. — DRAUGHTSMEN'S AND ALLIED TECHNICIANS
ASSOCIATION
Onslow Hall, Little Green, Richmond, Surrey
(Tel: 01–940 3341 and 8391)

E.T.U. — ELECTRICAL TRADES UNION
Hayes Court, West Common Road, Hayes, Bromley, Kent
(Tel: 01–462 6251)

N.A.O.P. — NATIONAL ASSOCIATION OF OPERATIVE PLASTERERS
1016, Harrow Road, Wembley, Middlesex
(Tel: 01–904 7794

N.F.B.T.O. — NATIONAL FEDERATION OF BUILDING TRADES
OPERATIVES
Federal House, Cedars Road, Clapham, London, S.W.4.
(Tel: 01–622 4451)

N.A.L.G.O. — NATIONAL AND LOCAL GOVERNMENT OFFICERS
ASSOCIATION
N.A.L.G.O. House, 8, Harewood Row, London, N.W.1.
(Tel: 01–262 8083)

N.T.F.M.F.S. — NATIONAL TILE, FAIENCE AND MOSAIC FIXERS'
SOCIETY
11, Camden High Street, London, N.W.1.
(Tel: 01–387 7747)

P.T.U. — PLUMBING TRADES UNION
15, Abbeville Road, Clapham, London, S.W.4.
(Tel: 01–673 8811/2)

W.P.W.U. — WALL PAPER WORKERS' UNION
223, Bury New Road, Whitefield, Manchester, Lancs.
(Tel: Whitefield 3645/6)

GENERAL BIBLIOGRAPHY

Aluminium for Architects, The British Aluminium Co. Ltd.,
Norfolk House, St James Square, London, S.W.1., Free to
architects
Architect and Contractors Yearbook, Architect and Contractors
Yearbook, 9 Paddington Street, London, W.1., Published
annually, Free to architects
Architects Standard Catalogues, The Standard Catalogue Co.
Ltd., 26 Bloomsbury Way, Holborn, London, W.C.1.,
published biennially, 5 vols
BRITISH STANDARDS INSTITUTION, British Standards summarised in *British Standards Handbook No. 3,* British Standards
Institution, 101 Pentonville Road, London, N.1., Amended
annually
BRITISH STANDARDS INSTITUTION, *British Standards Yearbook,*
British Standards Institution, 101 Pentonville Road, London,
N.1., Published annually. (Complete British Standards and
Codes of Practice are also obtainable from the British
Standards Institution at the above address)
Building Research Station, *Building Research Station Digests*
(First and second series), H.M.S.O.
Concrete Yearbook, Concrete Publications Ltd., 60 Buckingham
Gate, London, S.W.1., Published annually
DEPARTMENT OF EDUCATION AND SCIENCE, *Building Bulletins,*
H.M.S.O.
DIAMANT, R. M. E., *Industrialised Building,* Iliffe Books, an
imprint of the Butterworth Group, 88 Kingsway, London,
W.C.2., 3 vols (1965/68)
FAIRWEATHER, L. and SLIWA, J. A., *A. J. Metric Handbook,*
(3rd edn), Architectural Press, 9/13 Queen Anne's Gate,
London. S.W.1. (1968)
Laxton's Building Price Book, Kelly's Directories Ltd., Neville
House, Eden Street, Kingston-upon-Thames, Published
annually
MILLARD, PATRICIA, *Trade Associations and Professional Bodies
of the U.K.,* Pergamon Press Ltd., 4 Fitzroy Square, London,
W.1. (4th edn) (1969)
MINISTRY OF HOUSING AND LOCAL GOVERNMENT, *The Building
Regulations, 1965,* H.M.S.O. (1965)
MINISTRY OF HOUSING AND LOCAL GOVERNMENT, *Design Bulletins,*
H.M.S.O.
MINISTRY OF HOUSING AND LOCAL GOVERNMENT, *Homes for
Today and Tomorrow* (Parker Morris Report), H.M.S.O.
(1961)
MINISTRY OF HOUSING AND LOCAL GOVERNMENT, *Planning
Bulletins,* H.M.S.O.
MINISTRY OF PUBLIC BUILDING AND WORKS, *Advisory Leaflets,*
H.M.S.O.
MINISTRY OF PUBLIC BUILDING AND WORKS, *Dimensional Coordination for Building: Recommended Dimensions,* H.M.S.O.
(1967)
MINISTRY OF PUBLIC BUILDING AND WORKS, *Research and Development Bulletins,* H.M.S.O.
ROYAL INSTITUTE OF BRITISH ARCHITECTS, *R.I.B.A. Directory,*
The Institute, 66 Portland Place, London, W.1., Published
annually
ROYAL INSTITUTE OF BRITISH ARCHITECTS, *CI/Sfb Construction
Indexing Manual,* The Institute, 66 Portland Place, London,
W.1. (1969)
ROYAL INSTITUTE OF BRITISH ARCHITECTS, *CI/Sfb Classified List,*
The Institute, 66 Portland Place, London, W.1. (1969)
Specification, The Architectural Press, 9/13 Queen Anne's
Gate, London, S.W.1., Published annually, 2 vols
Street Furniture from the Design Index, Council of Industrial
Design, 28 Haymarket, London, S.W.1., Published biennially

96

9 METRICATION AND SI UNITS

METRICATION

Metrication is the name that has been coined to describe the changeover from imperial units to a system of metric units, that system being the 'Système Internationale d'Unités' (SI for short). As will be seen, this system differs in a number of important respects from the 'existing' metric system.

The Construction Industry was one of the first to become involved in the changeover to metric units, and a programme covering this transition was published in February 1967 by the B.S.I. (P.D. 6030). The change to the production of working drawings in metric terms for new contracts, which started in 1969, is expected to be effectively complete in the construction industry by the end of 1972.

Although, in what follows, a series of factors and tables are given for converting imperial units to SI units, it must not be expected that, when the changeover has been fully implemented, direct conversions can in general be applied. The opportunity is being taken to bring out a new set of Standards (in SI units), which will be applicable in all countries adopting SI units, and which will have the effect of reducing the number of sizes available in the light of present industrial needs. Furthermore, in the case of the construction industry, advantage is being taken of the changeover to introduce 'dimensional co-ordination'. The B.S.I. is busily engaged on the production of new specifications, starting with the basic commodities used in production throughout industry: semi-finished materials of all kinds (rod, bar, wire, sheet, tube, etc.), small components and shaping tools. Many of these have already been published and relevant ones should be consulted.

SI UNITS

1. The SI has six arbitrary basic units: kilogramme, metre, second, ampere, degree Kelvin (for thermodynamics), and the candela.

2. All other SI units are derived from these. The system is coherent, which means that the effect of multiplying two or more of the basic units together, or introducing as a quotient one or more basic units, or a combination of these operations, produces a derived unit—which is also unity. Thus 1 ampere × 1 second = 1 coulomb.

3. All multiples of SI units are in steps of a thousand (10^3) and sub-multiples in steps of a thousand (10^{-3}). Thus, the gramme, which was a basic unit in the earlier metric system, is no longer a basic unit in SI, having been replaced by the kilogramme. But as it is a thousandth part of a kilogramme it is an acceptable sub-multiple. Whereas, the centimetre, which has been replaced by the metre, is not an acceptable sub-multiple, and a measurement previously expressed in centimetres must now be expressed in metres or millimetres.

4. There is a new unit of force, the *newton*, which is independent of gravity. It is that force which gives a mass of one kilogramme an acceleration of one metre per second per second. The newton is often quoted as embodying a new concept, but the c.g.s. system had a unit of force independent of gravity, the dyne. The newton is equal to a hundred thousand dynes.

5. All of the expressions for work and energy, such as the ft lb, calorie, kilocalorie and Btu have been replaced by a single unit, the *joule*, which is a watt second.

6. All units of power, the rate of doing work, have been replaced by the joule per second or *watt*. Thus, horsepower, both British and French, disappears.

7. All of the practical units of electricity such as the ampere, volt, ohm, watt and farad are retained, but the c.g.s. electromagnetic and electrostatic units now officially disappear.

8. Certain 'supplementary' units are permitted, such as the year, day, hour, and minute and the angular degree, minute and second.

Table 9.1 BASIC SI UNITS

Physical quantity	Name of unit	Symbol for unit
length	metre	m
mass	kilogramme	kg
time	second	s
electric current	ampere	A
thermodynamic temperature	degree Kelvin	°K
luminous intensity	candela	cd

Notes

1. Symbols for units do not take a plural form.
2. The *metre* replaces the centimetre of the classical metric system and the use of the centimetre as a sub-multiple of the metre is deprecated.
3. The *kilogramme* replaces the gramme of the classical metric system.
4. The use of certain non-SI units, such as the day, hour and minute, is permitted, e.g., kilometres per hour.
5. Temperature difference and temperatures in 'everyday use' are expressed in degrees Celsius (centigrade) instead of degrees Kelvin. But the unit difference for Celsius and Kelvin are the same: 1 degree Celsius = 1 degree Kelvin; $0°K = -273·16°C$.

Table 9.2 SELECTED LIST OF SUPPLEMENTARY AND DERIVED SI UNITS
(These are extracted from B.S. 350: Part 1: 1959 and B.S. 3763: 1964, by kind permission of the British Standards Institution, 2, Park Street, London, W.1.)

Quantity	Unit	Symbol or abbreviation
area	square metre	m^2
volume	cubic metre	m^3
plane angle	radian	rad
solid angle	steradian	sr
velocity	metre per second	m/s
acceleration	metre per second squared	m/s^2
density (mass density)	kilogramme per cubic metre	kg/m^3
moment of inertia	kilogramme metre squared	$kg\ m^2$
force	newton	$N\ (kg\ m/s^2)$
pressure, stress	newton per square metre	N/m^2
energy (work, heat)	joule	J (N m)
power, heat flow rate	watt	W (J/s)
temperature (customary unit)	degree Celsius	°C
temperature interval	degree Kelvin	degK
	degree Celsius	degC
thermal coefficient of linear expansion	reciprocal degree (Kelvin or Celsius)	$degC^{-1}$, $°K^{-1}$, $°C^{-1}$
density of heat flow	watt per square metre	W/m^2
thermal conductivity	watt per metre degree Celsius	W/m degC
thermal conductance	watt per square metre degree Celsius	W/m^2 degC
luminous flux	lumen	lm (cd sr)
luminance	candela per square metre	cd/m^2
illumination	lux	$lx\ (lm/m^2)$

Notes

1. The abbreviations do not take 's' in the plural; e.g., the abbreviation for metres is not 'ms' but 'm', as for metre.
2. In symbols the use of a solidus (/) to indicate a quotient is preferred to the use of a negative index (except in sub-multiples of a basic unit): e.g., for watts per metre degree Celsius the symbol W/m degC is preferred to Wm^{-1} degC, although, at least initially, both forms are likely to be found.
   The solidus should not be duplicated in any one expression.
3. Practical units of electricity, such as the volt, ampere, watt, ohm, etc., remain unchanged.
4. Plane angles may still be expressed in degrees, minutes and seconds.
5. The decimal point will be used and not the continental comma.
6. Commas will not be used in thousands, i.e.: 1 512 415·621 342, not 1,512,415·621342. The figures will be grouped in threes either side of the decimal point.

Table 9.3 MULTIPLES OR SUB-MULTIPLES OF SI UNITS ARE FORMED BY
THE FOLLOWING PREFIXES

Multiplication factor	Prefix	Symbol
1 000 000 000 000 $= 10^{12}$	tera	T
1 000 000 000 $= 10^{9}$	giga	G
1 000 000 $= 10^{6}$	mega	M
1 000 $= 10^{3}$	kilo	k
100 $= 10^{2}$	hecto*	h
10 $= 10^{1}$	deca*	da
0·1 $= 10^{-1}$	deci*	d
0·01 $= 10^{-2}$	centi*	c
0·001 $= 10^{-3}$	milli	m
0·000 001 $= 10^{-6}$	micro	μ
0·000 000 001 $= 10^{-9}$	nano	n
0·000 000 000 001 $= 10^{-12}$	pico	p

Notes
1. *These multiples and sub-multiples are not part of SI but in practice will probably be encountered.
2. The use of multiple prefixes is not allowed. Thus, a thousandth of a millimetre must not be expressed as a milli-millimetre, but as a micrometre.

SELECTED CONVERSION FACTORS

The ultimate aim is to think and work in SI units and to forget the older units, but some time must elapse before this ideal is achieved. In the meantime, occasions will arise when it is necessary to use conversion factors. The following conversion factors have been specially selected as those likely to be required by architects, civil engineers and the construction industry.

LENGTH

1 inch	=	0·025 4 metre	1 chain	=	20·117 metre
1 foot	=	0·304 8 metre	1 furlong	=	201·68 metre
1 yard	=	0·914 4 metre	1 mile	=	1 609·344 metre

AREA

1 square inch	=	$6·451\ 6 \times 10^{-4}$	square metre
1 square foot	=	0·092 903	square metre
1 square yard	=	0·836 127	square metre
1 square mile	=	2·589 99	square kilometre
1 acre	=	4 046·9	square metre
	=	0·404 69	hectare (10 000 square metre)

VOLUME

1 cubic inch	=	$1·638\ 71 \times 10^{-5}$	cubic metre
1 cubic foot	=	0·028 317	cubic metre
1 cubic yard	=	0·764 55	cubic metre
1 fluid ounce	=	0·028 41	litre
1 imperial pint	=	0·568 24	litre
1 imperial gallon	=	4·546 0	litre

MASS

1 ounce (avdp)	=	28·350	gramme
1 pound (avdp)	=	0·453 59	kilogramme
1 stone	=	6·350 3	kilogramme
1 cwt	=	50·8	kilogramme
1 ton (2 240 lb)	=	1 016·05	kilogramme
	=	1·016	metric ton (tonne)

TEMPERATURE
Fahrenheit to Celsius (Centigrade) $°C = \frac{5}{9} (°F - 32)$

VELOCITY

1 foot per second	=	0·304 8	metre per second
	=	1·097 3	kilometre per hour
1 mile per hour	=	0·447 04	metre per second
	=	1·609 3	kilometre per hour
1 knot	=	0·514 8	metre per second
	=	1·853 2	kilometre per hour

DENSITY

1 pound per cubic inch	=	2·767 99 × 10⁴ kilogramme per cubic metre
1 pound per cubic foot	=	16·018 5 kilogramme per cubic metre

FORCE

1 poundal	=	0·138 255 newton
1 pound (force)	=	4·448 22 newton

PRESSURE, STRESS

1 pound-force per square inch	=	6 894·76 newton per square metre
		(1 millibar = 100 newton per square metre)
1 pound-force per square foot	=	4·882 4 kilogramme-force per square metre
	=	47·880 3 newton per square metre
1 ton-force per square inch	=	15·444 3 meganewtons per square metre

ENERGY (WORK, HEAT)

1 foot poundal	=	0·042 140 joule
1 foot pound-force	=	1·355 82 joule
	=	0·138 3 kilogramme-force metre
1 calorie	=	4·186 8 joule
1 kilowatt hour	=	3·6 × 10⁶ joule

POWER

1 horse-power (550 foot-pound–force per second)	=	745·7 watt
	=	76·04 kilogramme-force metre per second

MOMENTS

Moment of inertia	1 pound inch squared	=	2·926 4 kilogramme centimetre squared
Moment of section	1 in⁴	=	41·623 cm⁴

HEAT

1 British Thermal Unit	=	1 055·06 joule
1 International steam table calorie	=	4·186 8 joule

HEAT TRANSMISSION

1 British Thermal Unit per hour	=	0·293 1 watt
1 kilocalorie per hour	=	1·163 watt

HEAT TRANSFER COEFFICIENT

1 British Thermal Unit per square foot hour degree Fahrenheit	=	5·678 26 watts per square metre per degree Kelvin (Celsius)

THERMAL CONDUCTIVITY

British Thermal Unit per foot hour degree Fahrenheit	=	1·731 watts per metre degree Kelvin (Celsius)

HEAT FLUX

British Thermal Units per square foot hour	=	3·155 watt per square metre

SELECTED CONVERSION TABLES

The following tables (pp. 101–130) are extracted from B.S. 350: Part 2: 1962 and Supplement No. 1 (1967) to B.S. 350: Part 2: 1962, by kind permission of the British Standards Institution, 2, Park Street, London, W1A 2BS.

Table 9.4 LENGTH: FEET TO METRES

Basis: 1 ft = 0·3048 m (exactly)

feet	0	1	2	3	4	5	6	7	8	9
					metres					
0	—	0·3048	0·6096	0·9144	1·2192	1·5240	1·8288	2·1336	2·4384	2·7432
10	3·0480	3·3528	3·6576	3·9624	4·2672	4·5720	4·8768	5·1816	5·4864	5·7912
20	6·0960	6·4008	6·7056	7·0104	7·3152	7·6200	7·9248	8·2296	8·5344	8·8392
30	9·1440	9·4488	9·7536	10·0584	10·3632	10·6680	10·9728	11·2776	11·5824	11·8872
40	12·1920	12·4968	12·8016	13·1064	13·4112	13·7160	14·0208	14·3256	14·6304	14·9352
50	15·2400	15·5448	15·8496	16·1544	16·4592	16·7640	17·0688	17·3736	17·6784	17·9832
60	18·2880	18·5928	18·8976	19·2024	19·5072	19·8120	20·1168	20·4216	20·7264	21·0312
70	21·3360	21·6408	21·9456	22·2504	22·5552	22·8600	23·1648	23·4696	23·7744	24·0792
80	24·3840	24·6888	24·9936	25·2984	25·6032	25·9080	26·2128	26·5176	26·8224	27·1272
90	27·4320	27·7368	28·0416	28·3464	28·6512	28·9560	29·2608	29·5656	29·8704	30·1752
100	30·4800	30·7848	31·0896	31·3944	31·6992	32·0040	32·3088	32·6136	32·9184	33·2232
110	33·5280	33·8328	34·1376	34·4424	34·7472	35·0520	35·3568	35·6616	35·9664	36·2712
120	36·5760	36·8808	37·1856	37·4904	37·7952	38·1000	38·4048	38·7096	39·0144	39·3192
130	39·6240	39·9288	40·2336	40·5384	40·8432	41·1480	41·4528	41·7576	42·0624	42·3672
140	42·6720	42·9768	43·2816	43·5864	43·8912	44·1960	44·5008	44·8056	45·1104	45·4152
150	45·7200	46·0248	46·3296	46·6344	46·9392	47·2440	47·5488	47·8536	48·1584	48·4632
160	48·7680	49·0728	49·3776	49·6824	49·9872	50·2920	50·5968	50·9016	51·2064	51·5112
170	51·8160	52·1208	52·4256	52·7304	53·0352	53·3400	53·6448	53·9496	54·2544	54·5592
180	54·8640	55·1688	55·4736	55·7784	56·0832	56·3880	56·6928	56·9976	57·3024	57·6072
190	57·9120	58·2168	58·5216	58·8264	59·1312	59·4360	59·7408	60·0456	60·3504	60·6552
200	60·9600	61·2648	61·5696	61·8744	62·1792	62·4840	62·7888	63·0936	63·3984	63·7032
210	64·0080	64·3128	64·6176	64·9224	65·2272	65·5320	65·8368	66·1416	66·4464	66·7512
220	67·0560	67·3608	67·6656	67·9704	68·2752	68·5800	68·8848	69·1896	69·4944	69·7992
230	70·1040	70·4088	70·7136	71·0184	71·3232	71·6280	71·9328	72·2376	72·5424	72·8472
240	73·1520	73·4568	73·7616	74·0664	74·3712	74·6760	74·9808	75·2856	75·5904	75·8952
250	76·2000	76·5048	76·3096	77·1144	77·4192	77·7240	78·0288	78·3336	78·6384	78·9432
260	79·2480	79·5528	79·8576	80·1624	80·4672	80·7720	81·0768	81·3816	81·6864	81·9912
270	82·2960	82·6008	82·9056	83·2104	83·5152	83·8200	84·1248	84·4296	84·7344	85·0392
280	85·3440	85·6488	85·9536	86·2584	86·5632	86·8680	87·1728	87·4776	87·7824	88·0872
290	88·3920	88·6968	89·0016	89·3064	89·6112	89·9160	90·2208	90·5256	90·8304	91·1352
300	91·4400	91·7448	92·0496	92·3544	92·6592	92·9640	93·2688	93·5736	93·8784	94·1832
310	94·4880	94·7928	95·0976	95·4024	95·7072	96·0120	96·3168	96·6216	96·9264	97·2312
320	97·5360	97·8408	98·1456	98·4504	98·7552	99·0600	99·3648	99·6696	99·9744	100·279
330	100·584	100·889	101·194	101·498	101·803	102·108	102·413	102·718	103·022	103·327
340	103·632	103·937	104·242	104·546	104·851	105·156	105·461	105·766	106·070	106·375
350	106·680	106·985	107·290	107·594	107·899	108·204	108·509	108·814	109·118	109·423
360	109·728	110·033	110·338	110·642	110·947	111·252	111·557	111·862	112·166	112·471
370	112·776	113·081	113·386	113·690	113·995	114·300	114·605	114·910	115·214	115·519
380	115·824	116·129	116·434	116·738	117·043	117·348	117·653	117·958	118·262	118·567
390	118·872	119·177	119·482	119·786	120·091	120·396	120·701	121·006	121·310	121·615
400	121·920	122·225	122·530	122·834	123·139	123·444	123·749	124·054	124·358	124·663
410	124·968	125·273	125·578	125·882	126·187	126·492	126·797	127·102	127·406	127·711
420	128·016	128·321	128·626	128·930	129·235	129·540	129·845	130·150	130·454	130·759
430	131·064	131·369	131·674	131·978	132·283	132·588	132·893	133·198	133·502	133·807
440	134·112	134·417	134·722	135·026	135·331	135·636	135·941	136·246	136·550	136·855
450	137·160	137·465	137·770	138·074	138·379	138·684	138·989	139·294	139·598	139·903
460	140·208	140·513	140·818	141·122	141·427	141·732	142·037	142·342	142·646	142·951
470	143·256	143·561	143·866	144·170	144·475	144·780	145·085	145·390	145·694	145·999
480	146·304	146·609	146·914	147·218	147·523	147·828	148·133	148·438	148·742	149·047
490	149·352	149·657	149·962	150·266	150·571	150·876	151·181	151·486	151·790	152·095

continued

Table 9.4 LENGTH: FEET TO METRES *(continued)*

Basis: 1 ft = 0·3048 m (exactly)

feet	0	1	2	3	4	5	6	7	8	9
					metres					
500	152·400	152·705	153·010	153·314	153·619	153·924	154·229	154·534	154·838	155·143
510	155·448	155·753	156·058	156·362	156·667	156·972	157·277	157·582	157·886	158·191
520	158·496	158·801	159·106	159·410	159·715	160·020	160·325	160·630	160·934	161·239
530	161·544	161·849	162·154	162·458	162·763	163·068	163·373	163·678	163·982	164·287
540	164·592	164·897	165·202	165·506	165·811	166·116	166·421	166·726	167·030	167·335
550	167·640	167·945	168·250	168·554	168·859	169·164	169·469	169·774	170·078	170·383
560	170·688	170·993	171·298	171·602	171·907	172·212	172·517	172·822	173·126	173·431
570	173·736	174·041	174·346	174·650	174·955	175·260	175·565	175·870	176·174	176·479
580	176·784	177·089	177·394	177·698	178·003	178·308	178·613	178·918	179·222	179·527
590	179·832	180·137	180·442	180·746	181·051	181·356	181·661	181·966	182·270	182·575
600	182·880	183·185	183·490	183·794	184·099	184·404	184·709	185·014	185·318	185·623
610	185·928	186·233	186·538	186·842	187·147	187·452	187·757	188·062	188·366	188·671
620	188·976	189·281	189·586	189·890	190·195	190·500	190·805	191·110	191·414	191·719
630	192·024	192·329	192·634	192·938	193·243	193·548	193·853	194·158	194·462	194·767
640	195·072	195·377	195·682	195·986	196·291	196·596	196·901	197·206	197·510	197·815
650	198·120	198·425	198·730	199·034	199·339	199·644	199·949	200·254	200·558	200·863
660	201·168	201·473	201·778	202·082	202·387	202·692	202·997	203·302	203·606	203·911
670	204·216	204·521	204·826	205·130	205·435	205·740	206·045	206·350	206·654	206·959
680	207·264	207·569	207·874	208·178	208·483	208·788	209·093	209·398	209·702	210·007
690	210·312	210·617	210·922	211·226	211·531	211·836	212·141	212·446	212·750	213·055
700	213·360	213·665	213·970	214·274	214·579	214·884	215·189	215·494	215·798	216·103
710	216·408	216·713	217·018	217·322	217·627	217·932	218·237	218·542	218·846	219·151
720	219·456	219·761	220·066	220·370	220·675	220·980	221·285	221·590	221·894	222·199
730	222·504	222·809	223·114	223·418	223·723	224·028	224·333	224·638	224·942	225·247
740	225·552	225·857	226·162	226·466	226·771	227·076	227·381	227·696	227·990	228·295
750	228·600	228·905	229·210	229·514	229·819	230·124	230·429	230·734	231·038	231·343
760	231·648	231·953	232·258	232·562	232·867	233·172	233·477	233·782	234·086	234·391
770	234·696	235·001	235·306	235·610	235·915	236·220	236·525	236·830	237·134	237·439
780	237·744	238·049	238·354	238·658	238·963	239·268	239·573	239·878	240·182	240·487
790	240·792	241·097	241·402	241·706	242·011	242·316	242·621	242·926	243·230	243·535
800	243·840	244·145	244·450	244·754	245·059	245·364	245·669	245·974	246·278	246·583
810	246·888	247·193	247·498	247·802	248·107	248·412	248·717	249·022	249·326	249·631
820	249·936	250·241	250·546	250·850	251·155	251·460	251·765	252·070	252·374	252·679
830	252·984	253·289	253·594	253·898	254·203	254·508	254·813	255·118	255·422	255·727
840	256·032	256·337	256·642	256·946	257·251	257·556	257·861	258·166	258·470	258·775
850	259·080	259·385	259·690	259·994	260·299	260·604	260·909	261·214	261·518	261·823
860	262·128	262·433	262·738	263·042	263·347	263·652	263·957	264·262	264·566	264·871
870	265·176	265·481	265·786	266·090	266·395	266·700	267·005	267·310	267·614	267·919
880	268·224	268·529	268·834	269·138	269·443	269·748	270·053	270·358	270·662	270·967
890	271·272	271·577	271·882	272·186	272·491	272·796	273·101	273·406	273·710	274·015
900	274·320	274·625	274·930	275·234	275·539	275·844	276·149	276·454	276·758	277·063
910	277·368	277·673	277·978	278·282	278·587	278·892	279·197	279·502	279·806	280·111
920	280·416	280·721	281·026	281·330	281·635	281·940	282·245	282·550	282·854	283·159
930	283·464	283·769	284·074	284·378	284·683	284·988	285·293	285·598	285·902	286·207
940	286·512	286·817	287·122	287·426	287·731	288·036	288·341	288·646	288·950	289·255
950	289·560	289·865	290·170	290·474	290·779	291·084	291·389	291·694	291·998	292·303
960	292·608	292·913	293·218	293·522	293·827	294·132	294·437	294·742	295·046	295·351
970	295·656	295·961	296·266	296·570	296·875	297·180	297·485	297·790	298·094	298·399
980	298·704	299·009	299·314	299·618	299·923	300·228	300·533	300·838	301·142	301·447
990	301·752	302·057	302·362	302·666	302·971	303·276	303·581	303·886	304·190	304·495
1000	304·800	—	—	—	—	—	—	—	—	—

Table 9.5 FORCE: POUNDS FORCE TO NEWTONS

Basis: 1 lbf = 0·453 592 37 kgf
1 kgf = 9·806 65 N

pounds force	0	1	2	3	4	5	6	7	8	9
					newtons					
0	0·00000	4·44822	8·89644	13·3447	17·7929	22·2411	26·6893	31·1376	35·5858	40·0340
10	44·4822	48·9304	53·3787	57·8269	62·2751	66·7233	71·1715	75·6198	80·0680	84·5162
20	88·9644	93·4127	97·8609	102·309	106·757	111·206	115·654	120·102	124·550	128·998
30	133·447	137·895	142·343	146·791	151·240	155·688	160·136	164·584	169·032	173·481
40	177·929	182·377	186·825	191·274	195·722	200·170	204·618	209·066	213·515	217·963
50	222·411	226·859	231·308	235·756	240·204	244·652	249·100	253·549	257·997	262·445
60	266·893	271·342	275·790	280·238	284·686	289·134	293·583	298·031	302·479	306·927
70	311·376	315·824	320·272	324·720	329·168	333·617	338·065	342·513	346·961	351·410
80	355·858	360·306	364·754	369·202	373·651	378·099	382·547	386·995	391·444	395·892
90	400·340	404·788	409·236	413·685	418·133	422·581	427·029	431·477	435·926	440·374
100	444·822	449·270	453·719	458·167	462·615	467·063	471·511	475·960	480·408	484·856
110	489·304	493·753	498·201	502·649	507·097	511·545	515·994	520·442	524·890	529·338
120	533·787	538·235	542·683	547·131	551·579	556·028	560·476	564·924	569·372	573·821
130	578·269	582·717	587·165	591·613	596·062	600·510	604·958	609·406	613·855	618·303
140	622·751	627·199	631·647	636·096	640·544	644·992	649·440	653·889	658·337	662·785
150	667·233	671·681	676·130	680·578	685·026	689·474	693·923	698·371	702·819	707·267
160	711·715	716·164	720·612	725·060	729·508	733·957	738·405	742·853	747·301	751·749
170	756·198	760·646	765·094	769·542	773·991	778·439	782·887	787·335	791·783	796·232
180	800·680	805·128	809·576	814·025	818·473	822·921	827·369	831·817	836·266	840·714
190	845·162	849·610	854·059	858·507	862·955	867·403	871·851	876·300	880·748	885·196
200	889·644	894·093	898·541	902·989	907·437	911·885	916·334	920·782	925·230	929·678
210	934·127	938·575	943·023	947·471	951·919	956·368	960·816	965·264	969·712	974·161
220	978·609	983·057	987·505	991·953	996·402	1000·85	1005·30	1009·75	1014·19	1018·64
230	1023·09	1027·54	1031·99	1036·44	1040·88	1045·33	1049·78	1054·23	1058·68	1063·12
240	1067·57	1072·02	1076·47	1080·92	1085·37	1089·81	1094·26	1098·71	1103·16	1107·61
250	1112·06	1116·50	1120·95	1125·40	1129·85	1134·30	1138·74	1143·19	1147·64	1152·09
260	1156·54	1160·99	1165·43	1169·88	1174·33	1178·78	1183·23	1187·68	1192·12	1196·57
270	1201·02	1205·47	1209·92	1214·36	1218·81	1223·26	1227·71	1232·16	1236·61	1241·05
280	1245·50	1249·95	1254·40	1258·85	1263·29	1267·74	1272·19	1276·64	1281·09	1285·54
290	1289·98	1294·43	1298·88	1303·33	1307·78	1312·23	1316·67	1321·12	1325·57	1330·02
300	1334·47	1338·91	1343·36	1347·81	1352·26	1356·71	1361·16	1365·60	1370·05	1374·50
310	1378·95	1383·40	1387·85	1392·29	1396·74	1401·19	1405·64	1410·09	1414·53	1418·98
320	1423·43	1427·88	1432·33	1436·78	1441·22	1445·67	1450·12	1454·57	1459·02	1463·46
330	1467·91	1472·36	1476·81	1481·26	1485·71	1490·15	1494·60	1499·05	1503·50	1507·95
340	1512·40	1516·84	1521·29	1525·74	1530·19	1534·64	1539·08	1543·53	1547·98	1552·43
350	1556·88	1561·33	1565·77	1570·22	1574·67	1579·12	1583·57	1588·02	1592·46	1596·91
360	1601·36	1605·81	1610·26	1614·70	1619·15	1623·60	1628·05	1632·50	1636·95	1641·39
370	1645·84	1650·29	1654·74	1659·19	1663·63	1668·08	1672·53	1676·98	1681·43	1685·88
380	1690·32	1694·77	1699·22	1703·67	1708·12	1712·57	1717·01	1721·46	1725·91	1730·36
390	1734·81	1739·25	1743·70	1748·15	1752·60	1757·05	1761·50	1765·94	1770·39	1774·84
400	1779·29	1783·74	1788·19	1792·63	1797·08	1801·53	1805·98	1810·43	1814·87	1819·32
410	1823·77	1828·22	1832·67	1837·12	1841·56	1846·01	1850·46	1854·91	1859·36	1863·80
420	1868·25	1872·70	1877·15	1881·60	1886·05	1890·49	1894·94	1899·39	1903·84	1908·29
430	1912·74	1917·18	1921·63	1926·08	1930·53	1934·98	1939·42	1943·87	1948·32	1952·77
440	1957·22	1961·67	1966·11	1970·56	1975·01	1979·46	1983·91	1988·36	1992·80	1997·25
450	2001·70	2006·15	2010·60	2015·04	2019·49	2023·94	2028·39	2032·84	2037·29	2041·73
460	2046·18	2050·63	2055·08	2059·53	2063·97	2068·42	2072·87	2077·32	2081·77	2086·22
470	2090·66	2095·11	2099·56	2104·01	2108·46	2112·91	2117·35	2121·80	2126·25	2130·70
480	2135·15	2139·59	2144·04	2148·49	2152·94	2157·39	2161·84	2166·28	2170·73	2175·18
490	2179·63	2184·08	2188·53	2192·97	2197·42	2201·87	2206·32	2210·77	2215·21	2219·66

continued

Table 9.5 FORCE: POUNDS FORCE TO NEWTONS *(continued)*

Basis: 1 lbf = 0·453 592 37 kgf
1 kgf = 9·806 65 N

pounds force	0	1	2	3	4	5	6	7	8	9
					newtons					
500	2224·11	2228·56	2233·01	2237·46	2241·90	2246·35	2250·80	2255·25	2259·70	2264·14
510	2268·59	2273·04	2277·49	2281·94	2286·39	2290·83	2295·28	2299·73	2304·18	2308·63
520	2313·08	2317·52	2321·97	2326·42	2330·87	2335·32	2339·76	2344·21	2348·66	2353·11
530	2357·56	2362·01	2366·45	2370·90	2375·35	2379·80	2384·25	2388·70	2393·14	2397·59
540	2402·04	2406·49	2410·94	2415·38	2419·83	2424·28	2428·73	2433·18	2437·63	2442·07
550	2446·52	2450·97	2455·42	2459·87	2464·31	2468·76	2473·21	2477·66	2482·11	2486·56
560	2491·00	2495·45	2499·90	2504·35	2508·80	2513·25	2517·69	2522·14	2526·59	2531·04
570	2535·49	2539·93	2544·38	2548·83	2553·28	2557·73	2562·18	2566·62	2571·07	2575·52
580	2579·97	2584·42	2588·86	2593·31	2597·76	2602·21	2606·66	2611·11	2615·55	2620·00
590	2624·45	2628·90	2633·35	2637·80	2642·24	2646·69	2651·14	2655·59	2660·04	2664·48
600	2668·93	2673·38	2677·83	2682·28	2686·73	2691·17	2695·62	2700·07	2704·52	2708·97
610	2713·42	2717·86	2722·31	2726·76	2731·21	2735·66	2740·10	2744·55	2749·00	2753·45
620	2757·90	2762·35	2766·79	2771·24	2775·69	2780·14	2784·59	2789·03	2793·48	2797·93
630	2802·38	2806·83	2811·28	2815·72	2820·17	2824·62	2829·07	2833·52	2837·97	2842·41
640	2846·86	2851·31	2855·76	2860·21	2864·65	2869·10	2873·55	2878·00	2882·45	2886·90
650	2891·34	2895·79	2900·24	2904·69	2909·14	2913·59	2918·03	2922·48	2926·93	2931·38
660	2935·83	2940·27	2944·72	2949·17	2953·62	2958·07	2962·52	2966·96	2971·41	2975·86
670	2980·31	2984·76	2989·20	2993·65	2998·10	3002·55	3007·00	3011·45	3015·89	3020·34
680	3024·79	3029·24	3033·69	3038·14	3042·58	3047·03	3051·48	3055·93	3060·38	3064·82
690	3069·27	3073·72	3078·17	3082·62	3087·07	3091·51	3095·96	3100·41	3104·86	3109·31
700	3113·76	3118·20	3122·65	3127·10	3131·55	3136·00	3140·44	3144·89	3149·34	3153·79
710	3158·24	3162·69	3167·13	3171·58	3176·03	3180·48	3184·93	3189·37	3193·82	3198·27
720	3202·72	3207·17	3211·62	3216·06	3220·51	3224·96	3229·41	3233·86	3238·31	3242·75
730	3247·20	3251·65	3256·10	3260·55	3264·99	3269·44	3273·89	3278·34	3282·79	3287·24
740	3291·68	3296·13	3300·58	3305·03	3309·48	3313·93	3318·37	3322·82	3327·27	3331·72
750	3336·17	3340·61	3345·06	3349·51	3353·96	3358·41	3362·86	3367·30	3371·75	3376·20
760	3380·65	3385·10	3389·54	3393·99	3398·44	3402·89	3407·34	3411·79	3416·23	3420·68
770	3425·13	3429·58	3434·03	3438·48	3442·92	3447·37	3451·82	3456·27	3460·72	3465·16
780	3469·61	3474·06	3478·51	3482·96	3487·41	3491·85	3496·30	3500·75	3505·20	3509·65
790	3514·10	3518·54	3522·99	3527·44	3531·89	3536·34	3540·78	3545·23	3549·68	3554·13
800	3558·58	3563·03	3567·47	3571·92	3576·37	3580·82	3585·27	3589·71	3594·16	3598·61
810	3603·06	3607·51	3611·96	3616·40	3620·85	3625·30	3629·75	3634·20	3638·65	3643·09
820	3647·54	3651·99	3656·44	3660·89	3665·33	3669·78	3674·23	3678·68	3683·13	3687·58
830	3692·02	3696·47	3700·92	3705·37	3709·82	3714·27	3718·71	3723·16	3727·61	3732·06
840	3736·51	3740·95	3745·40	3749·85	3754·30	3758·75	3763·20	3767·64	3772·09	3776·54
850	3780·99	3785·44	3789·88	3794·33	3798·78	3803·23	3807·68	3812·13	3816·57	3821·02
860	3825·47	3829·92	3834·37	3838·82	3843·26	3847·71	3852·16	3856·61	3861·06	3865·50
870	3869·95	3874·40	3878·85	3883·30	3887·75	3892·19	3896·64	3901·09	3905·54	3909·99
880	3914·44	3918·88	3923·33	3927·78	3932·23	3936·68	3941·12	3945·57	3950·02	3954·47
890	3958·92	3963·37	3967·81	3972·26	3976·71	3981·16	3985·61	3990·05	3994·50	3998·95
900	4003·40	4007·85	4012·30	4016·74	4021·19	4025·64	4030·09	4034·54	4038·99	4043·43
910	4047·88	4052·33	4056·78	4061·23	4065·67	4070·12	4074·57	4079·02	4083·47	4087·92
920	4092·36	4096·81	4101·26	4105·71	4110·16	4114·60	4119·05	4123·50	4127·95	4132·40
930	4136·85	4141·29	4145·74	4150·19	4154·64	4159·09	4163·54	4167·98	4172·43	4176·88
940	4181·33	4185·78	4190·22	4194·67	4199·12	4203·57	4208·02	4212·47	4216·91	4221·36
950	4225·81	4230·26	4234·71	4239·16	4243·60	4248·05	4252·50	4256·95	4261·40	4265·84
960	4270·29	4274·74	4279·19	4283·64	4288·09	4292·53	4296·98	4301·43	4305·88	4310·33
970	4314·77	4319·22	4323·67	4328·12	4332·57	4337·02	4341·46	4345·91	4350·36	4354·81
980	4359·26	4363·71	4368·15	4372·60	4377·05	4381·50	4385·95	4390·39	4394·84	4399·29
990	4403·74	4408·19	4412·64	4417·08	4421·53	4425·98	4430·43	4434·88	4439·33	4443·77
1000	4448·22	—	—	—	—	—	—	—	—	—

Table 9.6 UK TONS FORCE TO KILONEWTONS

Basis: 1 lbf = 0·453 592 37 kgf   1 UK ton = 2240 lb
1 kgf = 9·806 65 N

UK tons force	0	1	2	3	4	5	6	7	8	9
					kilonewtons					
0	0·00000	9·96401	19·9280	29·8920	39·8561	49·8201	59·7841	69·7481	79·7121	89·6761
10	99·6401	109·604	119·568	129·532	139·496	149·460	159·424	169·388	179·352	189·316
20	199·280	209·244	219·208	229·172	239·136	249·100	259·064	269·028	278·992	288·956
30	298·920	308·884	318·848	328·812	338·776	348·740	358·704	368·668	378·632	388·596
40	398·561	408·525	418·489	428·453	438·417	448·381	458·345	468·309	478·273	488·237
50	498·201	508·165	518·129	528·093	538·057	548·021	557·985	567·949	577·913	587·877
60	597·841	607·805	617·769	627·733	637·697	647·661	657·625	667·589	677·553	687·517
70	697·481	707·445	717·409	727·373	737·337	747·301	757·265	767·229	777·193	787·157
80	797·121	807·085	817·049	827·013	836·977	846·941	856·905	866·869	876·833	886·797
90	896·761	906·725	916·689	926·653	936·617	946·581	956·545	966·509	976·473	986·437
100	996·401	1006·37	1016·33	1026·29	1036·26	1046·22	1056·19	1066·15	1076·11	1086·08
110	1096·04	1106·01	1115·97	1125·93	1135·90	1145·86	1155·83	1165·79	1175·75	1185·72
120	1195·68	1205·65	1215·61	1225·57	1235·54	1245·50	1255·47	1265·43	1275·39	1285·36
130	1295·32	1305·29	1315·25	1325·21	1335·18	1345·14	1355·11	1365·07	1375·03	1385·00
140	1394·96	1404·93	1414·89	1424·85	1434·82	1444·78	1454·75	1464·71	1474·67	1484·64
150	1494·60	1504·57	1514·53	1524·49	1534·46	1544·42	1554·39	1564·35	1574·31	1584·28
160	1594·24	1604·21	1614·17	1624·13	1634·10	1644·06	1654·03	1663·99	1673·95	1683·92
170	1693·88	1703·85	1713·81	1723·77	1733·74	1743·70	1753·67	1763·63	1773·59	1783·56
180	1793·52	1803·49	1813·45	1823·41	1833·38	1843·34	1853·31	1863·27	1873·23	1883·20
190	1893·16	1903·13	1913·09	1923·05	1933·02	1942·98	1952·95	1962·91	1972·87	1982·84
200	1992·80	2002·77	2012·73	2022·69	2032·66	2042·62	2052·59	2062·55	2072·51	2082·48
210	2092·44	2102·41	2112·37	2122·33	2132·30	2142·26	2152·23	2162·19	2172·15	2182·12
220	2192·08	2202·05	2212·01	2221·97	2231·94	2241·90	2251·87	2261·83	2271·79	2281·76
230	2291·72	2301·69	2311·65	2321·61	2331·58	2341·54	2351·51	2361·47	2371·44	2381·40
240	2391·36	2401·33	2411·29	2421·26	2431·22	2441·18	2451·15	2461·11	2471·08	2481·04
250	2491·00	2500·97	2510·93	2520·90	2530·86	2540·82	2550·79	2560·75	2570·72	2580·68
260	2590·64	2600·61	2610·57	2620·54	2630·50	2640·46	2650·43	2660·39	2670·36	2680·32
270	2690·28	2700·25	2710·21	2720·18	2730·14	2740·10	2750·07	2760·03	2770·00	2779·96
280	2789·92	2799·89	2809·85	2819·82	2829·78	2839·74	2849·71	2859·67	2869·64	2879·60
290	2889·56	2899·53	2909·49	2919·46	2929·42	2939·38	2949·35	2959·31	2969·28	2979·24
300	2989·20	2999·17	3009·13	3019·10	3029·06	3039·02	3048·99	3058·95	3068·92	3078·88
310	3088·84	3098·81	3108·77	3118·74	3128·70	3138·66	3148·63	3158·59	3168·56	3178·52
320	3188·48	3198·45	3208·41	3218·38	3228·34	3238·30	3248·27	3258·23	3268·20	3278·16
330	3288·12	3298·09	3308·05	3318·02	3327·98	3337·94	3347·91	3357·87	3367·84	3377·80
340	3387·76	3397·73	3407·69	3417·66	3427·62	3437·58	3447·55	3457·51	3467·48	3477·44
350	3487·40	3497·37	3507·33	3517·30	3527·26	3537·22	3547·19	3557·15	3567·12	3577·08
360	3587·04	3597·01	3606·97	3616·94	3626·90	3636·86	3646·83	3656·79	3666·76	3676·72
370	3686·68	3696·65	3706·61	3716·58	3726·54	3736·50	3746·47	3756·43	3766·40	3776·36
380	3786·32	3796·29	3806·25	3816·22	3826·18	3836·14	3846·11	3856·07	3866·04	3876·00
390	3885·96	3895·93	3905·89	3915·86	3925·82	3935·79	3945·75	3955·71	3965·68	3975·64
400	3985·61	3995·57	4005·53	4015·50	4025·46	4035·43	4045·39	4055·35	4065·32	4075·28
410	4085·25	4095·21	4105·17	4115·14	4125·10	4135·07	4145·03	4154·99	4164·96	4174·92
420	4184·89	4194·85	4204·81	4214·78	4224·74	4234·71	4244·67	4254·63	4264·60	4274·56
430	4284·53	4294·49	4304·45	4314·42	4324·38	4334·35	4344·31	4354·27	4364·24	4374·20
440	4384·17	4394·13	4404·09	4414·06	4424·02	4433·99	4443·95	4453·91	4463·88	4473·84
450	4483·81	4493·77	4503·73	4513·70	4523·66	4533·63	4543·59	4553·55	4563·52	4573·48
460	4583·45	4593·41	4603·37	4613·34	4623·30	4633·27	4643·23	4653·19	4663·16	4673·12
470	4683·09	4693·05	4703·01	4712·98	4722·94	4732·91	4742·87	4752·83	4762·80	4772·76
480	4782·73	4792·69	4802·65	4812·62	4822·58	4832·55	4842·51	4852·47	4862·44	4872·40
490	4882·37	4892·33	4902·29	4912·26	4922·22	4932·19	4942·15	4952·11	4962·08	4972·04

continued

Table 9.6 FORCE: UK TONS FORCE TO KILONEWTONS (*continued*)

Basis: 1 lbf = 0·453 592 37 kgf   1 UK ton = 2240 lb
1 kgf = 9·806 65 N

UK tons force	0	1	2	3	4	5	6	7	8	9
					kilonewtons					
500	4982·01	4991·97	5001·93	5011·90	5021·86	5031·83	5041·79	5051·75	5061·72	5071·68
510	5081·65	5091·61	5101·57	5111·54	5121·50	5131·47	5141·43	5151·39	5161·36	5171·32
520	5181·29	5191·25	5201·21	5211·18	5221·14	5231·11	5241·07	5251·03	5261·00	5270·96
530	5280·93	5290·89	5300·85	5310·82	5320·78	5330·75	5340·71	5350·67	5360·64	5370·60
540	5380·57	5390·53	5400·49	5410·46	5420·42	5430·39	5440·35	5450·32	5460·28	5470·24
550	5480·21	5490·17	5500·14	5510·10	5520·06	5530·03	5539·99	5549·96	5559·92	5569·88
560	5579·85	5589·81	5599·78	5609·74	5619·70	5629·67	5639·63	5649·60	5659·56	5669·52
570	5679·49	5689·45	5699·42	5709·38	5719·34	5729·31	5739·27	5749·24	5759·20	5769·16
580	5779·13	5789·09	5799·06	5809·02	5818·98	5828·95	5838·91	5848·88	5858·84	5868·80
590	5878·77	5888·73	5898·70	5908·66	5918·62	5928·59	5938·55	5948·52	5958·48	5968·44
600	5978·41	5988·37	5998·34	6008·30	6018·26	6028·23	6038·19	6048·16	6058·12	6068·08
610	6078·05	6088·01	6097·98	6107·94	6117·90	6127·87	6137·83	6147·80	6157·76	6167·72
620	6177·69	6187·65	6197·62	6207·58	6217·54	6227·51	6237·47	6247·44	6257·40	6267·36
630	6277·33	6287·29	6297·26	6307·22	6317·18	6327·15	6337·11	6347·08	6357·04	6367·00
640	6376·97	6386·93	6396·90	6406·86	6416·82	6426·79	6436·75	6446·72	6456·68	6466·64
650	6476·61	6486·57	6496·54	6506·50	6516·46	6526·43	6536·39	6546·36	6556·32	6566·28
660	6576·25	6586·21	6596·18	6606·14	6616·10	6626·07	6636·03	6646·00	6655·96	6665·92
670	6675·89	6685·85	6695·82	6705·78	6715·74	6725·71	6735·67	6745·64	6755·60	6765·56
680	6775·53	6785·49	6795·46	6805·42	6815·38	6825·35	6835·31	6845·28	6855·24	6865·20
690	6875·17	6885·13	6895·10	6905·06	6915·02	6924·99	6934·95	6944·92	6954·88	6964·84
700	6974·81	6984·77	6994·74	7004·70	7014·67	7024·63	7034·59	7044·56	7054·52	7064·49
710	7074·45	7084·41	7094·38	7104·34	7114·31	7124·27	7134·23	7144·20	7154·16	7164·13
720	7174·09	7184·05	7194·02	7203·98	7213·95	7223·91	7233·87	7243·84	7253·80	7263·77
730	7273·73	7283·69	7293·66	7303·62	7313·59	7323·55	7333·51	7343·48	7353·44	7363·41
740	7373·37	7383·33	7393·30	7403·26	7413·23	7423·19	7433·15	7443·12	7453·08	7463·05
750	7473·01	7482·97	7492·94	7502·90	7512·87	7522·83	7532·79	7542·76	7552·72	7562·69
760	7572·65	7582·61	7592·58	7602·54	7612·51	7622·47	7632·43	7642·40	7652·36	7662·33
770	7672·29	7682·25	7692·22	7702·18	7712·15	7722·11	7732·07	7742·04	7752·00	7761·97
780	7771·93	7781·89	7791·86	7801·82	7811·79	7821·75	7831·71	7841·68	7851·64	7861·61
790	7871·57	7881·53	7891·50	7901·46	7911·43	7921·39	7931·35	7941·32	7951·28	7961·25
800	7971·21	7981·17	7991·14	8001·10	8011·07	8021·03	8030·99	8040·96	8050·92	8060·89
810	8070·85	8080·81	8090·78	8100·74	8110·71	8120·67	8130·63	8140·60	8150·56	8160·53
820	8170·49	8180·45	8190·42	8200·38	8210·35	8220·31	8230·27	8240·24	8250·20	8260·17
830	8270·13	8280·09	8290·06	8300·02	8309·99	8319·95	8329·91	8339·88	8349·84	8359·81
840	8369·77	8379·73	8389·70	8399·66	8409·63	8419·59	8429·55	8439·52	8449·48	8459·45
850	8469·41	8479·37	8489·34	8499·30	8509·27	8519·23	8529·19	8539·16	8549·12	8559·09
860	8569·05	8579·02	8588·98	8598·94	8608·91	8618·87	8628·84	8638·80	8648·76	8658·73
870	8668·69	8678·66	8688·62	8698·58	8708·55	8718·51	8728·48	8738·44	8748·40	8758·37
880	8768·33	8778·30	8788·26	8798·22	8808·19	8818·15	8828·12	8838·08	8848·04	8858·01
890	8867·97	8877·94	8887·90	8897·86	8907·83	8917·79	8927·76	8937·72	8947·68	8957·65
900	8967·61	8977·58	8987·54	8997·50	9007·47	9017·43	9027·40	9037·36	9047·32	9057·29
910	9067·25	9077·22	9087·18	9097·14	9107·11	9117·07	9127·04	9137·00	9146·96	9156·93
920	9166·89	9176·86	9186·82	9196·78	9206·75	9216·71	9226·68	9236·64	9246·60	9256·57
930	9266·53	9276·50	9286·46	9296·42	9306·39	9316·35	9326·32	9336·28	9346·24	9356·21
940	9366·17	9376·14	9386·10	9396·06	9406·03	9415·99	9425·96	9435·92	9445·88	9455·85
950	9465·81	9475·78	9485·74	9495·70	9505·67	9515·63	9525·60	9535·56	9545·52	9555·49
960	9565·45	9575·42	9585·38	9595·34	9605·31	9615·27	9625·24	9635·20	9645·16	9655·13
970	9665·09	9675·06	9685·02	9694·98	9704·95	9714·91	9724·88	9734·84	9744·80	9754·77
980	9764·73	9774·70	9784·66	9794·62	9804·59	9814·55	9824·52	9834·48	9844·44	9854·41
990	9864·37	9874·34	9884·30	9894·26	9904·23	9914·19	9924·16	9934·12	9944·08	9954·05
1000	9964·01	—	—	—	—	—	—	—	—	—

Table 9.7 PRESSURE, STRESS: UK TONS-FORCE PER SQUARE INCH TO MEGANEWTONS PER SQUARE METRE

Basis: 1 UK ton = 2240 lb   1 kgf = 9·806 65 N
       1 lbf = 0·453 592 37 kgf   1 in = 0·0254 m

UK tonf/in²	0	0·1	0·2	0·3	0·4	0·5	0·6	0·7	0·8	0·9
					meganewtons per square metre					
0	0·00000	1·54443	3·08885	4·63328	6·17770	7·72213	9·26655	10·8110	12·3554	13·8998
1	15·4443	16·9887	18·5331	20·0775	21·6220	23·1664	24·7108	26·2552	27·7997	29·3441
2	30·8885	32·4329	33·9774	35·5218	37·0662	38·6106	40·1551	41·6995	43·2439	44·7883
3	46·3328	47·8772	49·4216	50·9660	52·5105	54·0549	55·5993	57·1437	58·6882	60·2326
4	61·7770	63·3215	64·8659	66·4103	67·9547	69·4992	71·0436	72·5880	74·1324	75·6769
5	77·2213	78·7657	80·3101	81·8546	83·3990	84·9434	86·4878	88·0323	89·5767	91·1211
6	92·6655	94·2100	95·7544	97·2988	98·8432	100·388	101·932	103·477	105·021	106·565
7	108·110	109·654	111·199	112·743	114·287	115·832	117·376	118·921	120·465	122·010
8	123·554	125·098	126·643	128·187	129·732	131·276	132·821	134·365	135·909	137·454
9	138·998	140·543	142·087	143·632	145·176	146·720	148·265	149·809	151·354	152·898
10	154·443	155·987	157·531	159·076	160·620	162·165	163·709	165·254	166·798	168·342
11	169·887	171·431	172·976	174·520	176·065	177·609	179·153	180·698	182·242	183·787
12	185·331	186·876	188·420	189·964	191·509	193·053	194·598	196·142	197·686	199·231
13	200·775	202·320	203·864	205·409	206·953	208·497	210·042	211·586	213·131	214·675
14	216·220	217·764	219·308	220·853	222·397	223·942	225·486	227·031	228·575	230·119
15	231·664	233·208	234·753	236·297	237·842	239·386	240·930	242·475	244·019	245·564
16	247·108	248·635	250·197	251·741	253·286	254·830	256·375	257·919	259·464	261·008
17	262·552	264·097	265·641	267·186	268·730	270·274	271·819	273·363	274·908	276·452
18	277·997	279·541	281·085	282·630	284·174	285·719	287·263	288·808	290·352	291·896
19	293·441	294·985	296·530	298·074	299·619	301·163	302·707	304·252	305·796	307·341
20	308·885	310·430	311·974	313·518	315·063	316·607	318·152	319·696	321·241	322·785
21	324·329	325·874	327·418	328·963	330·507	332·052	333·596	335·140	336·685	338·229
22	339·774	341·318	342·862	344·407	345·951	347·496	349·040	350·585	352·129	353·673
23	355·218	356·762	358·307	359·851	361·396	362·940	364·484	366·029	367·573	369·118
24	370·662	372·207	373·751	375·295	376·840	378·384	379·929	381·473	383·018	384·562
25	386·106	387·651	389·195	390·740	392·284	393·829	395·373	396·917	398·462	400·006
26	401·551	403·095	404·640	406·184	407·728	409·273	410·817	412·362	413·906	415·450
27	416·995	418·539	420·084	421·628	423·173	424·717	426·261	427·806	429·350	430·895
28	432·439	433·984	435·528	437·072	438·617	440·161	441·706	443·250	444·795	446·339
29	447·883	449·428	450·972	452·517	454·061	455·606	457·150	458·694	460·239	461·783
30	463·328	464·872	466·417	467·961	469·505	471·050	472·594	474·139	475·683	477·228
31	478·772	480·316	481·861	483·405	484·950	486·494	488·039	489·583	491·127	492·672
32	494·216	495·761	497·305	498·849	500·394	501·938	503·483	505·027	506·572	508·116
33	509·660	511·205	512·749	514·294	515·838	517·383	518·927	520·471	522·016	523·560
34	525·105	526·649	528·194	529·738	531·282	532·827	534·371	535·916	537·460	539·005
35	540·549	542·093	543·638	545·182	546·727	548·271	549·816	551·360	552·904	554·449
36	555·993	557·538	559·082	560·627	562·171	563·715	565·260	566·804	568·349	569·893
37	571·437	572·982	574·526	576·071	577·615	579·160	580·704	582·248	583·793	585·337
38	586·882	588·426	589·971	591·515	593·059	594·604	596·148	597·693	599·237	600·782
39	602·326	603·870	605·415	606·959	608·504	610·048	611·593	613·137	614·681	616·226
40	617·770	619·315	620·859	622·404	623·948	625·492	627·037	628·581	630·126	631·670
41	633·215	634·759	636·303	637·848	639·392	640·937	642·481	644·025	645·570	647·114
42	648·659	650·203	651·748	653·292	654·836	656·381	657·925	659·470	661·014	662·559
43	664·103	665·647	667·192	668·736	670·281	671·825	673·370	674·914	676·458	678·003
44	679·547	681·092	682·636	684·181	685·725	687·269	688·814	690·358	691·903	693·447
45	694·992	696·536	698·080	699·625	701·169	702·714	704·258	705·803	707·347	708·891
46	710·436	711·980	713·525	715·069	716·613	718·158	719·702	721·247	722·791	724·336
47	725·880	727·424	728·969	730·513	732·058	733·602	735·147	736·691	738·235	739·780
48	741·324	742·869	744·413	745·958	747·502	749·046	750·591	752·135	753·680	755·224
49	756·769	758·313	759·857	761·402	762·946	764·491	766·035	767·580	769·124	770·668

continued

Table 9.7 PRESSURE, STRESS: UK TONS-FORCE PER SQUARE INCH TO MEGANEWTONS PER SQUARE METRE *(continued)*

Basis: 1 UK ton = 2240 lb   1 kgf = 9·806 65 N
1 lbf = 0·453 592 37 kgf   1 in = 0·0254 m

UK tonf/in²	0	0·1	0·2	0·3	0·4	0·5	0·6	0·7	0·8	0·9
					meganewtons per square metre					
50	772·213	773·757	775·302	776·846	778·391	779·935	781·479	783·024	784·568	786·113
51	787·657	789·201	790·746	792·290	793·835	795·379	796·924	798·468	800·012	801·557
52	803·101	804·646	806·190	807·735	809·279	810·823	812·368	813·912	815·457	817·001
53	818·546	820·090	821·634	823·179	824·723	826·268	827·812	829·357	830·901	832·445
54	833·990	835·534	837·079	838·623	840·168	841·712	843·256	844·801	846·345	847·890
55	849·434	850·979	852·523	854·067	855·612	857·156	858·701	860·245	861·790	863·334
56	864·878	866·423	867·967	869·512	871·056	872·600	874·145	875·689	877·234	878·778
57	880·323	881·867	883·411	884·956	886·500	888·045	889·589	891·134	892·678	894·222
58	895·767	897·311	898·856	900·400	901·945	903·489	905·033	906·578	908·122	909·667
59	911·211	912·756	914·300	915·844	917·389	918·933	920·478	922·022	923·567	925·111
60	926·655	928·200	929·744	931·289	932·833	934·378	935·922	937·466	939·011	940·555
61	942·100	943·644	945·188	946·733	948·277	949·822	951·366	952·911	954·455	955·999
62	957·544	959·088	960·633	962·177	963·722	965·266	966·810	968·355	969·899	971·444
63	972·988	974·533	976·077	977·621	979·166	980·710	982·255	983·799	985·344	986·888
64	988·432	989·977	991·521	993·066	994·610	996·155	997·699	999·243	1000·79	1002·33
65	1003·88	1005·42	1006·97	1008·51	1010·05	1011·60	1013·14	1014·69	1016·23	1017·78
66	1019·32	1020·87	1022·41	1023·95	1025·50	1027·04	1028·59	1030·13	1031·68	1033·22
67	1034·77	1036·31	1037·85	1039·40	1040·94	1042·49	1044·03	1045·58	1047·12	1048·67
68	1050·21	1051·75	1053·30	1054·84	1056·39	1057·93	1059·48	1061·02	1062·56	1064·11
69	1065·65	1067·20	1068·74	1070·29	1071·83	1073·38	1074·92	1076·46	1078·01	1079·55
70	1081·10	1082·64	1084·19	1085·73	1087·28	1088·82	1090·36	1091·91	1093·45	1095·00
71	1096·54	1098·09	1099·63	1101·18	1102·72	1104·26	1105·81	1107·35	1108·90	1110·44
72	1111·99	1113·53	1115·08	1116·62	1118·16	1119·71	1121·25	1122·80	1124·34	1125·89
73	1127·43	1128·98	1130·52	1132·06	1133·61	1135·15	1136·70	1138·24	1139·79	1141·33
74	1142·87	1144·42	1145·96	1147·51	1149·05	1150·60	1152·14	1153·69	1155·23	1156·77
75	1158·32	1159·86	1161·41	1162·95	1164·50	1166·04	1167·59	1169·13	1170·67	1172·22
76	1173·76	1175·31	1176·85	1178·40	1179·94	1181·49	1183·03	1184·57	1186·12	1187·66
77	1189·21	1190·75	1192·30	1193·84	1195·39	1196·93	1198·47	1200·02	1201·56	1203·11
78	1204·65	1206·20	1207·74	1209·29	1210·83	1212·37	1213·92	1215·46	1217·01	1218·55
79	1220·10	1221·64	1223·19	1224·73	1226·27	1227·82	1229·36	1230·91	1232·45	1234·00
80	1235·54	1237·08	1238·63	1240·17	1241·72	1243·26	1244·81	1246·35	1247·90	1249·44
81	1250·98	1252·53	1254·07	1255·62	1257·16	1258·71	1260·25	1261·80	1263·34	1264·88
82	1266·43	1267·97	1269·52	1271·06	1272·61	1274·15	1275·70	1277·24	1278·78	1280·33
83	1281·87	1283·42	1284·96	1286·51	1288·05	1289·60	1291·14	1292·68	1294·23	1295·77
84	1297·32	1298·86	1300·41	1301·95	1303·50	1305·04	1306·58	1308·13	1309·67	1311·22
85	1312·76	1314·31	1315·85	1317·40	1318·94	1320·48	1322·03	1323·57	1325·12	1326·66
86	1328·21	1329·75	1331·29	1332·84	1334·38	1335·93	1337·47	1339·02	1340·56	1342·11
87	1343·65	1345·19	1346·74	1348·28	1349·83	1351·37	1352·92	1354·46	1356·01	1357·55
88	1359·09	1360·64	1362·18	1363·73	1365·27	1366·82	1368·36	1369·91	1371·45	1372·99
89	1374·54	1376·08	1377·63	1379·17	1380·72	1382·26	1383·81	1385·35	1386·89	1388·44
90	1389·98	1391·53	1393·07	1394·62	1396·16	1397·71	1399·25	1400·79	1402·34	1403·88
91	1405·43	1406·97	1408·52	1410·06	1411·61	1413·15	1414·69	1416·24	1417·78	1419·33
92	1420·87	1422·42	1423·96	1425·50	1427·05	1428·59	1430·14	1431·68	1433·23	1434·77
93	1436·32	1437·86	1439·40	1440·95	1442·49	1444·04	1445·58	1447·13	1448·67	1450·22
94	1451·76	1453·30	1454·85	1456·39	1457·94	1459·48	1461·03	1462·57	1464·12	1465·66
95	1467·20	1468·75	1470·29	1471·84	1473·38	1474·38	1476·47	1478·02	1479·56	1481·10
96	1482·65	1484·19	1485·74	1487·28	1488·83	1490·37	1491·92	1493·46	1495·00	1496·55
97	1498·09	1499·64	1501·18	1502·73	1504·27	1505·81	1507·36	1508·90	1510·45	1511·99
98	1513·54	1515·08	1516·63	1518·17	1519·71	1521·26	1522·80	1524·35	1525·89	1527·44
99	1528·98	1530·53	1532·07	1533·61	1535·16	1536·70	1538·25	1539·79	1541·34	1542·88
100	1544·43	—	—	—	—	—	—	—	—	—

Table 9.8 PRESSURE, STRESS: POUNDS FORCE PER SQUARE INCH TO KILONEWTONS PER SQUARE METRE

Basis: 1 lbf = 0·453 592 37 kgf   1 in = 0·0254 m
1 kgf = 9·806 65 N

lbf/in²	0	1	2	3	4	5	6	7	8	9
				kilonewtons per square metre						
0	0·00000	6·89476	13·7895	20·6843	27·5790	34·4738	41·3685	48·2633	55·1581	62·0528
10	68·9476	75·8423	82·7371	89·6318	96·5266	103·421	110·316	117·211	124·106	131·000
20	137·895	144·790	151·685	158·579	165·474	172·389	179·264	186·158	193·053	199·948
30	206·843	213·737	220·632	227·527	234·422	241·317	248·211	255·106	262·001	268·896
40	275·790	282·685	289·580	296·475	303·369	310·264	317·159	324·054	330·948	337·843
50	344·738	351·633	358·527	365·422	372·317	379·212	386·106	393·001	399·896	406·791
60	413·685	420·580	427·475	434·370	441·264	448·159	455·054	461·949	468·843	475·733
70	482·633	489·528	496·423	503·317	510·212	517·107	524·002	530·896	537·791	544·686
80	551·581	558·475	565·370	572·265	579·160	586·054	592·949	599·844	606·739	613·633
90	620·528	627·423	634·318	641·212	648·107	655·002	661·897	668·791	675·686	682·581
100	689·476	696·370	703·265	710·160	717·055	723·950	730·844	737·739	744·634	751·529
110	758·423	765·318	772·213	779·108	786·002	792·897	799·792	806·687	813·581	820·476
120	827·371	834·266	841·160	848·055	854·950	861·845	868·739	875·634	882·529	889·424
130	896·318	903·213	910·108	917·003	923·897	930·792	937·687	944·582	951·477	958·371
140	965·266	972·161	979·056	985·950	992·845	999·740	1006·63	1013·53	1020·42	1027·32
150	1034·21	1041·11	1048·00	1054·90	1061·79	1068·69	1075·58	1082·48	1089·37	1096·27
160	1103·16	1110·06	1116·95	1123·85	1130·74	1137·63	1144·53	1151·42	1158·32	1165·21
170	1172·11	1179·00	1185·90	1192·79	1199·69	1206·58	1213·48	1220·37	1227·27	1234·16
180	1241·06	1247·95	1254·85	1261·74	1268·64	1275·53	1282·42	1289·32	1296·21	1303·11
190	1310·00	1316·90	1323·79	1330·69	1337·58	1344·48	1351·37	1358·27	1365·16	1372·06
200	1378·95	1385·85	1392·74	1399·64	1406·53	1413·43	1420·32	1427·21	1434·11	1441·00
210	1447·90	1454·79	1461·69	1468·58	1475·48	1482·37	1489·27	1496·16	1503·06	1509·25
220	1516·85	1523·74	1530·64	1537·53	1544·43	1551·32	1558·22	1565·11	1572·00	1578·90
230	1585·79	1592·69	1599·58	1606·48	1613·37	1620·27	1627·16	1634·06	1640·95	1647·85
240	1654·74	1661·64	1668·53	1675·43	1682·32	1689·22	1696·11	1703·01	1709·90	1716·79
250	1723·69	1730·58	1737·48	1744·37	1751·27	1758·16	1765·06	1771·95	1778·85	1785·74
260	1792·64	1799·53	1806·43	1813·32	1820·22	1827·11	1834·01	1840·90	1847·79	1854·69
270	1861·58	1868·48	1875·37	1882·27	1889·16	1896·06	1902·95	1909·85	1916·74	1923·64
280	1930·53	1937·43	1944·32	1951·22	1958·11	1965·01	1971·90	1978·80	1985·69	1992·58
290	1999·48	2006·37	2013·27	2020·16	2027·06	2033·95	2040·85	2047·74	2054·64	2061·53
300	2068·43	2075·32	2082·22	2089·11	2096·01	2102·90	2109·80	2116·69	2123·59	2130·48
310	2137·37	2144·27	2151·16	2158·06	2164·95	2171·85	2178·74	2185·64	2192·53	2199·43
320	2206·32	2213·22	2220·11	2227·01	2233·90	2240·80	2247·69	2254·59	2261·48	2268·38
330	2275·27	2282·16	2289·06	2295·95	2302·85	2309·74	2316·64	2323·53	2330·43	2337·32
340	2344·22	2351·11	2358·01	2364·90	2371·80	2378·69	2385·59	2392·48	2399·38	2406·27
350	2413·17	2420·06	2426·95	2433·85	2440·74	2447·64	2454·53	2461·43	2468·32	2475·22
360	2482·11	2489·01	2495·90	2502·80	2509·69	2516·59	2523·48	2530·38	2537·27	2544·17
370	2551·06	2557·95	2564·85	2571·74	2578·64	2585·53	2592·43	2599·32	2606·22	2613·11
380	2620·01	2626·90	2633·80	2640·69	2647·59	2654·48	2661·38	2668·27	2675·17	2682·06
390	2688·96	2695·85	2702·74	2709·64	2716·53	2723·43	2730·32	2737·22	2744·11	2751·01
400	2757·90	2764·80	2771·69	2778·59	2785·48	2792·38	2799·27	2806·17	2813·06	2819·96
410	2826·85	2833·75	2840·64	2847·53	2854·43	2861·32	2868·22	2875·11	2882·01	2888·90
420	2895·80	2902·69	2909·59	2916·48	2923·38	2930·27	2937·17	2944·06	2950·96	2957·85
430	2964·75	2971·64	2978·54	2985·43	2992·32	2999·22	3006·11	3013·01	3019·90	3026·80
440	3033·69	3040·59	3047·48	3054·38	3061·27	3068·17	3075·06	3081·96	3088·85	3095·75
450	3102·64	3109·54	3116·43	3123·33	3130·22	3137·11	3144·01	3150·90	3157·80	3164·69
460	3171·59	3178·48	3185·38	3192·27	3199·17	3206·06	3212·96	3219·85	3226·75	3233·64
470	3240·54	3247·43	3254·33	3261·22	3268·11	3275·01	3281·90	3288·80	3295·69	3302·59
480	3309·48	3316·38	3323·27	3330·17	3337·06	3343·96	3350·85	3357·75	3364·64	3371·54
490	3378·43	3385·33	3392·22	3399·12	3406·01	3412·90	3419·80	3426·69	3433·59	3440·48

continued

Table 9.8 PRESSURE, STRESS: POUNDS FORCE PER SQUARE INCH TO KILONEWTONS PER SQUARE METRE *(continued)*

Basis: 1 lbf = 0·453 592 37 kgf   1 in = 0·0254 m
1 kgf = 9·806 65 N

lbf/in²	0	1	2	3	4	5	6	7	8	9
					kilonewtons per square metre					
500	3447·38	3454·27	3461·17	3468·06	3474·96	3481·85	3488·75	3495·64	3502·54	3509·43
510	3516·33	3523·22	3530·12	3537·01	3543·91	3550·80	3557·69	3564·59	3571·48	3578·38
520	3585·27	3592·17	3599·06	3605·96	3612·85	3619·75	3626·64	3633·54	3640·43	3647·33
530	3654·22	3661·12	3668·01	3674·91	3681·80	3688·70	3695·59	3702·48	3709·38	3716·27
540	3723·17	3730·06	3736·96	3743·85	3750·75	3757·64	3764·54	3771·43	3778·33	3785·22
550	3792·12	3799·01	3805·91	3812·80	3819·70	3826·59	3833·49	3840·38	3847·27	3854·17
560	3861·06	3867·96	3874·85	3881·75	3888·64	3895·54	3902·43	3909·33	3916·22	3923·12
570	3930·01	3936·91	3943·80	3950·70	3957·59	3964·49	3971·38	3978·27	3985·17	3992·06
580	3998·96	4005·85	4012·75	4019·64	4026·54	4033·43	4040·33	4047·22	4054·12	4061·01
590	4067·91	4074·80	4081·70	4088·59	4095·49	4102·38	4109·28	4116·17	4123·06	4129·96
600	4136·85	4143·75	4150·64	4157·54	4164·43	4171·33	4178·22	4185·12	4192·01	4198·91
610	4205·80	4212·70	4219·59	4226·49	4233·38	4240·28	4247·17	4254·07	4260·96	4267·85
620	4274·75	4281·64	4288·54	4295·43	4302·33	4309·22	4316·12	4323·01	4329·91	4336·80
630	4343·70	4350·59	4357·49	4364·38	4371·28	4378·17	4385·07	4391·96	4398·86	4405·75
640	4412·64	4419·54	4426·43	4433·33	4440·22	4447·12	4454·01	4460·91	4467·80	4474·70
650	4481·59	4488·49	4495·38	4502·28	4509·17	4516·07	4522·96	4529·86	4536·75	4543·65
660	4550·54	4557·43	4564·33	4571·22	4578·12	4585·01	4591·91	4598·80	4605·70	4612·59
670	4619·49	4626·38	4633·28	4640·17	4647·07	4653·96	4660·86	4667·75	4674·65	4681·54
680	4688·43	4695·33	4702·22	4709·12	4716·01	4722·91	4729·80	4736·70	4743·59	4750·49
690	4757·38	4764·28	4771·17	4778·07	4784·96	4791·86	4798·75	4805·65	4812·54	4819·44
700	4826·33	4833·22	4840·12	4847·01	4853·91	4860·80	4867·70	4874·59	4881·49	4888·38
710	4895·28	4902·17	4909·07	4915·96	4922·86	4929·75	4936·65	4943·54	4950·44	4957·33
720	4964·23	4971·12	4978·01	4984·91	4991·80	4998·70	5005·59	5012·49	5019·38	5026·28
730	5033·17	5040·07	5046·96	5053·86	5060·75	5067·65	5074·54	5081·44	5088·33	5095·23
740	5102·12	5109·02	5115·91	5122·80	5129·70	5136·59	5143·49	5150·38	5157·28	5164·17
750	5171·07	5177·96	5184·86	5191·75	5198·65	5205·54	5212·44	5219·33	5226·23	5233·12
760	5240·02	5246·91	5253·81	5260·70	5267·59	5274·49	5281·38	5288·28	5295·17	5302·07
770	5308·96	5315·86	5322·75	5329·65	5336·54	5343·44	5350·33	5357·23	5364·12	5371·02
780	5377·91	5384·81	5391·70	5398·59	5405·49	5412·38	5419·28	5426·17	5433·07	5439·96
790	5446·86	5453·75	5460·65	5467·54	5474·44	5481·33	5488·23	5495·12	5502·02	5508·91
800	5515·81	5522·70	5529·60	5536·49	5543·38	5550·28	5557·17	5564·07	5570·96	5577·86
810	5584·75	5591·65	5598·54	5605·44	5612·33	5619·23	5626·12	5633·02	5639·91	5646·81
820	5653·70	5660·60	5667·49	5674·39	5681·28	5688·17	5695·07	5701·96	5708·86	5715·75
830	5722·65	5729·54	5736·44	5743·33	5750·23	5757·12	5764·02	5770·91	5777·81	5784·70
840	5791·60	5798·49	5805·39	5812·28	5819·18	5826·07	5832·96	5839·86	5846·75	5853·65
850	5860·54	5867·44	5874·33	5881·23	5888·12	5895·02	5901·91	5908·81	5915·70	5922·60
860	5929·49	5936·39	5943·28	5950·18	5957·07	5963·97	5970·86	5977·75	5984·65	5991·54
870	5998·44	6005·33	6012·23	6019·12	6026·02	6032·91	6039·81	6046·70	6053·60	6060·49
880	6067·39	6074·28	6081·18	6088·07	6094·97	6101·86	6108·75	6115·65	6122·54	6129·44
890	6136·33	6143·23	6150·12	6157·02	6163·91	6170·81	6177·70	6184·60	6191·49	6198·39
900	6205·28	6212·18	6219·07	6225·97	6232·86	6239·76	6246·65	6253·54	6260·44	6267·33
910	6274·23	6281·12	6288·02	6294·91	6301·81	6308·70	6315·60	6322·49	6329·39	6336·28
920	6343·18	6350·07	6356·97	6363·86	6370·76	6377·65	6384·55	6391·44	6398·33	6405·23
930	6412·12	6419·02	6425·91	6432·81	6439·70	6446·60	6453·49	6460·39	6467·28	6474·18
940	6481·07	6487·97	6494·86	6501·76	6508·65	6515·55	6522·44	6529·34	6536·23	6543·12
950	6550·02	6556·91	6563·81	6570·70	6577·60	6584·49	6591·39	6598·28	6605·18	6612·07
960	6618·97	6625·86	6632·76	6639·65	6646·55	6653·44	6660·34	6667·23	6674·13	6681·02
970	6687·91	6694·81	6701·70	6708·60	6715·49	6722·39	6729·28	6736·18	6743·07	6749·97
980	6756·86	6763·76	6770·65	6777·55	6784·44	6791·34	6798·23	6805·13	6812·02	6818·91
990	6825·81	6832·70	6839·60	6846·49	6853·39	6860·28	6867·18	6874·07	6880·97	6887·86
1000	6894·76	—	—	—	—	—	—	—	—	—

Table 9.9 WORK, ENERGY: KILOWATT HOURS TO MEGAJOULES

Basis: 1 h = 3600s
1 W = 1 J/s

kWh	0	1	2	3	4	5	6	7	8	9
					megajoules					
0	0·00000	3·60000	7·20000	10·8000	14·4000	18·0000	21·6000	25·2000	28·8000	32·4000
10	36·0000	39·6000	43·2000	46·8000	50·4000	54·0000	57·6000	61·2000	64·8000	68·4000
20	72·0000	75·6000	79·2000	82·8000	86·4000	90·0000	93·6000	97·2000	100·800	104·400
30	108·000	111·600	115·200	118·800	122·400	126·000	129·600	133·200	136·800	140·400
40	144·000	147·600	151·200	154·800	158·400	162·000	165·600	169·200	172·800	176·400
50	180·000	183·600	187·200	190·800	194·400	198·000	201·600	205·200	208·800	212·400
60	216·000	219·600	223·200	226·800	230·400	234·000	237·600	241·200	244·800	248·400
70	252·000	255·600	259·200	262·800	266·400	270·000	273·600	277·200	280·800	284·400
80	288·000	291·600	295·200	298·800	302·400	306·000	309·600	313·200	316·800	320·400
90	324·000	327·600	331·200	334·800	338·400	342·000	345·600	349·200	352·800	356·400
100	360·000	363·600	367·200	370·800	374·400	378·000	381·600	385·200	388·800	392·400
110	396·000	399·600	403·200	406·800	410·400	414·000	417·600	421·200	424·800	428·400
120	432·000	435·600	439·200	442·800	446·400	450·000	453·600	457·200	460·800	464·400
130	468·000	471·600	475·200	478·800	482·400	486·000	489·600	493·200	496·800	500·400
140	504·000	507·600	511·200	514·800	518·400	522·000	525·600	529·200	532·800	536·400
150	540·000	543·600	547·200	550·800	554·400	558·000	561·600	565·200	568·800	572·400
160	576·000	579·600	583·200	586·800	590·400	594·000	597·600	601·200	604·800	608·400
170	612·000	615·600	619·200	622·800	626·400	630·000	633·600	637·200	640·800	644·400
180	648·000	651·600	655·200	658·800	662·400	666·000	669·600	673·200	676·800	680·400
190	684·000	687·600	691·200	694·800	698·400	702·000	705·600	709·200	712·800	716·400
200	720·000	723·600	727·200	730·800	734·400	738·000	741·600	745·200	748·800	752·400
210	756·000	759·600	763·200	766·800	770·400	774·000	777·600	781·200	784·800	788·400
220	792·000	795·600	799·200	802·800	806·400	810·000	813·600	817·200	820·800	824·400
230	828·000	831·600	835·200	838·800	842·400	846·000	849·600	853·200	856·800	860·400
240	864·000	867·600	871·200	874·800	878·400	882·000	885·600	889·200	892·800	896·400
250	900·000	903·600	907·200	910·800	914·400	918·000	921·600	925·200	928·800	932·400
260	936·000	939·600	943·200	946·800	950·400	954·000	957·600	961·200	964·800	968·400
270	972·000	975·600	979·200	982·800	986·400	990·000	993·600	997·200	1000·80	1004·40
280	1008·00	1011·60	1015·20	1018·80	1022·40	1026·00	1029·60	1033·20	1036·80	1040·40
290	1044·00	1047·60	1051·20	1054·80	1058·40	1062·00	1065·60	1069·20	1072·80	1076·40
300	1080·00	1083·60	1087·20	1090·80	1094·40	1098·00	1101·60	1105·20	1108·80	1112·40
310	1116·00	1119·60	1123·20	1126·80	1130·40	1134·00	1137·60	1141·20	1144·80	1148·40
320	1152·00	1155·60	1159·20	1162·80	1166·40	1170·00	1173·60	1177·20	1180·80	1184·40
330	1188·00	1191·60	1195·20	1198·80	1202·40	1206·00	1209·60	1213·20	1216·80	1220·40
340	1224·00	1227·60	1231·20	1234·80	1238·40	1242·00	1245·60	1249·20	1252·80	1256·40
350	1260·00	1263·60	1267·20	1270·80	1274·40	1278·00	1281·60	1285·20	1288·80	1292·40
360	1296·00	1299·60	1303·20	1306·80	1310·40	1314·00	1317·60	1321·20	1324·80	1328·40
370	1332·00	1335·60	1339·20	1342·80	1346·40	1350·00	1353·60	1357·20	1360·80	1364·40
380	1368·00	1371·60	1375·20	1378·80	1382·40	1386·00	1389·60	1393·20	1396·80	1400·40
390	1404·00	1407·60	1411·20	1414·80	1418·40	1422·00	1425·60	1429·20	1432·80	1436·40
400	1440·40	1443·60	1447·20	1450·80	1454·40	1458·00	1461·60	1465·20	1468·80	1472·40
410	1476·00	1479·60	1483·20	1486·80	1490·40	1494·00	1497·60	1501·20	1504·80	1508·40
420	1512·00	1515·60	1519·20	1522·80	1526·40	1530·00	1533·60	1537·20	1540·80	1544·40
430	1548·00	1551·60	1555·20	1558·80	1562·40	1566·00	1569·60	1573·20	1576·80	1580·40
440	1584·00	1587·60	1591·20	1594·80	1598·40	1602·00	1605·60	1609·20	1612·80	1616·40
450	1620·00	1623·60	1627·20	1630·80	1634·40	1638·00	1641·60	1645·20	1648·80	1652·40
460	1656·00	1659·60	1663·20	1666·80	1670·40	1674·00	1677·60	1681·20	1684·80	1688·40
470	1692·00	1695·60	1699·20	1702·80	1706·40	1710·00	1713·60	1717·20	1720·80	1724·40
480	1728·00	1731·60	1735·20	1738·80	1742·40	1746·00	1749·60	1753·20	1756·80	1760·40
490	1764·00	1767·60	1771·20	1774·80	1778·40	1782·00	1785·60	1789·20	1792·80	1796·40

continued

Table 9.9 WORK, ENERGY: KILOWATT HOURS TO MEGAJOULES *(continued)*

Basis: 1 h = 3600 s
1 W = 1 J/s

kWh	0	1	2	3	4	5	6	7	8	9
					megajoules					
500	1800·00	1803·60	1807·20	1810·80	1814·40	1818·00	1821·60	1825·20	1828·80	1832·40
510	1836·00	1839·60	1843·20	1846·80	1850·40	1854·00	1857·60	1861·20	1864·80	1868·40
520	1872·00	1875·60	1879·20	1882·80	1886·40	1890·00	1893·60	1897·20	1900·80	1904·40
530	1908·00	1911·60	1915·20	1918·80	1922·40	1926·00	1929·60	1933·20	1936·80	1940·40
540	1944·00	1947·60	1951·20	1954·80	1958·40	1962·00	1965·60	1969·20	1972·80	1976·40
550	1980·00	1983·60	1987·20	1990·80	1994·40	1998·00	2001·60	2005·20	2008·80	2012·40
560	2016·00	2019·60	2023·20	2026·80	2030·40	2034·00	2037·60	2041·20	2044·80	2048·40
570	2052·00	2055·60	2059·20	2062·80	2066·40	2070·00	2073·60	2077·20	2080·80	2084·40
580	2088·00	2091·60	2095·20	2098·80	2102·40	2106·00	2109·60	2113·20	2116·80	2120·40
590	2124·00	2127·60	2131·20	2134·80	2138·40	2142·00	2145·60	2149·20	2152·80	2156·40
600	2160·00	2163·60	2167·20	2170·80	2174·40	2178·00	2181·60	2185·20	2188·80	2192·40
610	2196·00	2199·60	2203·20	2206·80	2210·40	2214·00	2217·60	2221·20	2224·80	2228·40
620	2232·00	2235·60	2239·20	2242·80	2246·40	2250·00	2253·60	2257·20	2260·80	2264·40
630	2268·00	2271·60	2275·20	2278·80	2282·40	2286·00	2289·60	2293·20	2296·80	2300·40
640	2304·00	2307·60	2311·20	2314·80	2318·40	2322·00	2325·60	2329·20	2332·80	2336·40
650	2340·00	2343·60	2347·20	2350·80	2354·40	2358·00	2361·60	2365·20	2368·80	2372·40
660	2376·00	2379·60	2383·20	2386·80	2390·40	2394·00	2397·60	2401·20	2404·80	2408·40
670	2412·00	2415·60	2419·20	2422·80	2426·40	2430·00	2433·60	2437·20	2440·80	2444·40
680	2448·00	2451·60	2455·20	2458·80	2462·40	2466·00	2469·60	2473·20	2476·80	2480·40
690	2484·00	2487·60	2491·20	2494·80	2498·40	2502·00	2505·60	2509·20	2512·80	2516·40
700	2520·00	2523·60	2527·20	2530·80	2534·40	2538·00	2541·60	2545·20	2548·80	2552·40
710	2556·00	2559·60	2563·20	2566·80	2570·40	2574·00	2577·60	2581·20	2584·80	2588·40
720	2592·00	2595·60	2599·20	2602·80	2606·40	2610·00	2613·60	2617·20	2620·80	2624·40
730	2628·00	2631·60	2635·20	2638·80	2642·40	2646·00	2649·60	2653·20	2656·80	2660·40
740	2664·00	2667·60	2671·20	2674·80	2678·40	2682·00	2685·60	2689·20	2692·80	2696·40
750	2700·00	2703·60	2707·20	2710·80	2714·40	2718·00	2721·60	2725·20	2728·80	2732·40
760	2736·00	2739·60	2743·20	2746·80	2750·40	2754·00	2757·60	2761·20	2764·80	2768·40
770	2772·60	2775·60	2779·20	2782·80	2786·40	2790·00	2793·60	2797·20	2800·80	2804·40
780	2808·00	2811·60	2815·20	2818·80	2822·40	2826·00	2829·60	2833·20	2836·80	2840·40
790	2844·00	2847·60	2851·20	2854·80	2858·40	2862·00	2865·60	2869·20	2872·80	2876·40
800	2880·00	2883·60	2887·20	2890·80	2894·40	2898·00	2901·60	2905·20	2908·80	2912·40
810	2916·00	2919·60	2923·20	2926·80	2930·40	2934·00	2937·60	2941·20	2944·80	2948·40
820	2952·00	2955·60	2959·20	2962·80	2966·40	2970·00	2973·60	2977·20	2980·80	2984·40
830	2988·00	2991·60	2995·20	2998·80	3002·40	3006·00	3009·60	3013·20	3016·80	3020·40
840	3024·00	3027·60	3031·20	3034·80	3038·40	3042·00	3045·60	3049·20	3052·80	3056·40
850	3060·00	3063·60	3067·20	3070·80	3074·40	3078·00	3081·60	3085·20	3088·80	3092·40
860	3096·00	3099·60	3103·20	3106·80	3110·40	3114·00	3117·60	3121·20	3124·80	3128·40
870	3132·00	3135·60	3139·20	3142·80	3146·40	3150·00	3153·60	3157·20	3160·80	3164·40
880	3168·00	3171·60	3175·20	3178·80	3182·40	3186·00	3189·60	3193·20	3196·80	3200·40
890	3204·00	3207·60	3211·20	3214·80	3218·40	3222·00	3225·60	3229·20	3232·80	3236·40
900	3240·00	3243·60	3247·20	3250·80	3254·40	3258·00	3261·60	3265·20	3268·80	3272·40
910	3276·00	3279·60	3283·20	3286·80	3290·40	3294·00	3297·60	3301·20	3304·80	3308·40
920	3312·00	3315·60	3319·20	3322·80	3326·40	3330·00	3333·60	3337·20	3340·80	3344·40
930	3348·00	3351·60	3355·20	3358·80	3362·40	3366·00	3369·60	3373·20	3376·80	3380·40
940	3384·00	3387·60	3391·20	3394·80	3398·40	3402·00	3405·60	3409·20	3412·80	3416·40
950	3420·00	3423·60	3427·20	3430·80	3434·40	3438·00	3441·60	3445·20	3448·80	3452·40
960	3456·00	3459·60	3463·20	3466·80	3470·40	3474·00	3477·60	3481·20	3484·80	3488·40
970	3492·00	3495·60	3499·20	3502·80	3506·40	3510·00	3513·60	3517·20	3520·80	3524·40
980	3528·00	3531·60	3535·20	3538·80	3542·40	3546·00	3549·60	3553·20	3556·80	3560·40
990	3564·00	3567·60	3571·20	3574·80	3578·40	3582·00	3585·60	3589·20	3592·80	3596·40
1000	3600·00	—	—	—	—	—	—	—	—	—

Table 9.10 THERMAL CONDUCTANCE: BRITISH THERMAL UNITS PER SQUARE FOOT HOUR DEGREE FAHRENHEIT TO WATTS PER SQUARE METRE DEGREE CELSIUS

Basis: 1 ft = 0·3048 m   1 cal = 4·1868 J   1 h = 3600 s
9 Btu = 5 × 453·592 37 cal   1 W = 1 J/s

Btu/ft² h degF	0	100	200	300	400	500	600	700	800	900
				watts per square metre degree Celsius						
0	0·00000	567·826	1135·65	1703·48	2271·31	2839·13	3406·96	3974·78	4542·61	5110·44
1000	5678·26	6246·09	6813·92	7381·74	7949·57	8517·40	9085·22	9653·05	10220·9	10788·7
2000	11356·5	11924·4	12492·2	13060·0	13627·8	14195·7	14763·5	15331·3	15899·1	16467·0
3000	17034·8	17602·6	18170·4	18738·3	19306·1	19873·9	20441·7	21009·6	21577·4	22145·2
4000	22713·1	23280·9	23848·7	24416·5	24984·4	25552·2	26120·0	26687·8	27255·7	27823·5
5000	28391·3	28959·1	29527·0	30094·8	30662·6	21230·4	31798·3	32366·1	32933·9	33501·8
6000	34069·6	34637·4	35205·2	35773·1	36340·9	36908·7	37476·5	38044·4	38612·2	39180·0
7000	39747·8	40315·7	40883·5	41451·3	42019·1	42587·0	43154·8	43722·6	44290·5	44858·3
8000	45426·1	45993·9	46561·8	47129·6	47697·4	48265·2	48833·1	49400·9	49968·7	50536·5
9000	51104·4	51672·2	52240·0	52807·8	53375·7	53943·5	54511·3	55079·2	55647·0	56214·8
10000	56782·6	—	—	—	—	—	—	—	—	—

AUXILIARY TABLE

Btu/ft² h degF	0	10	20	30	40	50	60	70	80	90
				watts per square metre degree Celsius						
0	—	56·7826	113·565	170·348	227·131	283·913	340·696	397·478	454·261	511·044

Table 9.11 LENGTH: FRACTIONS OF AN INCH, IN SIXTY-FOURTHS, TO DECIMALS OF AN INCH AND TO MILLIMETRES

Basis: 1 in = 25·4 mm (exactly)   All values in this table are exact

inch	inch	millimetre	inch	inch	millimetre	inch	inch	millimetre
$\frac{1}{64}$	0·015 625	0·396 875	$\frac{23}{64}$	0·359 375	9·128 125	$\frac{45}{64}$	0·703 125	17·859 375
$\frac{1}{32}$	0·031 250	0·793 750	$\frac{3}{8}$	0·375 000	9·525 000	$\frac{23}{32}$	0·718 750	18·256 250
$\frac{3}{64}$	0·046 875	1·190 625	$\frac{25}{64}$	0·390 625	9·921 875	$\frac{47}{64}$	0·734 375	18·653 125
$\frac{1}{16}$	0·062·500	1·587 500	$\frac{13}{32}$	0·406 250	10·318 750	$\frac{3}{4}$	0·750 000	19·050 000
$\frac{5}{64}$	0·078 125	1·984 375	$\frac{27}{64}$	0·421 875	10·715 625	$\frac{49}{64}$	0·765 625	19·446 875
$\frac{3}{32}$	0·093 750	2·381 250	$\frac{7}{16}$	0·437 500	11·112 500	$\frac{25}{32}$	0·781 250	19·843 750
$\frac{7}{64}$	0·109 375	2·778 125	$\frac{29}{64}$	0·453 125	11·509 375	$\frac{51}{64}$	0·796 875	20·240 625
$\frac{1}{8}$	0·125 000	3·175 000	$\frac{15}{32}$	0·468 750	11·906 250	$\frac{13}{16}$	0·812 500	20·637 500
$\frac{9}{64}$	0·140 625	3·571 875	$\frac{31}{64}$	0·484 375	12·303 125	$\frac{53}{64}$	0·828 125	21·034 375
$\frac{5}{32}$	0·156 250	3·968 750	$\frac{1}{2}$	0·500 000	12·700 000	$\frac{27}{32}$	0·843 750	21·431 250
$\frac{11}{64}$	0·171 875	4·365 625	$\frac{33}{64}$	0·515 625	13·096 875	$\frac{55}{64}$	0·859 375	21·828 125
$\frac{3}{16}$	0·187 500	4·762 500	$\frac{17}{32}$	0·531 250	13·493 750	$\frac{7}{8}$	0·875 000	22·225 000
$\frac{13}{64}$	0·203 125	5·159 375	$\frac{35}{64}$	0·546 875	13·890 625	$\frac{57}{64}$	0·890 625	22·621 875
$\frac{7}{32}$	0·218 750	5·556·250	$\frac{9}{16}$	0·562 500	14·287 500	$\frac{29}{32}$	0·906 250	23·018 750
$\frac{15}{64}$	0·234 375	5·953 125	$\frac{37}{64}$	0·578 125	14·684 375	$\frac{59}{64}$	0·921 875	23·415 625
$\frac{1}{4}$	0·250 000	6·350 000	$\frac{19}{32}$	0·593 750	15·081 250	$\frac{15}{16}$	0·937 500	23·812 500
$\frac{17}{64}$	0·265 625	6·746 875	$\frac{39}{64}$	0·609 375	15·478 125	$\frac{61}{64}$	0·953 125	24·209 375
$\frac{9}{32}$	0·281 250	7·143 750	$\frac{5}{8}$	0·625 000	15·875 000	$\frac{31}{32}$	0·968 750	24·606 250
$\frac{19}{64}$	0·296 875	7·540 625	$\frac{41}{64}$	0·640 625	16·271 875	$\frac{63}{64}$	0·984 375	25·003 125
$\frac{5}{16}$	0·312 500	7·937 500	$\frac{21}{32}$	0·656 250	16·668 750	1	1·000 000	25·400 000
$\frac{21}{64}$	0·328 125	8·334 375	$\frac{43}{64}$	0·671 875	17·065 625			
$\frac{11}{32}$	0·343 750	8·731 250	$\frac{11}{16}$	0·687 500	17·462 500			

Table 9.12 LENGTH: INCHES AND FRACTIONS OF AN INCH TO MILLIMETRES

Basis: 1 in = 25·4 mm (exactly)

inches	0	1	2	3	4	5	6	7	8	9	10	11
						millimetres						
—	—	25·400	50·800	76·200	101·600	127·000	152·400	177·800	203·200	228·600	254·000	279·400
1/32	0·794	26·194	51·594	76·994	102·394	127·794	153·194	178·594	203·994	229·394	254·794	280·194
1/16	1·588	26·988	52·388	77·788	103·188	128·588	153·988	179·388	204·788	230·188	255·588	280·988
3/32	2·381	27·781	53·181	78·581	103·981	129·381	154·781	180·181	205·581	230·981	256·381	281·781
1/8	3·175	28·575	53·975	79·375	104·775	130·175	155·575	180·975	206·375	231·775	257·175	282·575
5/32	3·969	29·369	54·769	80·169	105·569	130·969	156·369	181·769	207·169	232·569	257·969	283·369
3/16	4·762	30·162	55·562	80·962	106·362	131·762	157·162	182·562	207·962	233·362	258·762	284·162
7/32	5·556	30·956	56·356	81·756	107·156	132·556	157·956	183·356	208·756	234·156	259·556	284·956
1/4	6·350	31·750	57·150	82·550	107·950	133·350	158·750	184·150	209·550	234·950	260·350	285·750
9/32	7·144	32·544	57·944	83·344	108·744	134·144	159·544	184·944	210·344	235·744	261·144	286·544
5/16	7·938	33·338	58·738	84·138	109·538	134·938	160·338	185·738	211·138	236·538	261·938	287·338
11/32	8·731	34·131	59·531	84·931	110·331	135·731	161·131	186·531	211·931	237·331	262·731	288·131
3/8	9·525	34·925	60·325	85·725	111·125	136·525	161·925	187·325	212·725	238·125	263·525	288·925
13/32	10·319	35·719	61·119	86·519	111·919	137·319	162·719	188·119	213·519	238·919	264·319	289·719
7/16	11·112	36·512	61·912	87·312	112·712	138·112	163·512	188·912	214·312	239·712	265·112	290·512
15/32	11·906	37·306	62·706	88·106	113·506	138·906	164·306	189·706	215·106	240·506	265·906	291·306
1/2	12·700	38·100	63·500	88·900	114·300	139·700	165·100	190·500	215·900	241·300	266·700	292·100
17/32	13·494	38·894	64·294	89·694	115·094	140·494	165·894	191·294	216·694	242·094	267·494	292·894
9/16	14·288	39·688	65·088	90·488	115·888	141·288	166·688	192·088	217·488	242·888	268·288	293·688
19/32	15·081	40·481	65·881	91·281	116·681	142·081	167·481	192·881	218·281	243·681	269·081	294·481
5/8	15·875	41·275	66·675	92·075	117·475	142·875	168·275	193·675	219·075	244·475	269·875	295·275
21/32	16·669	42·069	67·469	92·869	118·269	143·669	160·069	194·469	219·869	245·269	270·669	296·069
11/16	17·462	42·862	68·262	93·662	119·062	144·462	169·862	195·262	220·662	246·062	271·462	296·862
23/32	18·256	43·656	69·056	94·456	119·856	145·256	170·656	196·056	221·456	246·856	272·256	297·656
3/4	19·050	44·450	69·850	95·250	120·650	146·050	171·450	196·850	222·250	247·650	273·050	298·450
25/32	19·844	45·244	70·644	96·044	121·444	146·844	172·244	197·644	223·044	248·444	273·844	299·244
13/16	20·638	46·038	71·438	96·838	122·238	147·638	173·038	198·438	223·838	249·238	274·638	300·038
27/32	21·431	46·831	72·231	97·631	123·031	148·431	173·831	199·231	224·631	250·031	275·431	300·831
7/8	22·225	47·625	73·025	98·425	123·825	149·225	174·625	200·025	225·425	250·825	276·225	301·625
29/32	23·019	48·419	73·819	99·219	124·619	150·019	175·419	200·819	226·219	251·619	277·019	302·419
15/16	23·812	49·212	74·612	100·012	125·412	150·812	176·212	201·612	227·012	252·412	277·812	303·212
31/32	24·606	50·006	75·406	100·806	126·206	151·606	177·006	202·406	227·806	253·206	278·606	304·006

12 in = 304·800 mm

Table 9.13 LENGTH: FEET AND INCHES TO METRES

Basis: 1 in = 25·4 mm (exactly)   All values in this table are exact, except for those for fractions of an inch

	inches												Differences for sixteenths of an inch	
	0	**1**	**2**	**3**	**4**	**5**	**6**	**7**	**8**	**9**	**10**	**11**		
	metres													
feet														
0	—	0·0254	0·0508	0·0762	0·1016	0·1270	0·1524	0·1778	0·2032	0·2286	0·2540	0·2794		
1	0·3048	0·3302	0·3556	0·3810	0·4064	0·4318	0·4572	0·4826	0·5080	0·5334	0·5588	0·5842		
2	0·6096	0·6350	0·6604	0·6858	0·7112	0·7366	0·7620	0·7874	0·8128	0·8382	0·8636	0·8890	1	0·0016
3	0·9144	0·9398	0·9652	0·9906	1·0160	1·0414	1·0668	1·0922	1·1176	1·1430	1·1684	1·1938		
4	1·2192	1·2446	1·2700	1·2954	1·3208	1·3462	1·3716	1·3970	1·4224	1·4478	1·4732	1·4986		
5	1·5240	1·5494	1·5748	1·6002	1·6256	1·6510	1·6764	1·7018	1·7272	1·7526	1·7780	1·8034	2	0·0032
6	1·8288	1·8542	1·8796	1·9050	1·9304	1·9558	1·9812	2·0066	2·0320	2·0574	2·0828	2·1082		
7	2·1336	2·1590	2·1844	2·2098	2·2352	2·2606	2·2860	2·3114	2·3368	2·3622	2·3876	2·4130		
8	2·4384	2·4638	2·4892	2·5146	2·5400	2·5654	2·5908	2·6162	2·6416	2·6670	2·6924	2·7178	3	0·0048
9	2·7432	2·7686	2·7940	2·8194	2·8448	2·8702	2·8956	2·9210	2·9464	2·9718	2·9972	3·0226		
10	3·0480	3·0734	3·0988	3·1242	3·1496	3·1750	3·2004	3·2258	3·2512	3·2766	3·3020	3·3274		
11	3·3528	3·3782	3·4036	3·4290	3·4544	3·4798	3·5052	3·5306	3·5560	3·5814	3·6068	3·6322	4	0·0064
12	3·6576	3·6830	3·7084	3·7338	3·7592	3·7846	3·8100	3·8354	3·8608	3·8862	3·9116	3·9370		
13	3·9624	3·9878	4·0132	4·0386	4·0640	4·0894	4·1148	4·1402	4·1656	4·1910	4·2164	4·2418		
14	4·2672	4·2926	4·3180	4·3434	4·3688	4·3942	4·4196	4·4450	4·4704	4·4958	4·5212	4·5466	5	0·0079
15	4·5720	4·5974	4·6228	4·6482	4·6736	4·6990	4·7244	4·7498	4·7752	4·8006	4·8260	4·8514		
16	4·8768	4·9022	4·9276	4·9530	4·9784	5·0038	5·0292	5·0546	5·0800	5·1054	5·1308	5·1562		
17	5·1816	5·2070	5·2324	5·2578	5·2832	5·3086	5·3340	5·3594	5·3848	5·4102	5·4356	5·4610	6	0·0095
18	5·4864	5·5118	5·5372	5·5626	5·5880	5·6134	5·6388	5·6642	5·6896	5·7150	5·7404	5·7658		
19	5·7912	5·8166	5·8420	5·8674	5·8928	5·9182	5·9436	5·9690	5·9944	6·0198	6·0452	6·0706		
20	6·0960	6·1214	6·1468	6·1722	6·1976	6·2230	6·2484	6·2738	6·2992	6·3246	6·3500	6·3754	7	0·0111
21	6·4008	6·4262	6·4516	6·4770	6·5024	6·5278	6·5532	6·5786	6·6040	6·6294	6·6548	6·6802		
22	6·7056	6·7310	6·7564	6·7818	6·8072	6·8326	6·8580	6·8834	6·9088	6·9342	6·9596	6·9850		
23	7·0104	7·0358	7·0612	7·0866	7·1120	7·1374	7·1628	7·1882	7·2136	7·2390	7·2644	7·2898	8	0·0127
24	7·3152	7·3406	7·3660	7·3914	7·4168	7·4422	7·4676	7·4930	7·5184	7·5438	7·5692	7·5946		
25	7·6200	7·6454	7·6708	7·6962	7·7216	7·7470	7·7724	7·7978	7·8232	7·8486	7·8740	7·8994		
26	7·9248	7·9502	7·9756	8·0010	8·0264	8·0518	8·0772	8·1026	8·1280	8·1534	8·1788	8·2042	9	0·0143
27	8·2296	8·2550	8·2804	8·3058	8·3312	8·3566	8·3820	8·4074	8·4328	8·4582	8·4836	8·5090		
28	8·5344	8·5598	8·5852	8·6106	8·6360	8·6614	8·6868	8·7122	8·7376	8·7630	8·7884	8·8138		
29	8·8392	8·8646	8·8900	8·9154	8·9408	8·9662	8·9916	9·0170	9·0424	9·0678	9·0932	9·1186	10	0·0159
30	9·1440	9·1694	9·1948	9·2202	9·2456	9·2710	9·2964	9·3218	9·3472	9·3726	9·3980	9·4234		
31	9·4488	9·4742	9·4996	9·5250	9·5504	9·5758	9·6012	9·6266	9·6520	9·6774	9·7028	9·7282		
32	9·7536	9·7790	9·8044	9·8298	9·8552	9·8806	9·9060	9·9314	9·9568	9·9822	10·0076	10·0330	11	0·0175
33	10·0584	10·0838	10·1092	10·1346	10·1600	10·1854	10·2108	10·2362	10·2616	10·2870	10·3124	10·3378		
34	10·3632	10·3886	10·4140	10·4394	10·4648	10·4902	10·5156	10·5410	10·5664	10·5918	10·6172	10·6426		
35	10·6680	10·6934	10·7188	10·7442	10·7696	10·7950	10·8204	10·8458	10·8712	10·8966	10·9220	10·9474	12	0·0190
36	10·9728	10·9982	11·0236	11·0490	11·0744	11·0998	11·1252	11·1506	11·1760	11·2014	11·2268	11·2522		
37	11·2776	11·3030	11·3284	11·3538	11·3792	11·4046	11·4300	11·4554	11·4808	11·5062	11·5316	11·5570		
38	11·5824	11·6078	11·6332	11·6586	11·6840	11·7094	11·7348	11·7602	11·7856	11·8110	11·8364	11·8618	13	0·0206
39	11·8872	11·9126	11·9380	11·9634	11·9888	12·0142	12·0396	12·0650	12·0904	12·1158	12·1412	12·1666		
40	12·1920	12·2174	12·2428	12·2682	12·2936	12·3190	12·3444	12·3698	12·3952	12·4206	12·4460	12·4714		
41	12·4968	12·5222	12·5476	12·5730	12·5984	12·6238	12·6492	12·6746	12·7000	12·7254	12·7508	12·7762	14	0·0222
42	12·8016	12·8270	12·8524	12·8778	12·9032	12·9286	12·9540	12·9794	13·0048	13·0302	13·0556	13·0810		
43	13·1064	13·1318	13·1572	13·1826	13·2080	13·2334	13·2588	13·2842	13·3096	13·3350	13·3604	13·3858		
44	13·4112	13·4366	13·4620	13·4874	13·5128	13·5382	13·5636	13·5890	13·6144	13·6398	13·6652	13·6906	15	0·0238
45	13·7160	13·7414	13·7668	13·7922	13·8176	13·8430	13·8684	13·8938	13·9192	13·9446	13·9700	13·9954		
46	14·0208	14·0462	14·0716	14·0970	14·1224	14·1478	14·1732	14·1986	14·2240	14·2494	14·2748	14·3002		
47	14·3256	14·3510	14·3764	14·4018	14·4272	14·4526	14·4780	14·5034	14·5288	14·5542	14·5796	14·6050		
48	14·6304	14·6558	14·6812	14·7066	14·7320	14·7574	14·7828	14·8082	14·8336	14·8590	14·8844	14·9098		
49	14·9352	14·9606	14·9860	15·0114	15·0368	15·0622	15·0876	15·1130	15·1384	15·1638	15·1892	15·2146		

continued

Table 9.13 LENGTH: FEET AND INCHES TO METRES *(continued)*

Basis: 1 in = 25·4 mm (exactly)   All values in this table are exact, except those for fractions of an inch

feet	0	1	2	3	4	5	6	7	8	9	10	11	Differences for sixteenths of an inch	
							inches							
							metres							
50	15·2400	15·2654	15·2908	15·3162	15·3416	15·3670	15·3924	15·4178	15·4432	15·4686	15·4940	15·5194		
51	15·5448	15·5702	15·5956	15·6210	15·6464	15·6718	15·6972	15·7226	15·7480	15·7734	15·7988	15·8242		
52	15·8496	15·8750	15·9004	15·9258	15·9512	15·9766	16·0020	16·0274	16·0528	16·0782	16·1036	16·1290	1	0·0016
53	16·1544	16·1798	16·2052	16·2306	16·2560	16·2814	16·3068	16·3322	16·3576	16·3830	16·4084	16·4338		
54	16·4592	16·4846	16·5100	16·5354	16·5608	16·5862	16·6116	16·6370	16·6624	16·6878	16·7132	16·7386		
55	16·7640	16·7894	16·8148	16·8402	16·8656	16·8910	16·9164	16·9418	16·9672	16·9926	17·0180	17·0434	2	0·0032
56	17·0688	17·0942	17·1196	17·1450	17·1704	17·1958	17·2212	17·2466	17·2720	17·2974	17·3228	17·3482		
57	17·3736	17·3990	17·4244	17·4498	17·4752	17·5006	17·5260	17·5514	17·5768	17·6022	17·6276	17·6530		
58	17·6784	17·7038	17·7292	17·7546	17·7800	17·8054	17·8308	17·8562	17·8816	17·9070	17·9324	17·9578	3	0·0048
59	17·9832	18·0086	18·0340	18·0594	18·0848	18·1102	18·1356	18·1610	18·1864	18·2118	18·2372	18·2626		
60	18·2880	18·3134	18·3388	18·3642	18·3896	18·4150	18·4404	18·4658	18·4912	18·5166	18·5420	18·5674		
61	18·5928	18·6182	18·6436	18·6690	18·6944	18·7198	18·7452	18·7706	18·7960	18·8214	18·8468	18·8722	4	0·0064
62	18·8976	18·9230	18·9484	18·9738	18·9992	19·0246	19·0500	19·0754	19·1008	19·1262	19·1516	19·1770		
63	19·2024	19·2278	19·2532	19·2786	19·3040	19·3294	19·3548	19·3802	19·4056	19·4310	19·4564	19·4818		
64	19·5072	19·5326	19·5580	19·5834	19·6088	19·6342	19·6596	19·6850	19·7104	19·7358	19·7612	19·7866	5	0·0079
65	19·8120	19·8374	19·8628	19·8882	19·9136	19·9390	19·9644	19·9898	20·0152	20·0406	20·0660	20·0914		
66	20·1168	20·1422	20·1676	20·1930	20·2184	20·2438	20·2692	20·2946	20·3200	20·3454	20·3708	20·3962		
67	20·4216	20·4470	20·4724	20·4978	20·5232	20·5486	20·5740	20·5994	20·6248	20·6502	20·6756	20·7010	6	0·0095
68	20·7264	20·7518	20·7772	20·8026	20·8280	20·8534	20·8788	20·9042	20·9296	20·9550	20·9804	21·0058		
69	21·0312	21·0566	21·0820	21·1074	21·1328	21·1582	21·1836	21·2090	21·2344	21·2598	21·2852	21·3106		
70	21·3360	21·3614	21·3868	21·4122	21·4376	21·4630	21·4884	21·5138	21·5392	21·5646	21·5900	21·6154	7	0·0111
71	21·6408	21·6662	21·6916	21·7170	21·7424	21·7678	21·7932	21·8186	21·8440	21·8694	21·8948	21·9202		
72	21·9456	21·9710	21·9964	22·0218	22·0472	22·0726	22·0980	22·1234	22·1488	22·1742	22·1996	22·2250		
73	22·2504	22·2758	22·3012	22·3266	22·3520	22·3774	22·4028	22·4282	22·4536	22·4790	22·5044	22·5298	8	0·0127
74	22·5552	22·5806	22·6060	22·6314	22·6568	22·6822	22·7076	22·7330	22·7584	22·7838	22·8092	22·8346		
75	22·8600	22·8854	22·9108	22·9362	22·9616	22·9870	23·0124	23·0378	23·0632	23·0886	23·1140	23·1394		
76	23·1648	23·1902	23·2156	23·2410	23·2664	23·2918	23·3172	23·3426	23·3680	23·3934	23·4188	23·4442	9	0·0143
77	23·4696	23·4950	23·5204	23·5458	23·5712	23·5966	23·6220	23·6474	23·6728	23·6982	23·7236	23·7490		
78	23·7744	23·7998	23·8252	23·8506	23·8760	23·9014	23·9268	23·9522	23·9776	24·0030	24·0284	24·0538		
79	24·0792	24·1046	24·1300	24·1554	24·1808	24·2062	24·2316	24·2570	24·2824	24·3078	24·3332	24·3586	10	0·0159
80	24·3840	24·4094	24·4348	24·4602	24·4856	24·5110	24·5364	24·5618	24·5872	24·6126	24·6380	24·6634		
81	24·6888	24·7142	24·7396	24·7650	24·7904	24·8158	24·8412	24·8666	24·8920	24·9174	24·9428	24·9682		
82	24·9936	25·0190	25·0444	25·0698	25·0952	25·1206	25·1460	25·1714	25·1968	25·2222	25·2476	25·2730	11	0·0175
83	25·2984	25·3238	25·3492	25·3746	25·4000	25·4254	25·4508	25·4762	25·5016	25·5270	25·5524	25·5778		
84	25·6032	25·6286	25·6540	25·6794	25·7048	25·7302	25·7556	25·7810	25·8064	25·8318	25·8572	25·8826		
85	25·9080	25·9334	25·9588	25·9842	26·0096	26·0350	26·0604	26·0858	26·1112	26·1366	26·1620	26·1874	12	0·0190
86	26·2128	26·2382	26·2636	26·2890	26·3144	26·3398	26·3652	26·3906	26·4160	26·4414	26·4668	26·4922		
87	26·5176	26·5430	26·5684	26·5938	26·6192	26·6446	26·6700	26·6954	26·7208	26·7462	26·7716	26·7970		
88	26·8224	26·8478	26·8732	26·8986	26·9240	26·9494	26·9748	27·0002	27·0256	27·0510	27·0764	27·1018	13	0·0206
89	27·1272	27·1526	27·1780	27·2034	27·2288	27·2542	27·2796	27·3050	27·3304	27·3558	27·3812	27·4066		
90	27·4320	27·4574	27·4828	27·5082	27·5336	27·5590	27·5844	27·6098	27·6352	27·6606	27·6860	27·7114		
91	27·7368	27·7622	27·7876	27·8130	27·8384	27·8638	27·8892	28·9146	27·9400	27·9654	27·9908	28·0162	14	0·0222
92	28·0416	28·0670	28·0924	28·1178	28·1432	28·1686	28·1940	28·2194	28·2448	28·2702	28·2956	28·3210		
93	28·3464	28·3718	28·3972	28·4226	28·4480	28·4734	28·4988	28·5242	28·5496	28·5750	28·6004	28·6258		
94	28·6512	28·6766	28·7020	28·7274	28·7528	28·7782	28·8036	28·8290	28·8544	28·8798	28·9052	28·9306	15	0·0238
95	28·9560	28·9814	29·0068	29·0322	29·0576	29·0830	29·1084	29·1338	29·1592	29·1846	29·2100	29·2354		
96	29·2608	29·2862	29·3116	29·3370	29·3624	29·3878	29·4132	29·4386	29·4640	29·4894	29·5148	29·5402		
97	29·5656	29·5910	29·6164	29·6418	29·6672	29·6926	29·7180	29·7434	29·7688	29·7942	29·8196	29·8450		
98	29·8704	29·8958	29·9212	29·9466	29·9720	29·9974	30·0228	30·0482	30·0736	30·0990	30·1244	30·1498		
99	30·1752	30·2006	30·2260	30·2514	30·2768	30·3022	30·3276	30·3530	30·3784	30·4038	30·4292	30·4546		
100	30·4800	—					—		—			—		

Table 9.14 LENGTH: YARDS TO METRES

Basis: 1 yd = 0·9144 m (exactly)   Values given to four decimal places are exact

yards	0	1	2	3	4	5	6	7	8	9
					metres					
0	—	0·9144	1·8288	2·7432	3·6576	4·5720	5·4864	6·4008	7·3152	8·2296
10	9·1440	10·0584	10·9728	11·8872	12·8016	13·7160	14·6304	15·5448	16·4592	17·3736
20	18·2880	19·2024	20·1168	21·0312	21·9456	22·8600	23·7744	24·6888	25·6032	26·5176
30	27·4320	28·3464	29·2608	30·1752	31·0896	32·0040	32·9184	33·8328	34·7472	35·6616
40	36·5760	37·4904	38·4048	39·3192	40·2336	41·1480	42·0624	42·9768	43·8912	44·8056
50	45·7200	46·6344	47·5488	48·4632	49·3776	50·2920	51·2064	52·1208	53·0352	53·9496
60	54·8640	55·7784	56·6928	57·6072	58·5216	59·4360	60·3504	61·2648	62·1792	63·0936
70	64·0080	64·9224	65·8368	66·7512	67·6656	68·5800	69·4944	70·4088	71·3232	72·2376
80	73·1520	74·0664	74·9808	75·8952	76·8096	77·7240	78·6384	79·5528	80·4672	81·3816
90	82·2960	83·2104	84·1248	85·0392	85·9536	86·8680	87·7824	88·6968	89·6112	90·5256
100	91·4400	92·3544	93·2688	94·1832	95·0976	96·0120	96·9264	97·8408	98·7552	99·6696
110	100·584	101·498	102·413	103·327	104·242	105·156	106·070	106·985	107·899	108·814
120	109·728	110·642	111·557	112·471	113·386	114·300	115·214	116·129	117·043	117·958
130	118·872	119·786	120·701	121·615	122·530	123·444	124·358	125·273	126·187	127·102
140	128·016	128·930	129·845	130·759	131·674	132·588	133·502	134·417	135·331	136·246
150	137·160	138·074	138·989	139·903	140·818	141·732	142·646	143·561	144·475	145·390
160	146·304	147·218	148·133	149·047	149·962	150·876	151·790	152·705	153·619	154·534
170	155·448	156·362	157·277	158·191	159·106	160·020	160·934	161·849	162·763	163·678
180	164·592	165·506	166·421	167·335	168·250	169·164	170·078	170·993	171·907	172·822
190	173·736	174·650	175·565	176·479	177·394	178·308	178·222	180·137	181·051	181·966
200	182·880	183·794	184·709	185·623	186·538	187·452	188·366	189·281	190·195	191·110
210	192·024	192·938	193·853	194·767	195·682	196·596	197·510	198·425	199·339	200·254
220	201·168	202·082	202·997	203·911	204·826	205·740	206·654	207·569	208·483	209·398
230	210·312	211·226	212·141	213·055	213·970	214·884	215·798	216·713	217·627	218·542
240	219·456	220·370	221·285	222·199	223·114	224·028	224·942	225·857	226·771	227·686
250	228·600	229·514	230·429	231·343	232·258	233·172	234·086	235·001	235·915	236·830
260	237·744	238·658	239·573	240·487	241·402	242·316	243·230	244·145	245·059	245·974
270	246·888	247·802	248·717	249·631	250·546	251·460	252·374	253·289	254·203	255·118
280	256·032	256·946	257·861	258·775	259·690	260·604	261·518	262·433	263·347	264·262
290	265·176	266·090	267·005	267·919	268·834	269·748	270·662	271·577	272·491	273·406
300	274·320	275·234	276·149	277·063	277·978	278·892	279·806	280·721	281·635	282·550
310	283·464	284·378	285·293	286·207	287·122	288·036	288·950	289·865	290·779	291·694
320	292·608	293·522	294·437	295·351	296·266	297·180	298·094	299·009	299·923	300·838
330	301·752	302·666	303·581	304·495	305·410	306·324	307·238	308·153	309·067	309·982
340	310·896	311·810	312·725	313·639	314·554	315·468	316·382	317·297	318·211	319·126
350	320·040	320·954	321·869	322·783	323·698	324·612	325·526	326·441	327·355	328·270
360	329·184	330·098	331·013	331·927	332·842	333·756	334·670	335·585	336·499	337·414
370	338·328	339·242	340·157	341·071	341·986	342·900	343·814	344·729	345·643	346·558
380	347·472	348·386	349·301	350·215	351·130	352·044	352·958	353·873	354·787	355·702
390	356·616	357·530	358·445	359·359	360·274	361·188	362·102	363·017	363·931	364·846
400	365·760	366·674	367·589	368·503	369·418	370·332	371·246	372·161	373·075	373·990
410	374·904	375·818	376·733	377·647	378·562	379·476	380·390	381·305	382·219	383·134
420	384·048	384·962	385·877	386·791	387·706	388·620	389·534	390·449	391·363	392·278
430	393·192	394·106	395·021	395·935	396·850	397·764	398·678	399·593	400·507	401·422
440	402·336	403·250	404·165	405·079	405·994	406·908	407·822	408·737	409·651	410·566
450	411·480	412·394	413·309	414·223	415·138	416·052	416·966	417·881	418·795	419·710
460	420·624	421·538	422·453	423·367	424·282	425·196	426·110	427·025	427·939	428·854
470	429·768	430·682	431·597	432·511	433·426	434·340	435·254	436·169	437·083	437·998
480	438·912	439·826	440·741	441·655	442·570	443·484	444·398	445·313	446·227	447·142
490	448·056	448·970	449·885	450·799	451·714	452·628	453·542	454·457	455·371	456·286

continued

Table 9.14 LENGTH: YARDS TO METRES *(continued)*

Basis: 1 yd = 0·9144 m (exactly)

Values given to four decimal places are exact

yards	0	1	2	3	4	5	6	7	8	9
					metres					
500	457·200	458·114	459·029	459·943	460·858	461·772	462·686	463·601	464·515	465·430
510	466·344	467·258	468·173	469·087	470·002	470·916	471·830	472·745	473·659	474·574
520	475·488	476·402	477·317	478·231	479·146	480·060	480·974	481·889	482·803	483·718
530	484·632	485·546	486·461	487·375	488·290	489·204	490·118	491·033	491·947	492·862
540	493·776	494·690	495·605	496·519	497·434	498·348	499·262	500·177	501·091	502·006
550	502·920	503·834	504·749	505·663	506·578	507·492	508·406	509·321	510·235	511·150
560	512·064	512·978	513·893	514·807	515·722	516·636	517·550	518·465	519·379	520·294
570	521·208	522·122	523·037	523·951	524·866	525·780	526·694	527·609	528·523	529·438
580	530·352	531·266	532·181	533·095	534·010	534·924	535·838	536·753	537·667	538·582
590	539·496	540·410	541·325	542·239	543·154	544·068	544·982	545·897	546·811	547·726
600	548·640	549·554	550·469	551·383	552·298	553·212	554·126	555·041	555·955	556·870
610	557·784	558·698	559·613	560·527	561·442	562·356	563·270	564·185	565·099	566·014
620	566·928	567·842	568·757	569·671	570·586	571·500	572·414	573·329	574·243	575·158
630	576·072	576·986	577·901	578·815	579·730	580·644	581·558	582·473	583·387	584·302
640	585·216	586·130	587·045	587·959	588·874	589·788	590·702	591·617	592·531	593·446
650	594·360	595·274	596·189	597·103	598·018	598·932	599·846	600·761	601·675	602·590
660	603·504	604·418	605·333	606·247	607·162	608·076	608·990	609·905	610·819	611·734
670	612·648	613·562	614·477	615·391	616·306	617·220	618·134	619·049	619·963	620·878
680	621·792	622·706	623·621	624·535	625·450	626·364	627·278	628·193	629·107	630·022
690	630·936	631·850	632·765	633·679	634·594	635·508	636·422	637·337	638·251	639·166
700	640·080	640·994	641·909	642·823	643·738	644·652	645·566	646·481	647·395	648·310
710	649·224	650·138	651·053	651·967	652·882	653·796	654·710	655·625	656·539	657·454
720	658·368	659·282	660·197	661·111	662·026	662·940	663·854	664·769	665·683	666·598
730	667·512	668·426	669·341	670·255	671·170	672·084	672·998	673·913	674·827	675·742
740	676·656	677·570	678·485	679·399	680·314	681·228	682·142	683·057	683·971	684·886
750	685·800	686·714	687·629	688·543	689·458	690·372	691·286	692·201	693·115	694·030
760	694·944	695·858	696·773	697·687	698·602	699·516	700·430	701·345	702·259	703·174
770	704·088	705·002	705·917	706·831	707·746	708·660	709·574	710·489	711·403	712·318
780	713·232	714·146	715·061	715·975	716·890	717·804	718·718	719·633	720·547	721·462
790	722·376	723·290	724·205	725·119	726·034	726·948	727·862	728·777	729·691	730·606
800	731·520	732·434	733·349	734·263	735·178	736·092	737·006	737·921	738·835	739·750
810	740·664	741·578	742·493	743·407	744·322	745·236	746·150	747·065	747·979	748·894
820	749·808	750·722	751·637	752·551	753·466	754·380	755·294	756·209	757·123	758·038
830	758·952	759·866	760·781	761·695	762·610	763·524	764·438	765·353	766·267	767·182
840	768·096	769·010	769·925	770·839·	771·754	772·668	773·582	774·497	775·411	776·326
850	777·240	778·154	779·069	779·983	780·898	781·812	782·726	783·641	784·555	785·470
860	786·384	787·298	788·213	789·127	790·042	790·956	791·870	792·785	793·699	794·614
870	795·528	796·442	797·357	798·271	799·186	800·100	801·014	801·929	802·843	803·758
880	804·672	805·586	806·501	807·415	808·330	809·244	810·158	811·073	811·987	812·902
890	813·816	814·730	815·645	816·559	817·474	818·388	819·302	820·217	821·131	822·046
900	822·960	823·874	824·789	825·703	826·618	827·532	828·446	829·361	830·275	831·190
910	832·104	833·018	833·933	834·847	835;762	836·676	837·590	838·505	839·419	840·334
920	841·248	842·162	843·077	843·991	844·906	845·820	846·734	847·649	848·563	849·478
930	850·392	851·306	852·221	853·135	854·050	854·964	855·878	856·793	857·707	858·622
940	859·536	860·450	861·365	862·279	863·194	864·108	865·022	865·937	866·851	867·766
950	868·680	869·594	870·509	871·423	872·338	873·252	874·166	875·081	875·995	876·910
960	877·824	878·738	879·653	880·567	881·482	882·396	883·310	884·225	885·139	886·054
970	886·968	887·882	888·797	889·711	890·626	891·540	892·454	893·369	894·283	895·198
980	896·112	897·026	897·941	898·855	899·770	900·684	901·598	902·513	903·427	903·342
990	905·256	906·170	907·085	907·999	908·914	909·828	910·742	911·657	912·571	913·486
1000	914·400	—	—	—	—	—	—	—	—	—

Table 9.15 AREA: SQUARE INCHES TO SQUARE CENTIMETRES

Basis: 1 in² = 6·4516 cm² (exactly)

square inches	0	1	2	3	4	5	6	7	8	9
					square centimetres					
0	—	6·452	12·903	19·355	25·806	32·258	38·710	45·161	51·613	58·064
10	64·516	70·968	77·419	83·871	90·322	96·774	103·226	109·677	116·129	122·580
20	129·032	135·484	141·935	148·387	154·838	161·290	167·742	174·193	180·645	187·096
30	193·548	200·000	206·451	212·903	219·354	225·806	232·258	238·709	245·161	251·612
40	258·064	264·516	270·967	277·419	283·870	290·322	296·774	303·225	309·677	316·128
50	322·580	329·032	335·483	341·935	348·386	354·838	361·290	367·741	374·193	380·644
60	387·096	393·548	399·999	406·451	412·902	419·354	425·806	432·257	438·709	445·160
70	451·612	458·064	464·515	470·967	477·418	483·870	490·322	496·773	503·225	509·676
80	516·128	522·580	529·031	535·483	541·934	548·386	554·838	561·289	567·741	574·192
90	580·644	587·096	593·547	599·999	606·450	612·902	619·354	625·805	632·257	638·708
100	645·160	651·612	658·063	664·515	670·966	677·418	683·870	690·321	696·773	703·224
110	709·676	716·128	722·579	729·031	735·482	741·934	748·386	754·837	761·289	767·740
120	774·192	780·644	787·095	793·547	799·998	806·450	812·902	819·353	825·805	832·256
130	838·708	845·160	851·611	858·063	864·514	870·966	877·418	883·869	890·321	896·772
140	903·224	909·676	916·127	922·579	929·030	935·482	941·934	948·385	954·837	961·288
150	967·740	974·192	980·643	987·095	993·546	999·998	1006·45	1012·90	1019·35	1025·80
160	1032·26	1038·71	1045·16	1051·61	1058·06	1064·51	1070·97	1077·42	1083·87	1090·32
170	1096·77	1103·22	1109·68	1116·13	1122·58	1129·03	1135·48	1141·93	1148·38	1154·84
180	1161·29	1167·74	1174·19	1180·64	1187·09	1193·55	1200·00	1206·45	1212·90	1219·35
190	1225·80	1232·26	1238·71	1245·16	1251·61	1258·06	1264·51	1270·97	1277·42	1283·87
200	1290·32	1296·77	1303·22	1309·67	1316·13	1322·58	1329·03	1335·48	1341·93	1348·38
210	1354·84	1361·29	1367·74	1374·19	1380·64	1387·09	1393·55	1400·00	1406·45	1412·90
220	1419·35	1425·80	1432·26	1438·71	1445·16	1451·61	1458·06	1464·51	1470·96	1477·42
230	1483·87	1490·32	1496·77	1503·22	1509·67	1516·13	1522·58	1529·03	1535·48	1541·93
240	1548·38	1554·84	1561·29	1567·74	1574·19	1580·64	1587·09	1593·55	1600·00	1606·45
250	1612·90	1619·35	1625·80	1632·25	1638·71	1645·16	1651·61	1658·06	1664·51	1670·96
260	1677·42	1683·87	1690·32	1696·77	1703·22	1709·67	1716·13	1722·58	1729·03	1735·48
270	1741·93	1748·38	1754·84	1761·29	1767·14	1774·19	1780·64	1787·09	1793·54	1800·00
280	1806·45	1812·90	1819·35	1825·80	1832·25	1838·71	1845·16	1851·61	1858·06	1864·51
290	1870·96	1877·42	1883·87	1890·32	1896·77	1903·22	1909·67	1916·13	1922·58	1929·03
300	1935·48	1941·93	1948·38	1954·83	1961·29	1967·74	1974·19	1980·64	1987·09	1993·54
310	2000·00	2006·45	2012·90	2019·35	2025·80	2032·25	2038·71	2045·16	2051·61	2058·06
320	2064·51	2070·96	2077·42	2083·87	2090·32	2096·77	2103·22	2109·67	2116·12	2122·58
330	2129·03	2135·48	2141·93	2148·38	2154·83	2161·29	2167·74	2174·19	2180·64	2187·09
340	2193·54	2200·00	2206·45	2212·90	2219·35	2225·80	2232·25	2238·71	2245·16	2251·61
350	2258·06	2264·51	2270·96	2277·41	2283·87	2290·32	2296·77	2303·22	2309·67	2316·12
360	2322·58	2329·03	2335·48	2341·93	2348·38	2354·83	2361·29	2367·74	2374·19	2380·64
370	2387·09	2393·54	2400·00	2406·45	2412·90	2419·35	2425·80	2432·25	2438·70	2445·16
380	2451·61	2458·06	2464·51	2470·96	2477·41	2483·87	2490·32	2496·77	2503·22	2509·67
390	2516·12	2522·58	2529·03	2535·48	2541·93	2548·38	2554·83	2561·29	2567·74	2574·19
400	2580·64	2587·09	2593·54	2599·99	2606·45	2612·90	2619·35	2625·80	2632·25	2638·70
410	2645·16	2651·61	2658·06	2664·51	2670·96	2677·41	2683·87	2690·32	2696·77	2703·22
420	2709·67	2716·12	2722·58	2729·03	2735·48	2741·93	2748·38	2754·83	2761·28	2767·74
430	2774·19	2780·64	2787·09	2793·54	2799·99	2806·45	2812·90	2819·35	2825·80	2832·25
440	2838·70	2845·16	2851·61	2858·06	2864·51	2870·96	2877·41	2883·87	2890·32	2896·77
450	2903·22	2909·67	2916·12	2922·57	2929·03	2935·48	2941·93	2948·38	2954·83	2961·28
460	2967·74	2974·19	2980·64	2987·09	2993·54	2999·99	3006·45	3012·90	3019·35	3025·80
470	3032·25	3038·70	3045·16	3051·61	3058·06	3064·51	3070·96	3077·41	3083·86	3090·32
480	3096·77	3103·22	3109·67	3116·12	3122·57	3129·03	3135·48	3141·93	3148·38	3154·83
490	3161·28	3167·74	3174·19	3180·64	3187·09	3193·54	3199·99	3206·45	3212·90	3219·35

continued

Table 9.15 AREA: SQUARE INCHES TO SQUARE CENTIMETRES *(continued)*

Basis: 1 in² = 6·4516 cm² (exactly)

square inches	0	1	2	3	4	5	6	7	8	9
					square centimetres					
500	3225·80	3232·25	3238·70	3245·15	3251·61	3258·06	3264·51	3270·96	3277·41	3283·86
510	3290·32	3296·77	3303·22	3309·67	3316·12	3322·57	3329·03	3335·48	3341·93	3348·38
520	3354·83	3361·28	3367·74	3374·19	3380·64	3387·09	3393·54	3399·99	3406·44	3412·90
530	3419·35	3425·80	3432·25	3438·70	3445·15	3451·61	3458·06	3464·51	3470·96	3477·41
540	3483·86	3490·32	3496·77	3503·22	3509·67	3516·12	3522·57	3529·03	3535·48	3541·93
550	3548·38	3554·83	3561·28	3567·73	3574·19	3580·64	3587·09	3593·54	3599·99	3606·44
560	3612·90	3619·35	3625·80	3632·25	3638·70	3645·15	3651·61	3658·06	3664·51	3670·96
570	3677·41	3683·86	3690·32	3696·77	3703·22	3709·67	3716·12	3722·57	3729·02	3735·48
580	3741·93	3748·38	3754·83	3761·28	3767·73	3774·19	3780·64	3787·09	3793·54	3799·99
590	3806·44	3812·90	3819·35	3825·80	3832·25	3838·70	3845·15	3851·61	3858·06	3864·51
600	3870·96	3877·41	3883·86	3890·31	3896·77	3903·22	3909·67	3916·12	3922·57	3929·02
610	3935·48	3941·93	3948·38	3954·83	3961·28	3967·73	3974·19	3980·64	3987·09	3993·54
620	3999·99	4006·44	4012·90	4019·35	4025·80	4032·25	4038·70	4045·15	4051·60	4058·06
630	4064·51	4070·96	4077·41	4083·86	4090·31	4096·77	4103·22	4109·67	4116·12	4122·57
640	4129·02	4135·48	4141·93	4148·38	4154·83	4161·28	4167·73	4174·19	4180·64	4187·09
650	4193·54	4199·99	4206·44	4212·89	4219·35	4225·80	4232·25	4238·70	4245·15	4251·60
660	4258·06	4264·51	4270·96	4277·41	4283·86	4290·31	4296·77	4303·22	4309·67	4316·12
670	4322·57	4329·02	4335·48	4341·93	4348·38	4354·83	4361·28	4367·73	4374·18	4380·64
680	4387·09	4393·54	4399·99	4406·44	4412·89	4419·35	4425·80	4432·25	4438·70	4445·15
690	4451·60	4458·06	4464·51	4470·96	4477·41	4483·86	4490·31	4496·77	4503·22	4509·67
700	4516·12	4522·57	4529·02	4535·47	4541·93	4548·38	4554·83	4561·28	4567·73	4574·18
710	4580·64	4587·09	4593·54	4599·99	4606·44	4612·89	4619·35	4625·80	4632·25	4638·70
720	4645·15	4651·60	4658·06	4664·51	4670·96	4677·41	4683·86	4690·31	4696·76	4703·22
730	4709·67	4716·12	4722·57	4729·02	4735·47	4741·93	4748·38	4754·83	4761·28	4767·73
740	4774·18	4780·64	4787·09	4793·54	4799·99	4806·44	4812·89	4819·35	4825·80	4832·25
750	4838·70	4845·15	4851·60	4858·05	4864·51	4870·96	4877·41	4883·86	4890·31	4896·76
760	4903·22	4909·67	4916·12	4922·57	4929·02	4935·47	4941·93	4948·38	4954·83	4961·28
770	4967·73	4974·18	4980·64	4987·09	4993·54	4999·99	5006·44	5012·89	5019·34	5025·80
780	5032·25	5038·70	5045·15	5051·60	5058·05	5064·51	5070·96	5077·41	5083·86	5090·31
790	5096·76	5103·22	5109·67	5116·12	5122·57	5129·02	5135·47	5141·93	5148·38	5154·83
800	5161·28	5167·73	5174·18	5180·63	5187·09	5193·54	5199·99	5206·44	5212·89	5219·34
810	5225·80	5232·25	5238·70	5245·15	5251·60	5258·05	5264·51	5270·96	5277·41	5283·86
820	5290·31	5296·76	5303·22	5309·67	5316·12	5322·57	5329·02	5335·47	5341·92	5348·38
830	5354·83	5361·28	5367·73	5374·18	5380·63	5387·09	5393·54	5399·99	5406·44	5412·89
840	5419·34	5425·80	5432·25	5438·70	5445·15	5451·60	5458·05	5464·51	5470·96	5477·41
850	5483·86	5490·31	5496·76	5503·21	5509·67	5516·12	5522·57	5529·02	5535·47	5541·92
860	5548·38	5554·83	5561·28	5567·73	5574·18	5580·63	5587·09	5593·54	5599·99	5606·44
870	5612·89	5619·34	5625·80	5632·25	5638·70	5645·15	5651·60	5658·05	5664·50	5670·96
880	5677·41	5683·86	5690·31	5696·76	5703·21	5709·67	5716·12	5722·57	5729·02	5735·47
890	5741·92	5748·38	5754·83	5761·28	5767·73	5774·18	5780·63	5787·09	5793·54	5799·99
900	5806·44	5812·89	5819·34	5825·79	5832·25	5838·70	5845·15	5851·60	5858·05	5864·50
910	5870·96	5877·41	5883·86	5890·31	5896·76	5903·21	5909·67	5916·12	5922·57	5929·02
920	5935·47	5941·92	5948·38	5954·83	5961·28	5967·73	5974·18	5980·63	5987·08	5993·54
930	5999·99	6006·44	6012·89	6019·34	6025·79	6032·25	6038·70	6045·15	6051·60	6058·05
940	6064·50	6070·96	6077·41	6083·86	6090·31	6096·76	6103·21	6109·67	6116·12	6122·57
950	6129·02	6135·47	6141·92	6148·37	6154·83	6161·28	6167·73	6174·18	6180·63	6187·08
960	6193·54	6199·99	6206·44	6212·89	6219·34	6225·79	6232·25	6238·70	6245·15	6251·60
970	6258·05	6264·50	6270·96	6277·41	6283·86	6290·31	6296·76	6303·21	6309·66	6316·12
980	6322·57	6329·02	6335·47	6341·92	6348·37	6354·83	6361·28	6367·73	6374·18	6380·63
990	6387·08	6393·54	6399·99	6406·44	6412·89	6419·34	6425·79	6432·25	6438·70	6445·15
1000	6451·60	—	—	—	—	—	—	—	—	—

Table 9.16 AREA: SQUARE FEET TO SQUARE METRES

Basis: 1 ft² = 0·092 903 04 m² (exactly)

square feet	0	1	2	3	4	5	6	7	8	9
					square metres					
0	—	0·09290	0·18581	0·27871	0·37161	0·46452	0·55742	0·65032	0·74322	0·83613
10	0·92903	1·02193	1·11484	1·20774	1·30064	1·39355	1·48645	1·57935	1·67225	1·76516
20	1·85806	1·95096	2·04387	2·13677	2·22967	2·32258	2·41548	2·50838	2·60129	2·69419
30	2·78709	2·87999	2·97290	3·06580	3·15870	3·25161	3·34451	3·43741	3·53032	3·62322
40	3·71612	3·80902	3·90193	3·99483	4·08773	4·18064	4·27354	4·36644	4·45935	5·55225
50	4·64515	4·73806	4·83096	4·92386	5·01676	5·10967	5·20257	5·29547	5·38838	5·48128
60	5·57418	5·66709	5·75999	5·85289	5·94579	6·03870	6·13160	6·22450	6·31741	6·41031
70	6·50321	6·59612	6·68902	6·78192	6·87482	6·96773	7·06063	7·15353	7·24644	7·33934
80	7·43224	7·52515	7·61805	7·71095	7·80386	7·89676	7·98966	8·08256	8·17547	8·26837
90	8·36127	8·45418	8·54708	8·63998	8·73289	8·82579	8·91869	9·01159	9·10450	9·19740
100	9·29030	9·38321	9·47611	9·56901	9·66192	9·75482	9·84772	9·94063	10·0335	10·1264
110	10·2193	10·3122	10·4051	10·4980	10·5909	10·6838	10·7768	10·8697	10·9626	11·0555
120	11·1484	11·2413	11·3342	11·4271	11·5200	11·6129	11·7058	11·7987	11·8916	11·9845
130	12·0774	12·1703	12·2632	12·3561	12·4490	12·5419	12·6348	12·7277	12·8206	12·9135
140	13·0064	13·0993	13·1922	13·2851	13·3780	13·4709	13·5638	13·6567	13·7496	13·8426
150	13·9355	14·0284	14·1213	14·2142	14·3071	14·4000	14·4929	14·5858	14·6787	14·7716
160	14·8645	14·9574	15·0503	15·1432	15·2361	15·3290	15·4219	15·5148	15·6077	16·7006
170	15·7935	15·8864	15·9793	16·0722	16·1651	16·2580	16·3509	16·4438	16·5367	16·6296
180	16·7225	16·8155	16·9084	17·0013	17·0942	17·1871	17·2800	17·3729	17·4658	17·5587
190	17·6516	17·7445	17·8374	17·9303	18·0232	18·1161	18·2090	18·3019	18·3948	18·4877
200	18·5806	18·6735	18·7664	18·8593	18·9522	19·0451	19·1380	19·2309	19·3238	19·4167
210	19·5096	19·6025	19·6954	19·7883	19·8813	19·9742	20·0671	20·1600	20·2529	20·3458
220	20·4387	20·5316	20·6245	20·7174	20·8103	20·9032	20·9961	21·0890	21·1819	21·2748
230	21·3677	21·4606	21·5535	21·6464	21·7393	21·8322	21·9251	22·0180	22·1109	22·2038
240	22·2967	22·3896	22·4825	22·5754	22·6683	22·7612	22·8541	22·9471	23·0400	23·1329
250	23·2258	23·3187	23·4116	23·5045	23·5974	23·6903	23·7832	23·8761	23·9690	24·0619
260	24·1548	24·2477	24·3406	24·4335	24·5264	24·6193	24·7122	24·8051	24·8980	24·9909
270	25·0838	25·1767	25·2696	25·3625	25·4554	25·5483	25·6412	25·7341	25·8270	25·9199
280	26·0129	26·1058	26·1987	26·2916	26·3845	26·4774	26·5703	26·6632	26·7561	26·8490
290	26·9419	27·0348	27·1277	27·2206	27·3135	27·4064	27·4993	27·5922	27·6851	27·7780
300	27·8709	27·9638	28·0567	28·1496	28·2425	28·3354	28·4283	28·5212	28·6141	28·7070
310	28·7999	28·8928	28·9857	29·0787	29·1716	29·2645	29·3574	29·4503	29·5432	29·6361
320	29·7290	29·8219	29·9148	30·0077	30·1006	30·1935	30·2864	30·3793	30·4722	30·5651
330	30·6580	30·7509	30·8438	30·9367	21·0296	31·1225	31·2154	31·3083	31·4012	31·4941
340	31·5870	31·6799	31·7728	31·8657	31·9586	32·0515	32·1445	32·2374	32·3303	32·4232
350	32·5161	32·6090	32·7019	32·7948	32·8877	32·9806	33·0735	33·1664	33·2593	33·3522
360	33·4451	33·5380	33·6309	33·7238	33·8167	33·9096	34·0025	34·0954	34·1883	34·2812
370	34·3741	34·4670	34·5599	34·6528	34·7457	34·8386	34·9315	35·0244	35·1173	35·2103
380	35·3032	35·3961	35·4890	35·5819	35·6748	35·7677	35·8606	35·9535	36·0464	36·1393
390	36·2322	36·3251	36·4180	36·5109	36·6038	36·6967	36·7896	36·8825	36·9754	37·0683
400	37·1612	37·2541	37·3470	37·4399	37·5328	37·6257	37·7186	37·8115	37·9044	37·9973
410	38·0902	38·1831	38·2761	38·3690	38·4619	38·5548	38·6477	38·7406	38·8335	38·9264
420	39·0193	39·1122	39·2051	39·2980	39·3909	39·4838	39·5767	39·6696	39·7625	39·8554
430	39·9483	40·0412	40·1341	40·2270	40·3199	40·4128	40·5057	40·5986	40·6915	40·7844
440	40·8773	40·9702	41·0631	41·1560	41·2489	41·3419	41·4348	41·5277	41·6206	41·7135
450	41·8064	41·8993	41·9922	42·0851	42·1780	42·2709	42·3638	42·4567	42·5496	42·6425
460	42·7354	42·8283	42·9212	43·0141	43·1070	43·1999	43·2928	43·3857	43·4786	43·5715
470	43·6644	43·7573	43·8502	43·9431	44·0360	44·1289	44·2218	44·3148	44·4077	44·5006
480	44·5935	44·6864	44·7793	44·8722	44·9651	45·0580	45·1509	45·2438	45·3367	45·4296
490	45·5225	45·6154	45·7083	45·8012	45·8941	45·9870	46·0799	46·1728	46·2657	46·3586

continued

Table 9.16 AREA: SQUARE FEET TO SQUARE METRES *(continued)*

Basis: 1 ft² = 0·092 903 04 m² (exactly)

square feet	0	1	2	3	4	5	6	7	8	9
					square metres					
500	46·4515	46·5444	46·6373	46·7302	46·8231	46·9160	47·0089	47·1018	47·1947	47·2876
510	47·3806	47·4735	47·5664	47·6593	47·7522	47·8451	47·9380	48·0309	48·1238	48·2167
520	48·3096	48·4025	48·4954	48·5883	48·6812	48·7741	48·8670	48·9599	49·0528	49·1457
530	49·2386	49·3315	49·4244	49·5173	49·6102	49·7031	49·7960	49·8889	49·9818	50·0747
540	50·1676	50·2605	50·3534	50·4464	50·5393	50·6322	50·7251	50·8180	50·9109	51·0038
550	51·0967	51·1896	51·2825	51·3754	51·4683	51·5612	51·6541	51·7470	51·8399	51·9328
560	52·0257	52·1186	52·2115	52·3044	52·3973	52·4902	52·5831	52·6760	52·7689	52·8618
570	52·9547	53·0476	53·1405	53·2334	53·3263	53·4192	53·5122	53·6051	53·6980	53·7909
580	53·8838	53·9767	54·0696	54·1625	54·2554	54·3483	54·4412	54·5341	54·6270	54·7199
590	54·8128	54·9057	54·9986	55·0915	55·1844	55·2773	55·3702	55·4631	55·5560	55·6489
600	55·7418	55·8347	55·9276	56·0205	56·1134	56·2063	56·2992	56·3921	56·4850	56·5780
610	56·6709	56·7638	56·8567	56·9496	57·0425	57·1354	57·2283	57·3212	57·4141	57·5070
620	57·5999	57·6928	57·7857	57·8786	57·9715	58·0644	58·1573	58·2502	58·3431	58·4360
630	58·5289	58·6218	58·7147	58·8076	58·9005	58·9934	59·0863	59·1792	59·2721	59·3650
640	59·4579	59·5508	59·6438	59·7367	59·8296	59·9225	60·0154	60·1083	60·2012	60·2941
650	60·3870	60·4799	60·5728	60·6657	60·7586	60·8515	60·9444	61·0373	61·1302	61·2231
660	61·3160	61·4089	61·5018	61·5947	61·6876	61·7805	61·8734	61·9663	62·0592	62·1521
670	62·2450	62·3379	62·4308	62·5237	62·6166	62·7096	62·8025	62·8954	62·9883	63·0812
680	63·1741	63·2670	63·3599	63·4528	63·5457	63·6386	63·7315	63·8244	63·9173	64·0102
690	64·1031	64·1960	64·2889	64·3818	64·4747	64·5676	64·6605	64·7534	64·8463	64·9392
700	65·0321	65·1250	65·2179	65·3108	65·4037	65·4966	65·5895	65·6824	65·7754	65·8683
710	65·9612	66·0541	66·1470	66·2399	66·3328	66·4257	66·5186	66·6115	66·7044	66·7973
720	66·8902	66·9831	67·0760	67·1689	67·2618	67·3547	67·4476	67·5405	67·6334	67·7263
730	67·8192	67·9121	68·0050	68·0979	68·1908	68·2837	68·3766	68·4695	68·5624	68·6553
740	68·7482	68·8412	68·9341	69·0270	69·1199	69·2128	69·3057	69·3986	69·4915	69·5844
750	69·6773	69·7702	69·8631	69·9560	70·0489	70·1418	70·2347	70·3276	70·4205	70·5134
760	70·6063	70·6992	70·7921	70·8850	70·9779	71·0708	71·1637	71·2566	71·3495	71·4424
770	71·5353	71·6282	71·7211	71·8140	71·9070	71·9999	72·0928	72·1857	72·2786	72·3715
780	72·4644	72·5573	72·6502	72·7431	72·8360	72·9289	73·0218	73·1147	73·2076	73·3005
790	73·3934	73·4863	73·5792	73·6721	73·7650	73·8579	73·9508	74·0437	74·1366	74·2295
800	74·3224	74·4153	74·5082	74·6011	74·6940	74·7869	74·8799	74·9728	75·0657	75·1586
810	75·2515	75·3444	75·4373	75·5302	75·6231	75·7160	75·8089	75·9018	75·9947	76·0876
820	76·1805	76·2734	76·3663	76·4592	76·5521	76·6450	76·7379	76·8308	76·9237	77·0166
830	77·1095	77·2024	77·2953	77·3882	77·4811	77·5740	77·6669	77·7598	77·8527	77·9457
840	78·0386	78·1315	78·2244	78·3173	78·4102	78·5031	78·5960	78·6889	78·7818	78·8747
850	78·9676	79·0605	79·1534	79·2463	79·3392	79·4321	79·5250	79·6179	79·7108	79·8037
860	79·8966	79·9895	80·0824	80·1753	80·2682	80·3611	80·4540	80·5469	80·6398	80·7327
870	80·8256	80·9185	81·0115	81·1044	81·1973	81·2902	81·3831	81·4760	81·5689	81·6618
880	81·7547	81·8476	81·9405	82·0334	82·1263	82·2192	82·3121	82·4050	82·4979	82·5908
890	82·6837	82·7766	82·8695	82·9624	83·0553	83·1482	83·2411	83·3340	83·4269	83·5198
900	83·6127	83·7056	83·7985	83·8914	83·9843	84·0773	84·1702	84·2631	84·3560	84·4489
910	84·5418	84·6347	84·7276	84·8205	84·9134	85·0063	85·0992	85·1921	85·2850	85·3779
920	85·4708	85·5637	85·6566	85·7495	85·8424	85·9353	86·0282	86·1211	86·2140	86·3069
930	86·3998	86·4927	86·5856	86·6785	86·7714	86·8643	86·9572	87·0501	87·1431	87·2360
940	87·3289	87·4218	87·5147	87·6076	87·7005	87·7934	87·8863	87·9792	88·0721	88·1650
950	88·2579	88·3508	88·4437	88·5366	88·6295	88·7224	88·8153	88·9082	89·0011	89·0940
960	89·1869	89·2798	89·3727	89·4656	89·5585	89·6514	89·7443	89·8372	89·9301	90·0230
970	90·1159	90·2089	90·3018	90·3947	90·4876	90·5805	90·6734	90·7663	90·8592	90·9521
980	91·0450	91·1379	91·2308	91·3237	91·4166	91·5095	91·6024	91·6953	91·7882	91·8811
990	91·9740	92·0669	92·1598	92·2527	92·3456	92·4385	92·5314	92·6243	92·7172	92·8101
1000	92·9030	—	—	—	—	—	—	—	—	—

Table 9.17 AREA: SQUARE YARDS TO SQUARE METRES

Basis: 1 yd² = 0·836 127 36 m² (exactly)

square yards	0	1	2	3	4	5	6	7	8	9
					square metres					
0	—	0·8361	1·6723	2·5084	3·3445	4·1806	5·0168	5·8529	6·6890	7·5251
10	8·3613	9·1974	10·0335	10·8697	11·7058	12·5419	13·3780	14·2142	15·0503	15·8864
20	16·7225	17·5587	18·3948	19·2309	20·0671	20·9032	21·7393	22·5754	23·4116	24·2477
30	25·0838	25·9199	26·7561	27·5922	28·4283	29·2645	30·1006	30·9367	31·7728	32·6090
40	33·4451	34·2812	35·1173	35·9535	36·7896	37·6257	38·4619	39·2980	40·1341	40·9702
50	41·8064	42·6425	43·4786	44·3148	45·1509	45·9870	46·8231	47·6593	48·4954	49·3315
60	50·1676	51·0038	51·8399	52·6760	53·5122	54·3483	55·1844	56·0205	56·8567	57·6928
70	58·5289	59·3650	60·2012	61·0373	61·8734	62·7096	63·5457	64·3818	65·2179	66·0541
80	66·8902	67·7263	68·5624	69·3986	70·2347	71·0708	71·9070	72·7431	73·5792	74·4153
90	75·2515	76·0876	76·9237	77·7598	78·5960	79·4321	80·2682	81·1044	81·9405	82·7766
100	83·6127	84·4489	85·2850	86·1211	86·9572	87·7934	88·6295	89·4656	90·3018	91·1379
110	91·9740	92·8101	93·6463	94·4824	95·3185	96·1546	96·9908	97·8269	98·6630	99·4992
120	100·335	101·171	102·008	102·844	103·680	104·516	105·352	106·188	107·024	107·860
130	108·697	109·533	110·369	111·205	112·041	112·877	113·713	114·549	115·386	116·222
140	117·058	117·894	118·730	119·566	120·402	121·238	122·075	122·911	123·747	124·583
150	125·419	126·255	127·091	127·927	128·764	129·600	130·436	131·272	132·108	132·944
160	133·780	134·617	135·453	136·289	137·125	137·961	138·797	139·633	140·469	141·306
170	142·142	142·978	143·814	144·650	145·486	146·322	147·158	147·995	148·831	149·667
180	150·503	151·339	152·175	153·011	153·847	154·684	155·520	156·356	157·192	158·028
190	158·864	159·700	160·536	161·373	162·209	163·045	163·881	164·717	165·553	166·389
200	167·225	168·062	168·898	169·734	170·570	171·406	172·242	173·078	173·914	174·751
210	175·587	176·423	177·259	178·095	178·931	179·767	180·604	181·440	182·276	183·112
220	183·948	184·784	185·620	186·456	187·293	188·129	188·965	189·801	190·637	191·473
230	192·309	193·145	193·982	194·818	195·654	196·490	197·326	198·162	198·998	199·834
240	200·671	201·507	202·343	203·179	204·015	204·851	205·687	206·523	207·360	208·196
250	209·032	209·868	210·704	211·540	212·376	213·212	214·049	214·885	215·721	216·557
260	217·393	218·229	219·065	219·901	220·738	221·574	222·410	223·246	224·082	224·918
270	225·754	226·591	227·427	228·263	229·099	229·935	230·771	231·607	232·443	233·280
280	234·116	234·952	235·788	236·624	237·460	238·296	239·132	239·969	240·805	241·641
290	242·477	243·313	244·149	244·985	245·821	246·658	247·494	248·330	249·166	250·002
300	250·838	251·674	252·510	253·347	254·183	255·019	255·855	256·691	257·527	258·363
310	259·199	260·036	260·872	261·708	262·544	263·380	264·216	265·052	265·889	266·725
320	267·561	268·397	269·233	270·069	270·905	271·741	272·578	273·414	274·250	275·086
330	275·922	276·758	277·594	278·430	279·267	280·103	280·939	281·775	282·611	283·447
340	284·283	285·119	285·956	286·792	287·628	288·464	289·300	290·136	290·972	291·808
350	292·645	293·481	294·317	295·153	295·989	296·825	297·661	298·497	299·334	300·170
360	301·006	301·842	302·678	303·514	304·350	305·186	306·023	306·859	307·695	308·531
370	309·367	310·203	311·039	311·876	312·712	313·548	314·384	315·220	316·056	316·892
380	317·728	318·565	319·401	320·237	321·073	321·909	322·745	323·581	324·417	325·254
390	326·090	326·926	327·762	328·598	329·434	330·270	331·106	331·943	332·779	333·615
400	334·451	335·287	336·123	336·959	337·795	338·632	339·468	340·304	341·140	341·976
410	342·812	343·648	344·484	345·321	346·157	346·993	347·829	348·665	349·501	350·337
420	351·173	352·010	352·846	353·682	354·518	355·354	356·190	357·026	357·863	358·699
430	359·535	360·371	361·207	362·043	362·879	363·715	364·552	365·388	366·224	367·060
440	367·896	368·732	369·568	370·404	371·241	372·077	372·913	373·749	374·585	375·421
450	376·257	377·093	377·930	378·766	379·602	380·438	381·274	382·110	382·946	383·782
460	384·619	385·455	386·291	387·127	387·963	388·799	389·635	390·471	391·308	392·144
470	392·980	393·816	394·652	395·488	396·324	397·160	397·997	398·833	399·669	400·505
480	401·341	402·177	403·013	403·850	404·686	405·522	406·358	407·194	408·030	408·866
490	409·702	410·539	411·375	412·211	413·047	413·883	414·719	415·555	416·391	417·228

continued

Table 9.17 AREA: SQUARE YARDS TO SQUARE METRES *(continued)*

Basis: 1 yd² = 0·836 127 36 m² (exactly)

square yards	0	1	2	3	4	5	6	7	8	9
					square metres					
500	418·064	418·900	419·736	420·572	421·408	422·244	423·080	423·917	424·753	425·589
510	426·425	427·261	428·097	428·933	429·769	430·606	431·442	432·278	433·114	433·950
520	434·786	435·622	436·458	437·295	438·131	438·967	439·803	440·639	441·475	442·311
530	443·148	443·984	444·820	445·656	446·492	447·328	448·164	449·000	449·837	450·673
540	451·509	452·345	453·181	454·017	454·853	455·689	456·526	457·362	458·198	459·034
550	459·870	460·706	461·542	462·378	463·215	464·051	464·887	465·723	466·559	467·395
560	468·231	469·067	469·904	470·740	471·576	472·412	473·248	474·084	474·920	475·756
570	476·593	477·429	478·265	479·101	479·937	480·773	481·609	482·445	483·282	484·118
580	484·954	485·790	486·626	487·462	488·298	489·135	489·971	490·807	491·643	492·479
590	493·315	494·151	494·987	495·824	496·660	497·496	498·332	499·168	500·004	500·840
600	501·676	502·513	503·349	504·185	505·021	505·857	506·693	507·529	508·365	509·202
610	510·038	510·874	511·710	512·546	513·382	514·218	515·054	515·891	516·727	517·563
620	518·399	519·235	520·071	520·907	521·743	522·580	523·416	524·252	525·088	525·924
630	526·760	527·596	528·432	529·269	530·105	530·941	531·777	532·613	533·449	534·285
640	535·122	535·958	536·794	537·630	538·466	539·302	540·138	540·974	541·811	542·647
650	543·483	544·319	545·155	545·991	546·827	547·663	548·500	549·336	550·172	551·008
660	551·844	552·680	553·516	554·352	555·189	556·025	556·861	557·697	558·533	559·369
670	560·205	561·041	561·878	562·714	563·550	564·386	565·222	566·058	566·894	567·730
680	568·567	569·403	570·239	571·075	571·911	572·747	573·583	574·419	575·256	576·092
690	576·928	577·764	578·600	579·436	580·272	581·109	581·945	582·781	583·617	584·453
700	585·289	586·125	586·961	587·798	588·634	589·470	590·306	591·142	591·978	592·814
710	593·650	594·487	595·323	596·159	596·995	597·831	598·667	599·503	600·339	601·176
720	602·012	602·848	603·684	604·520	605·356	606·192	607·028	607·865	608·701	609·537
730	610·373	611·209	612·045	612·881	613·717	614·554	615·390	616·226	617·062	617·898
740	618·734	619·570	620·407	621·243	622·079	622·915	623·751	624·587	625·423	626·259
750	627·096	627·932	628·768	629·604	630·440	631·276	632·112	632·948	633·785	634·621
760	635·457	636·293	637·129	637·965	638·801	639·637	640·474	641·310	642·146	642·982
770	643·818	644·654	645·490	646·326	647·163	647·999	648·835	649·671	650·507	651·343
780	652·179	653·015	653·852	654·688	655·524	656·360	657·196	658·032	658·868	659·704
790	660·541	661·377	662·213	663·049	663·885	664·721	665·557	666·394	667·230	668·066
800	668·902	669·738	670·574	671·410	672·246	673·083	673·919	674·755	675·591	676·427
810	677·263	678·099	678·935	679·772	680·608	681·444	682·280	683·116	683·952	684·788
820	685·624	686·461	687·297	688·133	688·969	689·805	690·641	691·477	692·313	693·150
830	693·986	694·822	695·658	696·494	697·330	698·166	699·002	699·839	700·675	701·511
840	702·347	703·183	704·019	704·855	705·691	706·528	707·364	708·200	709·036	709·872
850	710·708	711·544	712·381	713·217	714·053	714·889	715·725	716·561	717·397	718·233
860	719·070	719·906	720·742	721·578	722·414	723·250	724·086	724·922	725·759	726·595
870	727·431	728·267	729·103	729·939	730·775	731·611	732·448	733·284	734·120	734·956
880	735·792	736·628	737·464	738·300	739·137	739·973	740·809	741·645	742·481	743·317
890	744·153	744·989	745·826	746·662	747·498	748·334	749·170	750·006	750·842	751·678
900	752·515	753·351	754·187	755·023	755·859	756·695	757·531	758·368	759·204	760·040
910	760·876	761·712	762·548	763·384	764·220	765·057	765·893	766·729	767·565	768·401
920	769·237	770·073	770·909	771·746	772·582	773·418	774·254	775·090	775·926	776·762
930	777·598	778·435	779·271	780·107	780·943	781·779	782·615	783·451	784·287	785·124
940	785·960	786·796	787·632	788·468	789·304	790·140	790·976	791·813	792·649	793·485
950	794·321	795·157	795·993	796·829	797·666	798·502	799·338	800·174	801·010	801·846
960	802·682	803·518	804·355	805·191	806·027	806·863	807·699	808·535	809·371	810·207
970	811·044	811·880	812·716	813·552	814·388	815·224	816·060	816·896	817·733	818·569
980	819·405	820·241	821·077	821·913	822·749	823·585	824·422	825·258	826·094	826·930
990	827·766	828·602	829·438	830·274	831·111	831·947	832·783	833·619	834·455	835·291
1000	836·127	—	—	—	—	—	—	—	—	—

Table 9.18 VOLUME: CUBIC FEET TO CUBIC METRES

Basis: 1 ft = 0·3048 m (exactly)

cubic feet	0	1	2	3	4	5	6	7	8	9
					cubic metres					
0	—	0·02832	0·05663	0·08495	0·11327	0·14158	0·16990	0·19822	0·22653	0·25485
10	0·28317	0·31149	0·33980	0·36812	0·39644	0·42475	0·45307	0·48139	0·50970	0·53802
20	0·56634	0·59465	0·62297	0·65129	0·67960	0·70792	0·73624	0·76455	0·79287	0·82119
30	0·84951	0·87782	0·90614	0·93446	0·96277	0·99109	1·01941	1·04772	1·07604	1·10436
40	1·13267	1·16099	1·18931	1·21762	1·24594	1·27426	1·30257	1·33089	1·35921	1·38753
50	1·41584	1·44416	1·47248	1·50079	1·52911	1·55743	1·58574	1·61406	1·64238	1·67069
60	1·69901	1·72733	1·75564	1·78396	1·81228	1·84060	1·86891	1·89723	1·92555	1·95386
70	1·98218	2·01050	2·03881	2·06713	2·09545	2·12376	2·15208	2·18040	2·20871	2·23703
80	2·26535	2·29366	2·32198	2·35030	2·37862	2·40693	2·43525	2·46357	2·49188	2·52020
90	2·54852	2·57683	2·60515	2·63347	2·66178	2·69010	2·71842	2·74673	2·77505	2·80337
100	2·83168	2·86000	2·88832	2·91664	2·94495	2·97327	3·00159	3·02990	3·05822	3·08654
110	3·11485	3·14317	3·17149	3·19980	3·22812	3·25644	3·28475	3·31307	3·34139	3·36970
120	3·39802	3·42634	3·45466	3·48297	3·51129	3·53961	3·56792	3·59624	3·62456	3·65287
130	3·68119	3·70951	3·73782	3·76614	3·79446	3·82277	3·85109	3·87941	3·90772	3·93604
140	3·96436	3·99268	4·02099	4·04931	4·07763	4·10594	4·13426	4·16258	4·19089	4·21921
150	4·24753	4·27584	4·30416	4·33248	4·36079	4·38911	4·41743	4·44574	4·47406	4·50238
160	4·53070	4·55901	4·58733	4·61565	4·64396	4·67228	4·70060	4·72891	4·75723	4·78555
170	4·81386	4·84218	4·87050	4·89881	4·92713	4·95545	4·98377	5·01208	5·04040	5·06872
180	5·09703	5·12535	5·15367	5·18198	5·21030	5·23862	5·26693	5·29525	5·32357	5·35188
190	5·38020	5·40852	5·43683	5·46515	5·49347	5·52179	5·55010	5·57842	5·60674	5·63505
200	5·66337	5·69169	5·72000	5·74832	5·77664	5·80495	5·83327	5·86159	5·88990	5·91822
210	5·94654	5·97485	6·00317	6·03149	6·05981	6·08812	6·11644	6·14476	6·17307	6·20139
220	6·22971	6·25802	6·28634	6·31466	6·34297	6·37129	6·39961	6·42792	6·45624	6·48456
230	6·51287	6·54119	6·56951	6·59783	6·62614	6·65446	6·68278	6·71109	6·73941	6·76773
240	6·79604	6·82436	6·85268	6·88099	6·90931	6·93763	6·96594	6·99426	7·02258	7·05089
250	7·07921	7·10753	7·13585	7·16416	7·19248	7·22080	7·24911	7·27743	7·30575	7·33406
260	7·36238	7·39070	7·41901	7·44733	7·47565	7·50396	7·53228	7·56060	7·58891	7·61723
270	7·64555	7·67387	7·70218	7·73050	7·75882	7·78713	7·81545	7·84377	7·87208	7·90040
280	7·92872	7·95703	7·98535	8·01367	8·04198	8·07030	8·09862	8·12693	8·15525	8·18357
290	8·21189	8·24020	8·26852	8·29684	8·32515	8·35347	8·38179	8·41010	8·43842	8·46674
300	8·49505	8·52337	8·55169	8·58000	8·60832	8·63664	8·66496	8·69327	8·72159	8·74991
310	8·77822	8·80654	8·83486	8·86317	8·89149	8·91981	8·94812	8·97644	9·00476	9·03307
320	9·06139	9·08971	9·11802	9·14634	9·17466	9·20298	9·23129	9·25961	9·28793	9·31624
330	9·34456	9·37288	9·40119	9·42951	9·45783	9·48614	9·51446	9·54278	9·57109	9·59941
340	9·62773	9·65604	9·68436	9·71268	9·74100	9·76931	9·79763	9·82595	9·85426	9·88258
350	9·91090	9·93921	9·96753	9·99585	10·0242	10·0525	10·0808	10·1091	10·1374	10·1657
360	10·1941	10·2224	10·2507	10·2790	10·3073	10·3356	10·3640	10·3923	10·4206	10·4489
370	10·4772	10·5056	10·5339	10·5622	10·5905	10·6188	10·6471	10·6755	10·7038	10·7321
380	10·7604	10·7887	10·8170	10·8454	10·8737	10·9020	10·9303	10·9586	10·9869	11·0153
390	11·0436	11·0719	11·1002	11·1285	11·1568	11·1852	11·2135	11·2418	11·2701	11·2984
400	11·3267	11·3551	11·3834	11·4117	11·4400	11·4683	11·4966	11·5250	11·5533	11·5816
410	11·6099	11·6382	11·6665	11·6949	11·7232	11·7515	11·7798	11·8081	11·8364	11·8648
420	11·8931	11·9214	11·9497	11·9780	12·0063	12·0347	12·0630	12·0913	12·1196	12·1479
430	12·1762	12·2046	12·2329	12·2612	12·2895	12·3178	12·3461	12·3745	12·4028	12·4311
440	12·4594	12·4877	12·5160	12·5444	12·5727	12·6010	12·6293	12·6576	12·6859	12·7143
450	12·7426	12·7709	12·7992	12·8275	12·8558	12·8842	12·9125	12·9408	12·9691	12·9974
460	13·0257	13·0541	13·0824	13·1107	13·1390	13·1673	13·1957	13·2240	13·2523	13·2806
470	13·3089	13·3372	13·3656	13·3939	13·4222	13·4505	13·4788	13·5071	13·5355	13·5638
480	13·5921	13·6204	13·6487	13·6770	13·7054	13·7337	13·7620	13·7903	13·8186	13·8469
490	13·8753	13·9036	13·9319	13·9602	13·9885	14·0168	14·0452	14·0735	14·1018	14·1301

continued

Table 9.18 VOLUME: CUBIC FEET TO CUBIC METRES *(continued)*

Basis: 1 ft = 0·3048 m (exactly)

cubic feet	0	1	2	3	4	5	6	7	8	9
					cubic metres					
500	14·1584	14·1867	14·2151	14·2434	14·2717	14·3000	14·3283	14·3566	14·3850	14·4133
510	14·4416	14·4699	14·4982	14·5265	14·5549	14·5832	14·6115	14·6398	14·6681	14·6964
520	14·7248	14·7531	14·7814	14·8097	14·8380	14·8663	14·8947	14·9230	14·9513	14·9796
530	15·0079	15·0362	15·0646	15·0929	15·1212	15·1495	15·1778	15·2061	15·2345	15·2628
540	15·2911	15·3194	15·3477	15·3760	15·4044	15·4327	15·4610	15·4893	15·5176	15·5459
550	15·5743	15·6026	15·6309	15·6592	15·6875	15·7158	15·7442	15·7725	15·8008	15·8291
560	15·8574	15·8858	15·9141	15·9424	15·9707	15·9990	16·0273	16·0557	16·0840	16·1123
570	16·1406	16·1689	16·1972	16·2256	16·2539	16·2822	16·3105	16·3388	16·3671	16·3955
580	·16·4238	16·4521	16·4804	16·5087	16·5370	16·5654	16·5937	16·6220	16·6503	16·6786
590	16·7069	16·7353	16·7636	16·7919	16·8202	16·8485	16·8768	16·9052	16·9335	16·9618
600	16·9901	17·0184	17·0467	17·0751	17·1034	17·1317	17·1600	17·1883	17·2166	17·2450
610	17·2733	17·3016	17·3299	17·3582	17·3865	17·4149	17·4432	17·4715	17·4998	17·5281
620	17·5564	17·5848	17·6131	17·6414	17·6697	17·6980	17·7263	17·7547	17·7830	17·8113
630	17·8396	17·8679	17·8962	17·9246	17·9529	17·9812	18·0095	18·0378	18·0661	18·0945
640	18·1228	18·1511	18·1794	18·2077	18·2360	18·2644	18·2927	18·3210	18·3493	18·3776
650	18·4060	18·4343	18·4626	18·4909	18·5192	18·5475	18·5759	18·6042	18·6325	18·6608
660	18·6891	18·7174	18·7458	18·7741	18·8024	18·8307	18·8590	18·8873	18·9157	18·9440
670	18·9723	19·0006	19·0289	19·0572	19·0856	19·1139	19·1422	19·1705	19·1988	19·2271
680	19·2555	19·2838	19·3121	19·3404	19·3687	19·3970	19·4254	19·4537	19·4820	19·5103
690	19·5386	19·5669	19·5953	19·6236	19·6519	19·6802	19·7085	19·7368	19·7652	19·7935
700	19·8218	19·8501	19·8784	19·9067	19·9351	19·9634	19·9917	20·0200	20·0483	20·0766
710	20·1050	20·1333	20·1616	20·1899	20·2182	20·2465	20·2749	20·3032	20·3315	20·3598
720	20·3881	20·4164	20·4448	20·4731	20·5014	20·5297	20·5580	20·5863	20·6147	20·6430
730	20·6713	20·6996	20·7279	20·7562	20·7846	20·8129	20·8412	20·8695	20·8978	20·9261
740	20·9545	20·9828	21·0111	21·0394	21·0677	21·0961	21·1244	21·1527	21·1810	21·2093
750	21·2376	21·2660	21·2943	21·3226	21·3509	21·3792	21·4075	21·4359	21·4642	21·4925
760	21·5208	21·5491	21·5774	21·6058	21·6341	21·6624	21·6907	21·7190	21·7473	21·7757
770	21·8040	21·8323	21·8606	21·8889	21·9172	21·9456	21·9739	22·0022	22·0305	22·0588
780	22·0871	22·1155	22·1438	22·1721	22·2004	22·2287	22·2570	22·2854	22·3137	22·3420
790	22·3703	22·3986	22·4269	22·4553	22·4836	22·5119	22·5402	22·5685	22·5968	22·6252
800	22·6535	22·6818	22·7101	22·7384	22·7667	22·7951	22·8234	22·8517	22·8800	22·9083
810	22·9366	22·9650	22·9933	23·0216	23·0499	23·0782	23·1065	23·1349	23·1632	23·1915
820	23·2198	23·2481	23·2764	23·3048	23·3331	23·3614	23·3897	23·4180	23·4463	23·4747
830	23·5030	23·5313	23·5596	23·5879	23·6163	23·6446	23·6729	23·7012	23·7295	23·7578
840	23·7862	23·8145	23·8428	23·8711	23·8994	23·9277	23·9561	23·9844	24·0127	24·0410
850	24·0693	24·0976	24·1260	24·1543	24·1826	24·2109	24·2392	24·2675	24·2959	24·3242
860	24·3525	24·3808	24·4091	24·4374	24·4658	24·4941	24·5224	24·5507	24·5790	24·6073
870	24·6357	24·6640	24·6923	24·7206	24·7489	24·7772	24·8056	24·8339	24·8622	24·8905
880	24·9188	24·9471	24·9755	25·0038	25·0321	25·0604	25·0887	25·1170	25·1454	25·1737
890	25·2020	25·2303	25·2586	25·2869	25·3153	25·3436	25·3719	25·4002	25·4285	25·4568
900	25·4852	25·5135	25·5418	25·5701	25·5984	25·6267	25·6551	25·6834	25·7117	25·7400
910	25·7683	25·7966	25·8250	25·8533	25·8816	25·9099	25·9382	25·9665	25·9949	26·0232
920	26·0515	26·0798	26·1081	26·1364	26·1648	26·1931	26·2214	26·2497	27·2780	26·3064
930	26·3347	26·3630	26·3913	26·4196	26·4479	26·4763	26·5046	26·5329	26·5612	26·5895
940	26·6178	26·6462	26·6745	26·7028	26·7311	26·7594	26·7877	26·8161	26·8444	26·8727
950	26·9010	26·9293	26·9576	26·9860	27·0143	27·0426	27·0709	27·0992	27·1275	27·1559
960	27·1842	27·2125	27·2408	27·2691	27·2974	27·3258	27·3541	27·3824	27·4107	27·4390
970	27·4673	27·4957	27·5240	27·5523	27·5806	27·6089	27·6372	27·6656	27·6939	27·7222
980	27·7505	27·7788	27·8071	27·8355	27·8638	27·8921	27·9204	27·9487	27·9770	28·0054
990	28·0337	28·0620	28·0903	28·1186	28·1469	28·1753	28·2036	28·2319	28·2602	28·2885
1000	28·3168	—	—	—	—	—	—	—	—	—

Table 9.19 VOLUME: CUBIC YARDS TO CUBIC METRES

Basis: 1 yd = 0·9144 m (exactly)

cubic yards	0	1	2	3	4	5	6	7	8	9
					cubic metres					
0	—	0·7646	1·5291	2·2937	3·0582	3·8228	4·5873	5·3519	6·1164	6·8810
10	7·6455	8·4101	9·1747	9·9392	10·7038	11·4683	12·2329	12·9974	13·7620	14·5265
20	15·2911	16·0557	16·8202	17·5848	18·3493	19·1139	19·8784	20·6430	21·4075	22·1721
30	22·9366	23·7012	24·4658	25·2303	25·9949	26·7594	27·5240	28·2885	29·0531	29·8176
40	30·5822	31·3467	32·1113	32·8759	33·6404	34·4050	35·1695	35·9341	36·6986	37·4632
50	38·2277	38·9923	39·7569	40·5214	41·2860	42·0505	42·8151	43·5796	44·3442	45·1087
60	45·8733	46·6378	47·4024	48·1670	48·9315	49·6961	50·4606	51·2252	51·9897	52·7543
70	53·5188	54·2834	55·0480	55·8125	56·5771	57·3416	58·1062	58·8707	59·6353	60·3998
80	61·1644	61·9289	62·6935	63·4581	64·2226	64·9872	65·7517	66·5163	67·2808	68·0454
90	68·8099	69·5745	70·3390	71·1036	71·8682	72·6327	73·3973	74·1618	74·9264	75·6909
100	76·4555	—	—	—	—	—	—	—	—	—

Table 9.20 VOLUME: UK GALLONS TO LITRES

Basis: 1 UK gal = 4·545 96 litres

UK gallons	0	1	2	3	4	5	6	7	8	9
					litres					
0	—	4·546	9·092	13·638	18·184	22·730	27·276	31·822	36·368	40·914
10	45·460	50·006	54·552	59·097	63·643	68·189	72·735	77·281	81·827	86·373
20	90·919	95·465	100·011	104·557	109·103	113·649	118·195	122·741	127·287	131·833
30	136·379	140·925	145·471	150·017	154·563	159·109	163·655	168·201	172·746	177·292
40	181·838	186·384	190·930	195·476	200·022	204·568	209·114	213·660	218·206	222·752
50	227·298	231·844	236·390	240·936	245·482	250·028	254·574	259·120	263·666	268·212
60	272·758	277·304	281·850	286·395	290·941	295·487	300·033	304·579	309·125	313·671
70	318·217	322·763	327·309	331·855	336·401	340·947	345·493	350·039	354·585	359·131
80	363·677	368·223	372·769	377·315	381·861	386·407	390·953	395·499	400·044	404·590
90	409·136	413·682	418·228	422·774	427·320	431·866	436·412	440·958	445·504	450·050
100	454·596	—	—	—	—	—	—	—	—	—

Table 9.21 MASS: POUNDS TO KILOGRAMMES

Basis: 1 lb = 0·453 592 37 kg (exactly)

pounds	0	1	2	3	4	5	6	7	8	9
					kilogrammes					
0	—	0·45359	0·90718	1·36078	1·81437	2·26796	2·72155	3·17515	3·62874	4·08233
10	4·53592	4·98952	5·44311	5·89670	6·35029	6·80389	7·25748	7·71107	8·16466	8·61826
20	9·07185	9·52544	9·97903	10·4326	10·8862	11·3398	11·7934	12·2470	12·7006	13·1542
30	13·6078	14·0614	14·5150	14·9685	15·4221	15·8757	16·3293	16·7829	17·2365	17·6901
40	18·1437	18·5973	19·0509	19·5045	19·9581	20·4117	20·8652	21·3188	21·7724	22·2260
50	22·6796	23·1332	23·5868	24·0404	24·4940	24·9476	25·4012	25·8548	26·3084	26·7619
60	27·2155	27·6691	28·1227	28·5763	29·0299	29·4835	29·9371	30·3907	30·8443	31·2979
70	31·7515	32·2051	32·6587	33·1122	33·5658	34·0194	34·4730	34·9266	35·3802	35·8338
80	36·2874	36·7410	37·1946	37·6482	38·1018	38·5554	39·0089	39·4625	39·9161	40·3697
90	40·8233	41·2769	41·7305	42·1841	42·6377	43·0913	43·5449	43·9985	44·4521	44·9056
100	45·3592	45·8128	46·2664	46·7200	47·1736	47·6272	48·0808	48·5344	48·9880	49·4416
110	49·8952	50·3488	50·8023	51·2559	51·7095	52·1631	52·6167	53·0703	53·5239	53·9775
120	54·4311	54·8847	55·3383	55·7919	56·2455	56·6990	57·1526	57·6062	58·0598	58·5134
130	58·9670	59·4206	59·8742	60·3278	60·7814	61·2350	61·6886	62·1422	62·5957	63·0493
140	63·5029	63·9565	64·4101	64·8637	65·3173	65·7709	66·2245	66·6781	67·1317	67·5853
150	68·0389	68·4924	68·9460	69·3996	69·8532	70·3068	70·7604	71·2140	71·6676	72·1212
160	72·5748	73·0284	73·4820	73·9356	74·3891	74·8427	75·2963	75·7499	76·2035	76·6571
170	77·1107	77·5643	78·0179	78·4715	78·9251	79·3787	79·8323	80·2858	80·7394	81·1930
180	81·6466	82·1002	82·5538	83·0074	83·4610	83·9146	84·3682	84·8218	85·2754	85·7290
190	86·1826	86·6361	87·0897	87·5433	87·9969	88·4505	88·9041	89·3577	89·8113	90·2649
200	90·7185	91·1721	91·6257	92·0793	92·5328	92·9864	93·4400	93·8936	94·3472	94·8008
210	95·2544	95·7080	96·1616	96·6152	97·0688	97·5224	97·9760	98·4295	98·8831	99·3367
220	99·7903	100·244	100·698	101·151	101·605	102·058	102·512	102·965	103·419	103·873
230	104·326	104·780	105·233	105·687	106·141	106·594	107·048	107·501	107·955	108·409
240	108·862	109·316	109·769	110·223	110·677	111·130	111·584	112·037	112·491	112·945
250	113·398	113·852	114·305	114·759	115·212	115·666	116·120	116·573	117·027	117·480
260	117·934	118·388	118·841	119·295	119·748	120·202	120·656	121·109	121·563	122·016
270	122·470	122·924	123·377	123·831	124·284	124·738	125·191	125·645	126·099	126·552
280	127·006	127·459	127·913	128·367	128·820	129·274	129·727	130·181	130·635	131·088
290	131·542	131·995	132·449	132·903	133·356	133·810	134·263	134·717	135·171	135·624
300	136·078	136·531	136·985	137·438	137·892	138·346	138·799	139·253	139·706	140·160
310	140·614	141·067	141·521	141·974	142·428	142·882	143·335	143·789	144·242	144·696
320	145·150	145·603	146·057	146·510	146·964	147·418	147·871	148·325	148·778	149·232
330	149·685	150·139	150·593	151·046	151·500	151·953	152·407	152·861	153·314	153·768
340	154·221	154·675	155·129	155·582	156·036	156·489	156·943	157·397	157·850	158·304
350	158·757	159·211	159·665	160·118	160·572	161·025	161·479	161·932	162·386	162·840
360	163·293	163·747	164·200	164·654	165·108	165·561	166·015	166·468	166·922	167·376
370	167·829	168·283	168·736	169·190	169·644	170·097	170·551	171·004	171·458	171·912
380	172·365	172·819	173·272	173·726	174·179	174·633	175·087	175·540	175·994	176·447
390	176·901	177·355	177·808	178·262	178·715	179·169	179·623	180·076	180·530	180·983
400	181·437	181·891	182·344	182·798	183·251	183·705	184·159	184·612	185·066	185·519
410	185·973	186·426	186·880	187·334	187·787	188·241	188·694	189·148	189·602	190·055
420	190·509	190·962	191·416	191·870	192·323	192·777	193·230	193·684	194·138	194·591
430	195·045	195·498	195·952	196·405	196·859	197·313	197·766	198·220	198·673	199·127
440	199·581	200·034	200·488	200·941	201·395	201·849	202·302	202·756	203·209	203·663
450	204·117	204·570	205·024	205·477	205·931	206·385	206·838	207·292	207·745	208·199
460	208·652	209·106	209·560	210·013	210·467	210·920	211·374	211·828	212·281	212·735
470	213·188	213·642	214·096	214·549	215·003	215·456	215·910	216·364	216·817	217·271
480	217·724	218·178	218·632	219·085	219·539	219·992	220·446	220·899	221·353	221·807
490	222·260	222·714	223·167	223·621	224·075	224·528	224·982	225·435	225·889	226·343

continued

Table 9.21 MASS: POUNDS TO KILOGRAMMES *(continued)*

Basis: 1 lb = 0·453 592 37 kg *(exactly)*

pounds	0	1	2	3	4	5	6	7	8	9
					kilogrammes					
500	226·796	227·250	227·703	228·157	228·611	229·064	229·518	229·971	230·425	230·879
510	231·332	231·786	232·239	232·693	233·146	233·600	234·054	234·507	234·961	235·414
520	235·868	236·322	236·775	237·229	237·682	238·136	238·590	239·043	239·497	239·950
530	240·404	240·858	241·311	241·765	242·218	242·672	243·126	243·579	244·033	244·486
540	244·940	245·393	245·847	246·301	246·754	247·208	247·661	248·115	248·569	249·022
550	249·476	249·929	250·383	250·837	251·290	251·744	252·197	252·651	253·105	253·558
560	254·012	254·465	254·919	255·373	255·826	256·280	256·733	257·187	257·640	258·094
570	258·548	259·001	259·455	259·908	260·362	260·816	261·269	261·723	262·176	262·630
580	263·084	263·537	263·991	264·444	264·898	265·352	265·805	266·259	266·712	267·166
590	267·619	268·073	268·527	268·980	269·434	269·887	270·341	270·795	271·248	271·702
600	272·155	272·609	273·063	273·516	273·970	274·423	274·877	275·331	275·784	276·238
610	276·691	277·145	277·599	278·052	278·506	278·959	279·413	279·866	280·320	280·774
620	281·227	281·681	282·134	282·588	283·042	283·495	283·949	284·402	284·856	285·310
630	285·763	286·217	286·670	287·124	287·578	288·031	288·485	288·938	289·392	289·846
640	290·299	290·753	291·206	291·660	292·113	292·567	293·021	293·474	293·928	294·381
650	294·835	295·289	295·742	296·196	296·649	297·103	297·557	298·010	298·464	298·917
660	299·371	299·825	300·278	300·732	301·185	301·639	302·093	302·546	303·000	303·453
670	303·907	304·360	304·814	305·268	305·721	306·175	306·628	307·082	307·536	307·989
680	308·443	308·896	309·350	309·804	310·257	310·711	311·164	311·618	312·072	312·525
690	312·979	313·432	313·886	314·340	314·793	315·247	315·700	316·154	316·607	317·061
700	317·515	317·968	318·422	318·875	319·329	319·783	320·236	320·690	321·143	321·597
710	322·051	322·504	322·958	323·411	323·865	324·319	324·772	325·226	325·679	326·133
720	326·587	327·040	327·494	327·947	318·401	328·854	329·308	329·762	330·215	330·669
730	331·122	331·576	332·030	332·483	332·937	333·390	333·844	334·298	334·751	335·205
740	335·658	336·112	336·566	337·019	337·473	337·926	338·380	338·834	339·287	339·741
750	340·194	340·648	341·101	341·555	342·009	342·462	342·916	343·369	343·823	344·277
760	344·730	345·184	345·637	346·091	346·545	346·998	347·452	347·905	348·359	348·813
770	349·266	349·720	350·173	350·627	351·080	351·534	351·988	352·441	352·895	353·348
780	353·802	354·256	354·709	355·163	355·616	356·070	356·524	356·977	357·431	357·884
790	358·338	358·792	359·245	359·699	360·152	360·606	361·060	361·513	361·967	362·420
800	362·874	363·327	363·781	364·235	364·688	365·142	365·595	366·049	366·503	366·956
810	367·410	367·863	368·317	368·771	369·224	369·678	370·131	370·585	371·039	371·492
820	371·946	372·399	372·853	373·307	373·760	374·214	374·667	375·121	375·574	376·028
830	376·482	376·935	377·389	377·842	378·296	378·750	379·203	379·657	380·110	380·564
840	381·018	381·471	381·925	382·378	382·832	383·286	383·739	384·193	384·646	385·100
850	385·554	386·007	386·461	386·914	387·368	387·821	388·275	388·729	389·182	389·636
860	390·089	390·543	390·997	391·450	391·904	392·357	392·811	393·265	393·718	394·172
870	394·625	395·079	395·533	395·986	396·440	396·893	397·347	397·801	398·254	398·708
880	399·161	399·615	400·068	400·522	400·976	401·429	401·883	402·336	402·790	403·244
890	403·697	404·151	404·604	405·058	405·512	405·965	406·419	406·872	407·326	407·780
900	408·233	408·687	409·140	409·594	410·048	410·501	410·955	411·408	411·862	412·315
910	412·769	413·223	413·676	414·130	414·583	415·037	415·491	415·944	416·398	416·851
920	417·305	417·759	418·212	418·666	419·119	419·573	420·027	420·480	420·934	421·387
930	421·841	422·294	422·748	423·202	423·655	424·109	424·562	425·016	425·470	425·923
940	426·377	426·830	427·284	427·738	428·191	428·645	429·098	429·552	430·006	430·459
950	430·913	431·366	431·820	432·274	432·727	433·181	433·634	434·088	434·541	434·995
960	435·449	435·902	436·356	436·809	437·263	437·717	438·170	438·624	439·077	439·531
970	439·985	440·438	440·892	441·345	441·799	442·253	442·706	443·160	443·613	444·067
980	444·521	444·974	445·428	445·881	446·335	446·788	447·242	447·696	448·149	448·603
990	449·056	449·510	449·964	450·417	450·871	451·324	451·778	452·232	452·685	453·139
1000	453·592	—	—	—	—	—	—	—	—	—

Table 9.22 MASS: UK TONS, HUNDREDWEIGHTS AND QUARTERS TO TONNES

Basis: 1 UK ton = 2240 lb
1 lb = 0·453 592 37 kg
1 tonne = 1000 kg

UK tons	0	1	2	3	4	5	6	7	8	9
					tonnes					
0	—	1·0160	2·0321	3·0481	4·0642	5·0802	6·0963	7·1123	8·1284	9·1444
10	10·1605	11·1765	12·1926	13·2086	14·2247	15·2407	16·2568	17·2728	18·2888	19·3049
20	20·3209	21·3370	22·3530	23·3691	24·3851	25·4012	26·4172	27·4333	28·4493	29·4654
30	30·4814	31·4975	32·5135	33·5295	34·5456	35·5616	36·5777	37·5937	38·6098	39·6258
40	40·6419	41·6579	42·6740	43·6900	44·7061	45·7221	46·7382	47·7542	48·7703	49·7863
50	50·8023	51·8184	52·8344	53·8505	54·8665	55·8826	56·8986	57·9147	58·9307	59·9468
60	60·9628	61·9789	62·9949	64·0110	65·0270	66·0430	67·0591	68·0751	69·0912	70·1072
70	71·1233	72·1393	73·1554	74·1714	75·1875	76·2035	77·2196	78·2356	79·2517	80·2677
80	81·2838	82·2998	83·3158	84·3319	85·3479	86·3640	87·3800	88·3961	89·4121	90·4282
90	91·4442	92·4603	93·4763	94·4924	95·5084	96·5245	97·5405	98·5566	99·5726	100·589
100	101·605	—	—	—	—	—	—	—	—	—

cwt	0	1	2	3	4	5	6	7	8	9
					tonne					
0	—	0·05080	0·10160	0·15241	0·20321	0·25401	0·30481	0·35562	0·40642	0·45722
10	0·50802	0·55883	0·60963	0·66043	0·71123	0·76204	0·81284	0·86364	0·91444	0·96524

quarters	0	1	2	3
			tonne	
0	—	0·01270	0·02540	0·03810

BIBLIOGRAPHY

Further information can be gained from the following:

MINISTRY OF TECHNOLOGY, NATIONAL PHYSICAL LABORATORY, *Changing to the Metric System. Conversion Factors and Symbols and Definitions,* H.M.S.O. (1967).
P.D. 5686, *The Use of SI Units,* British Standards Institution, London (December 1965).

B.S. 3763:1964. *The International System of Units (SI),* British Standards Institution, London.
B.S. 350 *Conversion Factors and Tables.* Part 1:1959. *Basis of tables. Conversion factors;* Part 2:1962. *Detailed conversion tables,* British Standards Institution, London.
NAFT, S. and SOLA, R. DE, *International Conversion Tables,* (revised and enlarged by P. H. Bigg), Cassell, London (1965).

INDEX

INDEX